Family Favorites

Potluck Picks

Sunday Suppers

Make-ahead Meals

Hurry!
To get your **free** gift of **Homestyle Casseroles**, detach and mail this survey today!

We need your help!

Please take a moment to fill out and return the brief survey below.

To show our thanks, we'll send you a

free gift
of **Homestyle Casseroles!**

An exclusive collection of 67 family-favorite meals, with our compliments

BONUS TEAR-OUT SECTION! storage and freezing charts

homestyle **Casseroles**

67 warm and welcoming meals *plus make-ahead dinner ideas*

Back by Popular Demand! $3.99 U.S. $4.99 Canada

heartfelt homespun comfort foods

GREAT RECIPES COLLECTION

crockery
dinners

Grand Avenue Books
Des Moines, Iowa

Grand Avenue Books
An imprint of Meredith® Corporation

Great Recipes Collection: Crockery Dinners
Contributing Editor: Lisa Kingsley
Senior Associate Art Director: Ken Carlson
Copy and Production Editor: Victoria Forlini
Contributing Designer: Joline Rivera
Copy Chief: Terri Fredrickson
Contributing Copy Editors: Gretchen Kauffmann, Vicki Sidey
Editorial Operations Manager: Karen Schirm
Manager, Book Production: Rick von Holdt
Electronic Production Coordinator: Paula Forest
Editorial and Design Assistants: Kaye Chabot, Mary Lee Gavin, Patricia Loder

Grand Avenue Books
Editor in Chief: Linda Raglan Cunningham
Design Director: Matt Strelecki
Managing Editor: Gregory H. Kayko
Executive Editor, Grand Avenue Books: Dan Rosenberg

Publisher: James D. Blume
Executive Director, Marketing: Jeffrey Myers
Executive Director, New Business Development: Todd M. Davis
Executive Director, Sales: Ken Zagor
Director, Operations: George A. Susral
Director, Production: Douglas M. Johnston

Vice President and General Manager: Douglas J. Guendel

Meredith Publishing Group
President, Publishing Group: Stephen M. Lacy
Vice President-Publishing Director: Bob Mate

Meredith Corporation
Chairman and Chief Executive Officer: William T. Kerr

Chairman of the Executive Committee: E.T. Meredith III

All of us at Grand Avenue Books are dedicated to providing you with the information you need to create delicious meals. If for any reason you are not satisfied with this book, or if you have other comments or suggestions, write to us at: Grand Avenue Books, Editorial Department LN-116, 1716 Locust Street, Des Moines, IA 50309-3023

introduction

More than 250 slow-cooker recipes for everything from appetizers to desserts give you variety, value—and guaranteed great taste.

There's nothing quite like walking in the door after a busy day away from home to the mouthwatering aroma and eager anticipation of a dinner that's ready and waiting. Your slow cooker lets you do just that. *Great Recipes Collection: Crockery Dinners* gives you a generous helping of opportunities to put that most humble and handy appliance to good use.

Crockery Dinners is chock-full of failproof recipes that will please everyone in your family. In the mood for comfort food? Try Chicken and Dumplings or Old-Fashioned Beef Stew. Need something to munch on while you watch the Sunday game? Toss Buffalo Wings in the slow cooker in the morning and serve them with Blue Cheese Dip (and lots of napkins) at kick-off. Need something just a little bit special for dinner guests? Look no further than Winter Night Osso Bucco

or Mustard-Sauced Lamb and Artichokes. Got a sweet tooth? Cozy up with a bowl of warm Apple-Cherry Cobbler or gooey and indulgent Chocolate-Peanut Butter Pudding Cake. In addition to the more than 250 family-pleasing recipes for appetizers and beverages, soups and stews, meats, poultry, vegetables and sides, and desserts, a special section called Slow Cooking 101 (see page 6) gives you everything you need to know about using your slow cooker safely and getting the best results. It also provides a few culinary tricks, such as how to make a spice bag for mulled beverages and how to fashion aluminum foil handles for lifting soufflés and meat loaves out of the slow cooker with ease.

Using your slow cooker has always been easy and convenient. With *Great Recipes Collection: Crockery Dinners*, it is now a lot more interesting and fun.

Kielbasa Stew, page 97

contents

slow cooking 101

Dinner that cooks by itself while you're at the office, at play, or working around the house is a dream come true to busy families who, despite their schedules, want to enjoy a delicious home-cooked meal together at the end of a long day.

The make-it-and-forget-it nature of crockery cooking is the main reason for the humble appliance's popularity—not to mention that it makes more economical cuts of meat butter-knife tender and fills the house with wonderful aromas as dinner simmers undisturbed. Before you rush into slow cooking, however, there are a few simple things you might need to know—starting with the types of slow cookers that are available.

Slow Cooker Models

The most common type of slow cooker is the continuous slow cooker. All of the recipes in this book were tested in this type of cooker, which continuously cooks foods slowly at a very low wattage. The heating coils or elements are wrapped around the sides of the cooker and stay on continuously. This type of cooker generally has fixed settings: low, which is about 200°F; high, which is about 300°F; and, in some models, automatic (these shift from high to low heat automatically). The ceramic liner may or may not be removable.

The other type of cooker—the intermittent cooker—is not recommended for the recipes in this cookbook. In intermittent cookers, the heating elements or coils are located below the food container and cycle on and off during operation. If your cooker has a dial indicating temperatures in degrees, this is the type of cooker you have. Because the recipes in this book need continuous slow temperatures, this cooker will not cook the food properly.

Slow cookers come in a range of sizes, but the most widely available—and most useful— have a capacity of $3\frac{1}{2}$, 4, 5, or 6 quarts. The recipes in this book recommend the size to use. Check the capacity of your cooker to see whether it fits the recommendation in the recipe. For best results the slow cooker must be at least half full and no more than two-thirds full. If your budget and storage space can afford it, it doesn't hurt to have two slow cookers—a smaller and a larger one —to be able to make nearly any recipe. Slow cookers also can be either round, which is perfect for soups and stews, or oval, which more easily accommodates roasts and cut-up whole chickens. A basic but good quality $3\frac{1}{2}$-quart model of either shape can be found for less than \$25, and the larger models for about \$40.

Cooking Times

If you want dinner to cook all day, use the low-heat setting of your cooker, and the corresponding recommended time for low heat. For a shorter cooking time, use the high-heat setting. Cooking times may vary depending on the cooker, but the recommended timings generally will work with all continuous slow cookers. When a recipe recommends only one cooking setting and time, do not use the other setting because your recipe may not turn out properly.

As good as something may smell, resist the temptation to lift the lid during cooking. Removing the lid—even for a moment—allows significant amounts of heat to escape and extends the cooking time. Because the slow cooker cooks at such low temperatures, it is unable to quickly recover the lost heat and return to the desired temperature. An uncovered cooker can lose up to 20 degrees of cooking heat in as little as 2 minutes. A quick peek will change the temperature by only 1 or 2 degrees. When a recipe calls for lifting the lid near the end of the cooking time, do so as quickly as possible, replacing the lid as soon as you can.

Safety First

Foods prepared in a slow cooker are safe to eat even though they cook at low temperatures. The long cooking time and the steam that forms in the tightly covered container destroy bacteria. To ensure that your food is safe to eat, though, take a few precautions. Clean the cooker and all utensils before you start. Always completely thaw raw meat or poultry before adding it to the cooker. Do not use the slow cooker for very large pieces of meat. Cut in half any roasts that are larger than $2\frac{1}{2}$ pounds.

Many cooks buy large-capacity slow cookers so they can cook once and have enough leftovers for another meal. Be sure to remove cooked food from the crockery cooker before storing it. If you store the warm food and the crockery liner in the refrigerator, the food may not cool down quickly enough. Cooling foods quickly is the key to keeping them safe from bacteria. Store leftovers in a storage container and refrigerate or freeze.

Time-Savers

If you need to leave early in the morning—or if your morning will be very busy—you can start your preparations the previous night. Place cleaned and chopped vegetables, seasonings, and liquids into a bowl or in the slow cooker liner if it is removable. Do not mix raw meat or poultry with other raw ingredients. Chill the vegetables. The following morning, assemble all of the ingredients in the cooker (in the order recommended in the recipe), cover, and spend the rest of the day as you like.

There may be times when you will be gone a bit longer than the recipe needs to cook. In these instances, you can use an automatic timer to start your cooker (some slow cooker models have timers on them already). These can be purchased at a hardware store.

When using the timer, prepare the recipe and thoroughly chill all of the ingredients. When you're ready to leave the house, fill the cooker, plug it into the timer, set the timer, and turn on the cooker. It's very important to remember that food should never stand more than two hours before it begins cooking. Also, do not use this method for recipes that include frozen fish.

Slow Cooking with Dairy Products

Milk, cream, and natural cheeses break down from long cooking times. Use substitutes such as reconstituted condensed soups and nonfat dry milk powder. You can also use evaporated milk, if you add it during the last 30 to 60 minutes of cooking time. Natural cheeses can be stirred into a finished dish just before serving.

Tricks of the Trade

There are a couple of techniques commonly used in slow cooking that are helpful to know how to do. Many hot beverages such as spiced cider and mulled wine call for using a spice bag. To make a spice bag, cut a double thickness of 100-percent-cotton cheesecloth in a 6-inch square. Place spices in the center of the square. Bring up the corners of the cheesecloth and tie with clean 100-percent-cotton string.

Foil handles make it easy to lift a soufflé dish or meat loaf out of the slow cooker. To make foil handles, tear off three 18×2-inch strips of heavy foil or use regular foil folded to double thickness. Crisscross the foil strips in a spoke design. (Place them on a large sheet of waxed paper if shaping meat loaf.) Place the soufflé dish or shaped meat loaf in the center of the spoke before cooking.

Slow Cooker Care

To keep your slow cooker in good condition and ensure that it will be around to make many satisfying meals for years to come, follow a few simple guidelines.

First, never put cold food or water into a hot cooker, or a hot cooker in the refrigerator. Sudden temperature changes can crack the ceramic liner. Also, never immerse the cooker or the cord in water—and always unplug the cooker before cleaning it.

To clean the slow cooker, wipe the liner with a soft cloth and hot soapy water only. Avoid using abrasive cleaners and cleansing pads. Removable ceramic liners can be washed in the dishwasher or by hand.

appetizers and beverages

Get the party started—and keep it going—with these snacks and beverages. Everything from creamy dips and Buffalo wings to mulled wine will keep your guests happy—and you enjoying them.

Almost-A-Meal Queso

The dried, smoked jalapeños called chipotle peppers have a spicy, almost chocolatey flavor. They give this hearty dip lots of zip. Look for them in the produce section of your supermarket.

Prep: 20 minutes **Cook:** 1 to 2 hours on high **Makes:** 8 cups (64, 2-tablespoon servings)

1 pound ground beef

1 large onion, chopped

2 cloves garlic, minced

2 pounds American cheese, cubed

½ of a 16-ounce link cooked kielbasa or smoked sausage, quartered lengthwise and sliced

1 14½-ounce can diced tomatoes

1 4-ounce can chopped green chiles

2 to 3 chipotle peppers in adobo sauce, drained and chopped (optional)

1 tablespoon chili powder

1½ teaspoons Worcestershire sauce

½ teaspoon ground black pepper

Tortilla chips

1. In a large skillet cook the ground beef, onion, and garlic until beef is no longer pink; drain. Add to a 3½- or 4-quart slow cooker. Stir in cheese, sausage, undrained tomatoes, undrained green chiles, chipotle peppers (if desired), chili powder, Worcestershire sauce, and ground black pepper.

2. Cover and cook on high-heat setting for 1 to 2 hours until cheese melts, stirring after 1 hour. To serve, keep warm on low-heat setting, stirring occasionally. Serve with tortilla chips.

Nutrition Facts per serving: 82 calories, 6 g total fat, 20 mg cholesterol, 258 mg sodium, 1 g carbohydrate, 5 g protein.

Supreme Pizza Fondue

For a truly supreme version of this savory fondue, use a combination of sausage, pepperoni, Canadian bacon, and 1/2 teaspoon each of basil and oregano.

Prep: 20 minutes **Cook:** 3 hours on low **Makes:** 5½ cups (10, ½-cup servings)

1. In a large skillet cook the sausage, onion, and garlic until meat is brown. Drain off fat.

2. In a 3½- or 4-quart slow cooker combine spaghetti sauce, mushrooms, pepperoni or Canadian-style bacon, and basil or oregano. Stir in the meat mixture.

3. Cover; cook on low-heat setting for 3 hours. If desired, stir in ripe olives and sweet pepper. Cover; cook on low-heat setting for 15 minutes more. To serve, spear the dippers with fondue forks and dip into the fondue.

Nutrition Facts per serving: 254 calories, 12 g total fat, 39 mg cholesterol, 738 mg sodium, 24 g carbohydrate, 13 g protein.

4 ounces bulk Italian sausage
1 small onion, finely chopped
1 clove garlic, minced
1 30-ounce jar meatless spaghetti sauce
1 cup sliced fresh mushrooms
⅔ cup chopped pepperoni or Canadian-style bacon
1 teaspoon dried basil or oregano, crushed
½ cup sliced pitted ripe olives (optional)
¼ cup chopped green sweet pepper (optional)
Dippers such as focaccia bread or Italian bread cubes, mozzarella or provolone cheese cubes, or cooked tortellini or ravioli

Cheeseburger Dip

America's favorite sandwich gets deconstructed in this fun dip. Serve it with cocktail buns for scooping, and you won't miss a thing from the real McCoy.

Prep: 15 minutes   **Cook:** 3 hours on low or 1½ hours on high   **Makes:** 5½ cups (22, ¼-cup servings)

  2 pounds lean ground beef
1½ cups chopped onion
  2 cloves garlic, minced
  1 15-ounce jar cheese dip
½ cup catsup
¼ cup yellow mustard
¼ cup sweet pickle relish
   Corn chip scoops, tortilla
   chips, or cocktail buns

1. In a large skillet cook beef, onion, and garlic until meat is brown. Drain off fat.

2. Stir cheese dip, catsup, mustard, and pickle relish into cooked meat mixture. Transfer meat mixture to a 3½-quart slow cooker. Cover; cook on low-heat setting for 3 to 4 hours or on high-heat setting for 1½ to 2 hours. Serve immediately or keep warm on low-heat setting for up to 2 hours. Serve with chips or buns.

Nutrition Facts per serving: 134 calories, 8 g total fat, 38 mg cholesterol, 447 mg sodium, 5 g carbohydrate, 10 g protein.

Cheesy Beer-Salsa Dip

Small toasted squares of corn bread make the perfect vehicle for enjoying this three-cheese and salsa extravaganza. Choose the level of heat by using either mild, medium, or hot salsa.

Prep: 15 minutes **Cook:** 3 hours on low or 1½ hours on high **Makes:** 5½ cups (22, ¼-cup servings)

1. In a 3½- or 4-quart slow cooker combine salsa, three cheeses, and beer.

2. Cover; cook on low-heat setting for 3 to 4 hours or on high-heat setting for 1½ to 2 hours. Serve immediately or keep warm on low-heat setting for up to 2 hours. Stir before serving. Serve with Corn Bread Dippers or tortilla chips.

Corn Bread Dippers: Prepare one 8½-ounce package corn muffin mix according to package directions. Spread in an 8×8×2-inch baking pan and bake in 400° oven for 20 minutes or until toothpick inserted in center comes out clean. Cool bread in pan on a wire rack for 5 minutes. Remove bread from pan; cool completely. Cut into ½-inch thick slices; cut each slice into three pieces. Place in single layer on a large baking sheet. Bake in a 425° oven for 10 minutes or until crisp, turning once. Cool on wire rack. Store in an airtight container up to 2 days. Makes about 42.

Nutrition Facts per serving: **211 calories, 15 g total fat, 47 mg cholesterol, 557 mg sodium, 10 g carbohydrate, 9 g protein.**

- 1 16-ounce jar salsa
- 4 cups shredded American cheese (1 pound)
- 2 cups shredded Monterey Jack cheese or American cheese (8 ounces)
- 1 8-ounce package cream cheese, cut up
- ⅔ cup beer or milk
  Corn Bread Dippers or tortilla chips

Hot Artichoke Dip

This classic is a surefire hit with any crowd. Serve it on toasted pita wedges or lavosh crackerbread.
Clean the leeks thoroughly by slicing them lengthwise and fanning the layers under running water.

Prep: 20 minutes   **Cook:** 3 hours on low   **Makes:** 5 cups (20, ¼-cup servings)

2 medium leeks, thinly sliced
(⅔ cup)
1 tablespoon olive oil
2 14-ounce cans artichoke
hearts, drained and
coarsely chopped
2 cups light mayonnaise
dressing (do not use
regular mayonnaise)
1 cup chopped red
sweet pepper
1 cup finely shredded
Parmesan cheese
1 teaspoon Mediterranean
seasoning or
lemon-pepper seasoning
Finely shredded
Parmesan cheese
Toasted pita wedges

1. In a large skillet cook leeks in hot olive oil over medium heat until tender. Place in a 3½- to 4-quart slow cooker. Stir in the artichoke hearts, light mayonnaise, sweet pepper, 1 cup Parmesan, and seasoning. Cover and cook on low-heat setting for 3 to 4 hours until cheese is melted and mixture is heated through.

2. To serve, stir mixture, sprinkle with additional Parmesan, and keep warm on low-heat setting for up to 1 hour. Serve on toasted pita wedges.

Nutrition Facts per serving: **129 calories, 10 g total fat, 14 mg cholesterol, 361 mg sodium, 6 g carbohydrate, 3 g protein.**

Tex-Mex Cheese Dip

If you like your Tex-Mex spicy, use hot salsa and tongue-tingling chorizo sausage—an authentic Mexican sausage fired up by chiles—in place of the ground beef.

Prep: 15 minutes   **Cook:** 3 hours on low or 1½ hours on high   **Makes:** 6 cups (24, ¼-cup servings)

1. In a skillet cook beef, chicken, or turkey, onion, and garlic until meat is brown. Drain off fat.

2. Transfer meat mixture to a 3½- or 4-quart slow cooker. Stir in cumin, coriander, and salsa. Cover; cook on low-heat setting for 3 to 4 hours or on high-heat setting for 1½ to 2 hours until heated through.

3. Stir in cheese. Cover; cook on high-heat setting for 5 to 10 minutes or until cheese melts. Serve with chips. The dip may be kept warm in slow cooker up to 2 hours on low-heat setting.

Nutrition Facts per ¼ cup dip without chips: **133 calories, 10 g total fat, 36 mg cholesterol, 341 mg sodium, 2 g carbohydrate, 10 g protein.**

1½ pounds lean ground beef
   or ground raw chicken
   or raw turkey
1 cup chopped onion
2 cloves garlic, minced
1 teaspoon ground cumin
1 teaspoon ground coriander
1 12-ounce jar chunky salsa
1 16-ounce package cheese
   with jalapeño peppers
   Tortilla chips or corn chips

Bacon-Horseradish Dip

Lip-tingling horseradish makes this dip a real kick. Use sharp cheddar for the most intense flavor. Save a little prep time by buying pre-cooked and crumbled bacon.

Prep: 25 minutes **Cook:** 4 hours on low or 2 hours on high **Makes:** 5 cups (20, ¼-cup servings)

3 8-ounce packages
  cream cheese, softened
  and cut up
3 cups shredded cheddar
  cheese (12 ounces)
1 cup half-and-half
  or light cream
⅓ cup chopped green onion
3 tablespoons prepared
  horseradish
1 tablespoon Worcestershire
  sauce
3 cloves garlic, minced
½ teaspoon coarse-ground
  pepper
12 slices bacon, crisp cooked,
  cooled, and finely crumbled
  (1 cup)
  Corn chips, toasted
  baguette slices,
  toasted pita wedges,
  or assorted crackers

1. In a 3½- or 4-quart slow cooker combine cream cheese, cheddar cheese, half-and-half, green onion, horseradish, Worcestershire sauce, garlic, and pepper. Cover and cook on low-heat setting for 4 to 5 hours or on high-heat setting for 2 to 2½ hours, stirring once halfway through cooking. Stir in the bacon. Serve with corn chips, baguette slices, pita wedges, or assorted crackers.

Nutrition Facts per serving: **227 calories, 21 g total fat, 63 mg cholesterol, 282 mg sodium, 2 g carbohydrate, 8 g protein.**

Spicy Sausage Pizza Dip

Deep-dish pizza has nothing on this tasty pot of dip. Stir it occasionally as it's served to keep the sausage evenly distributed throughout the tomato sauce.

Prep: 20 minutes **Cook:** 6 hours on low or 3 hours on high **Makes:** 3½ cups dip (14, ¼-cup servings)

1. In a large skillet cook Italian sausage, onion, and garlic until meat is brown and onion is tender; drain well.

2. In a 3½- or 4-quart slow cooker combine sausage mixture, tomato sauce, undrained tomatoes, tomato paste, oregano, basil, sugar, and red pepper. Stir all ingredients together. Cover; cook on low-heat setting for 6 to 8 hours or on high-heat setting for 3 to 4 hours.

3. Stir in olives. Sprinkle with grated Parmesan cheese. Serve with desired dippers.

Nutrition Facts per serving: **120 calories, 8 g total fat, 22 mg cholesterol, 378 mg sodium, 5 g carbohydrate, 6 g protein.**

1 pound bulk Italian sausage
1 small onion, chopped (⅓ cup)
2 cloves garlic, minced
1 15-ounce can tomato sauce
1 7½-ounce can tomatoes, cut up
½ of a 6-ounce can tomato paste (⅓ cup)
2 teaspoons dried oregano, crushed
1½ teaspoons dried basil, crushed
1 teaspoon sugar
⅛ teaspoon ground red pepper
¼ cup chopped black olives
2 tablespoons grated Parmesan cheese
Dippers: breadsticks, breaded mozzarella cheese sticks, and green sweet pepper strips

Asiago Cheese Dip

Keep this creamy, elegant dip warm in a slow cooker for up to two hours after cooking. Stir it just before serving so everyone gets a bit of tomato, mushroom, and green onion in every bite.

Prep: 15 minutes   **Cook:** 3 hours on low or 1½ hours on high   **Makes:** 7 cups (28, ¼-cup servings)

1 cup chicken broth or water
4 ounces dried tomatoes
4 8-ounce cartons dairy
   sour cream
1¼ cups mayonnaise
½ of an 8-ounce package
   cream cheese, cut up
1 cup sliced fresh mushrooms
1 cup thinly sliced green onion
6 ounces shredded Asiago
   cheese (1½ cups)
Thinly sliced green onion
Toasted baguette slices

1. In a medium saucepan bring the chicken broth or water to boiling. Remove from heat and add the dried tomatoes. Cover and let stand for 5 minutes. Drain, discard the liquid, and chop the tomatoes (about 1¼ cups).

2. Meanwhile, in a 3½- or 4-quart slow cooker combine the sour cream, mayonnaise, cream cheese, mushrooms, 1 cup green onion, and Asiago cheese. Stir in the chopped tomatoes. Cover and cook on low-heat setting for 3 to 4 hours or on high-heat setting for 1½ to 2 hours. Stir before serving and sprinkle with additional green onion. Keep warm on low-heat setting for 1 to 2 hours. Serve warm with toasted baguette slices.

Nutrition Facts per serving: 195 calories, 19 g total fat, 31 mg cholesterol, 242 mg sodium, 5 g carbohydrate, 4 g protein.

Reuben Spread

All the elements of the classic Reuben sandwich—spiced corned beef, tangy sauerkraut, Swiss cheese, and sweet Thousand Island dressing—mingle in this creamy, melted mélange.

Prep: 15 minutes **Cook:** 2½ hours on low **Makes:** 5 cups (20, ¼-cup servings)

1. In a 3½- or 4-quart slow cooker combine corned beef, sauerkraut, dressing, cheeses, horseradish, and caraway seed.

2. Cover; cook on low-heat setting for 2½ to 3 hours. Serve immediately or keep warm on low-heat setting for up to 2 hours. Stir well before serving. Serve with toasted bread slices or crackers.

Nutrition Facts per serving: **157 calories, 13 g total fat, 38 mg cholesterol, 531 mg sodium, 3 g carbohydrate, 7 g protein.**

1 pound cooked corned beef, finely chopped
1 16-ounce can sauerkraut, rinsed, drained, and snipped
1 cup Thousand Island salad dressing
1½ cups shredded Swiss cheese
1 3-oz. package cream cheese, cubed
1 tablespoon prepared horseradish
1 teaspoon caraway seed
Toasted cocktail rye bread slices or rye crackers

Apricot-Glazed Ham Balls

Cut the ham in 1-inch chunks before putting it in a food processor or blender to grind it to a fine texture. You can also ask the meat-counter attendant to grind it for you.

Prep: 20 minutes **Bake:** 20 minutes **Cook:** 4 hours on low or 1½ hours on high **Makes:** 30 meatballs

1 beaten egg

½ cup graham cracker crumbs
(7 squares)

2 tablespoons unsweetened
pineapple juice

1 teaspoon dry mustard

¼ teaspoon salt

½ pound ground fully
cooked ham

½ pound ground pork

½ cup snipped dried apricots

1 18-ounce jar apricot
preserves

⅓ cup unsweetened
pineapple juice

1 tablespoon cider vinegar

½ teaspoon ground ginger

1. For meatballs, in a large bowl combine egg, graham cracker crumbs, the 2 tablespoons pineapple juice, dry mustard, and salt. Add ground ham, ground pork, and snipped apricots; mix well. Shape into 30 meatballs. Place in a 15×10×1-inch baking pan. Bake, uncovered, in a 350° oven for 20 minutes. Remove from oven; drain.

2. Meanwhile, stir together apricot preserves, the ⅓ cup pineapple juice, vinegar, and ground ginger. Set aside.

3. Add cooked meatballs to 3½- or 4-quart slow cooker. Pour apricot preserve mixture over meatballs. Cover; cook on low-heat setting for 4 to 5 hours or on high-heat setting for 1½ to 2 hours. Serve immediately or cover and keep warm on low-heat setting for up to 2 hours. Gently stir before serving.

Nutrition Facts per meatball: 86 calories, 2 g total fat, 15 mg cholesterol, 151 mg sodium, 15 g carbohydrate, 3 g protein.

Tangy Cocktail Meatballs

If you can't find stuffing mix, use croutons that have been lightly crushed inside a sealable plastic bag with a rolling pin or the bottom of a mixing bowl.

Prep: 20 minutes **Bake:** 15 minutes **Cook:** 2 hours on high **Makes:** 50 meatballs

1. In a large bowl combine egg, soup, stuffing mix, and salt. Add ground beef; mix well. Shape into 1-inch meatballs. Place meatballs in a 15×10×1-inch baking pan. Bake in a 350° oven for 15 to 18 minutes or until done. Drain meatballs and transfer to a 3½-, 4-, or 5-quart slow cooker.

2. In a bowl combine catsup, tomato sauce, water, brown sugar, Worcestershire sauce, vinegar, and tapioca. Pour over meatballs; stir gently to coat.

3. Cover; cook on high-heat setting for 2 to 3 hours. Serve immediately or keep warm on low-heat setting up to 2 hours. Serve with toothpicks.

Nutrition Facts per meatball: 58 calories, 3 g total fat, 15 mg cholesterol, 191 mg sodium, 5 g carbohydrate, 4 g protein.

1 beaten egg
1 10½-ounce can condensed French onion soup
2 cups herb-seasoned stuffing mix
½ teaspoon seasoned salt
2 pounds ground beef
1 cup salsa-style catsup or regular catsup
1 8-ounce can tomato sauce
1 cup water
⅓ cup packed brown sugar
¼ cup Worcestershire sauce
¼ cup vinegar
2 tablespoons quick-cooking tapioca

Cranberry-Sauced Sausages

With beautifully hued, sweet-tart cranberry sauce and aromatic allspice, these saucy sausages are just the thing to serve at a casual holiday gathering.

Prep: 10 minutes **Cook:** 2 hours on high **Makes:** 16 servings

2 8-ounce cans jellied
   cranberry sauce
⅔ cup catsup
2 tablespoons lemon juice
1 teaspoon dry mustard
¼ teaspoon allspice
2 5.3-ounce packages
   small fully cooked
   smoked sausage links

1. In a 3½- or 4-quart slow cooker combine cranberry sauce, catsup, lemon juice, dry mustard, and allspice. Stir in the smoked sausage links. Cover and cook for about 2 hours on high setting or until heated through.

Nutrition Facts per serving: **119 calories, 6 g total fat, 13 mg cholesterol, 304 mg sodium, 14 g carbohydrate, 3 g protein.**

Sweet 'n' Sour Ham Balls

If you don't have time to make the meatballs, simply stir up the sweet 'n' sour sauce and add cocktail wieners or Polish sausage chunks—then cover and heat.

Prep: 30 minutes   **Cook:** 4 hours on low or 1½ hours on high   **Makes:** 30 meatballs

1. In a 3½- or 4-quart slow cooker stir together sweet and sour sauce, pineapple juice, brown sugar, and ground ginger. Set aside.

2. For meatballs, in a large bowl combine egg, graham cracker crumbs, and milk. Add ground ham and pork; mix well. Shape into 30 meatballs. Spray a 12-inch skillet with nonstick coating. Add meatballs and brown on all sides over medium heat.

3. Add browned meatballs to slow cooker. Cover; cook on low-heat setting for 4 to 5 hours or on high-heat setting for 1½ to 2 hours. Serve immediately or keep warm on low-heat setting for up to 2 hours.

Nutrition Facts per meatball: **51 calories, 1 g total fat, 13 mg cholesterol, 130 mg sodium, 7 g carbohydrate, 3 g protein.**

- 1 9- or 10-ounce bottle sweet and sour sauce
- ⅓ cup unsweetened pineapple juice
- ⅓ cup packed brown sugar
- ¼ teaspoon ground ginger
- 1 beaten egg
- ½ cup graham cracker crumbs
- 2 tablespoons milk
- ½ pound ground fully cooked ham
- ½ pound ground pork
  Nonstick spray coating

Hot Honeyed Spareribs

Party hearty with these ribs. They're perfect for an open house. They stay warm in the honeyed picante sauce and no one goes away hungry.

Prep: 20 minutes **Broil:** 10 minutes **Cook:** 6 hours on low or 3 hours on high **Makes:** 10 to 12 servings

3½ to 4 pounds pork baby back ribs, cut into 1-rib portions

2 cups bottled picante sauce or salsa

½ cup honey

1 tablespoon quick-cooking tapioca

1 teaspoon ground ginger

1. Preheat broiler. Place ribs on the unheated rack of a broiler pan. Broil 6 inches from the heat about 10 minutes or until brown, turning once. Transfer ribs to a 3½-, 4-, 5-, or 6-quart slow cooker.

2. In a medium bowl combine picante sauce or salsa, honey, tapioca, and ginger. Pour sauce over ribs.

3. Cover and cook on low-heat setting for 6 to 7 hours or on high-heat setting for 3 to 3½ hours. Skim off fat from sauce, if desired. Serve sauce with ribs.

Nutrition Facts per serving: **215 calories, 6 g total fat, 43 mg cholesterol, 246 mg sodium, 18 g carbohydrate, 20 g protein.**

Buffalo Wings with Blue Cheese Dip

Serve these spicy sports-bar favorites with their traditional accompaniments: crisp celery sticks and cold beer. The dip will hold up to two weeks in the refrigerator—if there's any left over.

Prep: 30 minutes **Broil:** 10 minutes **Cook:** 4 hours on low or 2 hours on high **Makes:** 32 servings

1. Cut off and discard wing tips. Cut each wing into 2 sections. Place chicken on the unheated rack of a broiler pan. Broil 4 to 5 inches from the heat about 10 minutes or until chicken is browned, turning once. Transfer chicken to a 3½- or 4-quart slow cooker. Combine chili sauce and hot pepper sauce; pour over chicken wings.

2. Cover; cook on low-heat setting for 4 to 5 hours or on high-heat setting for 2 to 2½ hours. Serve chicken wings with Blue Cheese Dip or ranch salad dressing.

Blue Cheese Dip: In a blender container combine one 8-ounce carton dairy sour cream; ½ cup mayonnaise or salad dressing; ½ cup crumbled blue cheese (2 ounces); 1 clove garlic, minced; and 1 tablespoon white wine vinegar or white vinegar. Cover and blend until smooth. Store dip, covered, in the refrigerator for up to 2 weeks. If desired, top dip with additional crumbled blue cheese before serving.

Nutrition Facts per piece with 1 tablespoon Blue Cheese Dip: **108 calories, 8 g total fat, 21 mg cholesterol, 217 mg sodium, 3 g carbohydrate, 6 g protein.**

16 chicken wings (about 3 pounds)
1½ cups bottled chili sauce
3 to 4 tablespoons bottled hot pepper sauce
1 recipe Blue Cheese Dip or bottled ranch salad dressing

Barbecue-Style Chicken Wings

Serve lots of napkins (maybe even some moist towelettes!) with these sweet and saucy wings.

Prep: 15 minutes **Broil:** 10 minutes **Cook:** 4 hours on low or 2 hours on high **Makes:** 32 servings

16 chicken wings
    (about 3 pounds)
1½ cups bottled
    barbecue sauce
¼ cup honey
 2 teaspoons prepared mustard
1½ teaspoons Worcestershire
    sauce

1. Cut off and discard wing tips. Cut each wing at joint to make 2 sections.

2. Place chicken on unheated rack of a broiler pan. Broil 4 to 5 inches from the heat about 10 minutes or until chicken is browned, turning once. Transfer to a 3½- or 4-quart slow cooker.

3. For sauce, combine barbecue sauce, honey, mustard, and Worcestershire sauce; pour over chicken wings. Cover; cook on low-heat setting for 4 to 5 hours or on high-heat setting for 2 to 2½ hours.

Nutrition Facts per serving: **67 calories, 4 g total fat, 14 mg cholesterol, 115 mg sodium, 4 g carbohydrate, 5 g protein.**

Five Spice Pecans

The slow cooker toasts nuts to a beautiful golden brown and enhances their flavor. Toast these Asian-flavored nibbles and freeze them in 1- to 2-cup batches up to 3 months before the holidays.

Prep: 10 minutes **Cook:** 2 hours on low and 15 minutes on high **Makes:** 4 cups (16, ¼-cup servings)

1. Place pecans in a 3½- or 4-quart slow cooker. In a bowl combine the melted margarine or butter, soy sauce, five-spice powder, garlic powder, ginger, and red pepper. Pour over nuts. Stir to coat nuts.

2. Cover; cook on low-heat setting for 2 hours. Uncover and stir. Turn to high-heat setting. Cover and continue cooking on high-heat setting for 15 to 30 minutes. Cool.

Nutrition Facts per serving: **217 calories, 22 g total fat, 8 mg cholesterol, 145 mg sodium, 6 g carbohydrate, 2 g protein.**

1 pound pecan halves (4 cups)
¼ cup margarine
 or butter, melted
2 tablespoons soy sauce
1 teaspoon five-spice powder
½ teaspoon garlic powder
½ teaspoon ground ginger
¼ teaspoon ground red pepper

Sugar-Roasted Almonds

When the hunger bug bites, these sweet and crunchy nuts hit the spot. They can be stored in the refrigerator for up to 1 week, if they last that long.

Prep: 20 minutes **Cook:** 4 hours on low **Makes:** 5½ cups (22, ¼-cup servings)

4 cups whole unblanched
   almonds or mixed nuts,
   toasted
1 egg white
1 teaspoon water
⅓ cup granulated sugar
⅓ cup packed brown sugar
2 teaspoons ground cinnamon
½ teaspoon salt

1. Place the nuts in a 3½- or 4-quart slow cooker. In a medium mixing bowl beat the egg white and water with a wire whisk or rotary beater until frothy. Stir in remaining ingredients. Pour over nuts and stir gently to coat.

2. Cover and cook on low-heat setting for 4 to 4½ hours, stirring once halfway through cooking. Spread on waxed paper, separating into small clusters to cool. Store in a tightly covered container in the refrigerator for up to 1 week.

Nutrition Facts per serving: **182 calories, 13 g total fat, 0 mg cholesterol, 57 mg sodium, 12 g carbohydrate, 6 g protein.**

Spicy Tomato Cocktail

Serve this warm libation with an assortment of specialty olives and an array of Italian cheeses.

Prep: 5 minutes **Cook:** 3 hours on low or 1 hour on high **Makes:** 8 (6-ounce) servings

1. In a 3½- or 4-quart slow cooker combine vegetable juice, celery, brown sugar, lemon juice, horseradish, Worcestershire sauce, and hot pepper sauce.

2. Cover; cook on low-heat setting for 3 to 4 hours or on high-heat setting for 1 to 1½ hours. Discard celery. Ladle beverage into cups. Float a lemon half slice on each serving, if desired.

Nutrition Facts per serving: 47 calories, 0 g total fat, 0 mg cholesterol, 612 mg sodium, 12 g carbohydrate, 1 g protein.

1 46-ounce can vegetable juice
1 stalk celery, halved (if necessary to fit)
2 tablespoons brown sugar
2 tablespoons lemon juice
1½ teaspoons prepared horseradish
1 teaspoon Worcestershire sauce
½ teaspoon bottled hot pepper sauce
Lemon slices, halved (optional)

Hot Buttered Cider

This spiced cider is the perfect fall warm-up after raking leaves or cheering at a football game.

Prep: 10 minutes   **Cook:** 7 hours on low or 3 hours on high   **Makes:** 10 (6-ounce) servings

4 inches stick cinnamon
1 teaspoon whole allspice
1 teaspoon whole cloves
  Peel from 1 lemon,
    cut into strips
8 cups apple cider
2 tablespoons brown sugar
2 tablespoons butter
  or margarine
  Cinnamon sticks (optional)

1. For a spice bag, tie cinnamon, allspice, cloves, and lemon peel in a 6-inch square of 100-percent-cotton cheesecloth. In a 3½-, 4-, 5-, or 6-quart slow cooker combine spice bag, apple cider, and brown sugar. Cover; cook on low-heat setting for 7 to 8 hours or on high-heat setting for 3 to 4 hours.

2. Discard spice bag. Ladle hot punch into cups; float about ½ teaspoon butter or margarine on each serving. Serve with a cinnamon stick stirrer, if desired.

Nutrition Facts per serving: **128 calories, 2 g total fat, 6 mg cholesterol, 30 mg sodium, 30 g carbohydrate, 0 g protein.**

Spiced Citrus Sipper

There's nothing like a tropical drink to take the chill away when the weather turns cold—especially when it's served warm. Stir up this sipper when you're longing for the sun.

Prep: 15 minutes   **Cook:** 4 hours on low or 2 hours on high   **Makes:** 12 (6-ounce) servings

1. Tie lemon peel, stick cinnamon, allspice, and cloves in a spice bag. In a 3½-, 4-, 5-, or 6-quart slow cooker combine spice bag, water, pineapple-orange juice concentrate, and honey. Stir in beer and vodka or rum.

2. Cover; cook on low-heat setting for 4 to 6 hours or on high-heat setting for 2 to 3 hours. Remove and discard spice bag.

Nutrition Facts per serving: **126 calories, 0 g total fat, 0 mg cholesterol, 15 mg sodium, 22 g carbohydrate, 1 g protein.**

Peel of 1 lemon, cut
   into strips
5 inches stick cinnamon,
   broken
1 teaspoon whole allspice
1 teaspoon whole cloves
4 cups water
1 12-ounce can frozen
   pineapple-orange juice
   concentrate
¼ cup honey
2 12-ounce cans beer
½ cup vodka or rum

Holiday Wassail

This lively concoction of fruit juices, aromatic spices, and a spark of lemon makes for a spirited drink, whether or not you add the real spirits!

Prep: 10 minutes **Cook:** 5 hours on low or 2½ hours on high **Makes:** 14 (6-ounce) servings

6 inches stick cinnamon, broken
12 whole cloves
8 cups water
½ of a 12-ounce can frozen cranberry juice cocktail concentrate (¾ cup)
½ of a 12-ounce can frozen raspberry juice blend concentrate (¾ cup)
1 6-ounce can frozen apple juice concentrate (¾ cup)
½ cup sugar
⅓ cup lemon juice
½ to ¾ cup brandy or rum or 6 tea bags (optional)
Orange slices (optional)

1. For spice bag, cut a double thickness of 100-percent-cotton cheesecloth into a 6-inch square. Place cinnamon and cloves in center of cheesecloth square. Bring up corners of cheesecloth and tie with a clean string.

2. In a 3½-, 4-, or 5-quart slow cooker combine water, cranberry juice cocktail concentrate, raspberry juice blend concentrate, apple juice concentrate, sugar, and lemon juice. Add the spice bag to juice mixture.

3. Cover; cook on low-heat setting for 5 to 6 hours or on high-heat setting for 2½ to 3 hours. Remove the spice bag and discard. If desired, about 5 minutes before serving, add brandy or rum or the tea bags to the slow cooker. Allow to stand for 5 minutes. Discard the tea bags, if using.

4. To serve, ladle beverage into cups. If desired, float an orange slice atop each serving.

Nutrition Facts per serving: **80 calories, 0 g total fat, 0 mg cholesterol, 8 mg sodium, 21 g carbohydrate, 0 g protein.**

Hot Buttered Apple Rum

When the air gets nippy and the snowflakes fly, this festive drink will warm you from head to toe.

Prep: 10 minutes   **Cook:** 7 hours on low or 3 hours on high   **Makes:** 10 (6-ounce) servings

1. Tie cinnamon, allspice, and cloves in a spice bag. In a 3½-, 4-, 5-, or 6-quart slow cooker combine spice bag, apple juice, rum, and brown sugar. Cover; cook on low-heat setting for 7 to 8 hours or on high-heat setting for 3 to 4 hours.

2. Discard spice bag. Ladle hot punch into cups; float about ½ teaspoon butter or margarine atop each serving.

Nutrition Facts per serving: **185 calories, 2 g total fat, 5 mg cholesterol, 29 mg sodium, 27 g carbohydrate, 0 g protein.**

4 inches stick cinnamon, broken
1 teaspoon whole allspice
1 teaspoon whole cloves
7 cups apple juice
1 to 1½ cups rum
⅓ cup packed brown sugar
Butter or margarine

Touchdown Toddy

Whether you're watching a game or reading a book, this mellow and mild drink warms up fall and winter afternoons. If you don't have Burgundy, any dry red wine will do.

Prep: 10 minutes   **Cook:** 4 hours on low or 3 hours on high   **Makes:** 11 (8-ounce) servings

16 whole cloves

4 inches stick cinnamon, broken

6 cups apple juice

4 cups water

1 cup Burgundy

⅔ cup instant lemon-flavored tea powder

1. Tie cloves and cinnamon in a spice bag. In a 3½-, 4-, 5-, or 6-quart slow cooker combine spice bag, apple juice, water, Burgundy, and tea powder. Cover; cook on low-heat setting for 4 to 6 hours or on high-heat setting for 3 to 4 hours. Discard spice bag.

Nutrition Facts per serving: **164 calories, 0 g total fat, 0 mg cholesterol, 9 mg sodium, 38 g carbohydrate, 0 g protein.**

Cardamom-Cranberry Warm-up

For a nonalcoholic drink, substitute 2½ cups white grape juice for the red wine and cranberry liqueur, and omit the honey. Crème de cassis is black currant liqueur.

Prep: 5 minutes **Cook:** 4 hours on low or 2 hours on high **Makes:** 9 (4-ounce) servings

1. Pinch cardamom pods to break open. Tie cardamom, cinnamon, and 6 whole cloves in a spice bag made from a double thickness of a small square of cheesecloth tied with a string.

2. In a 3½- or 4-quart slow cooker combine spice bag, wine, water, frozen juice concentrate, and honey. Add cranberry liqueur or crème de cassis, if desired. Cover; cook on low-heat setting for 4 to 6 hours or on high-heat setting for 2 to 2½ hours.

3. Remove and discard spice bag. If desired, stud orange slices with additional whole cloves. Ladle punch into cups and float an orange slice on each serving.

For 5- or 6-quart slow cooker: Double all ingredients. Prepare as above. Cook on low-heat setting for 6 to 8 hours or on high-heat setting 4 to 5 hours. Makes 18 (4-ounce) servings.

Nutrition Facts per serving: **95 calories, 0 g total fat, 0 mg cholesterol, 5 mg sodium, 16 g carbohydrate, 0 g protein.**

4 whole cardamom pods
8 inches stick cinnamon, broken
6 whole cloves
2 cups dry red wine
1⅓ cups water
1 6-ounce can frozen cranberry juice concentrate
3 tablespoons honey
½ cup cranberry liqueur or crème de cassis (optional)
Orange slices, halved (optional)
Whole cloves (optional)

Mulled Cider

**Be sure you use the processed cider found on the grocery shelf. The unprocessed cider found in the supermarket refrigerated section will separate and have a curdled appearance when heated.

Prep: 15 minutes **Cook:** 5 hours on low or 2½ hours on high **Makes:** 8 (8-ounce) servings

Peel from ½ orange,
 cut into pieces
6 inches stick cinnamon,
 broken*
1 1-inch piece ginger,
 peeled and thinly sliced
1 teaspoon whole allspice
8 cups apple cider
 or apple juice**
1 cup apple brandy (optional)
¼ cup honey or packed
 brown sugar

1. For spice bag, cut a double thickness of 100-percent-cotton cheesecloth into a 6- or 8-inch square. Place orange peel, cinnamon, ginger, and allspice in center of cheesecloth square. Bring up corners of cheesecloth and tie with a clean string.

2. In a 3½-, 4-, or 5-quart slow cooker combine apple cider or apple juice, apple brandy (if desired), and honey or brown sugar. Add spice bag to cider mixture.

3. Cover; cook on low-heat setting for 5 to 6 hours or on high-heat setting for 2½ to 3 hours. Remove spice bag and discard. Ladle cider into cups.

Note: To break cinnamon sticks, place in a heavy plastic bag and pound sticks with a meat mallet.

Nutrition Facts per serving: **149 calories, 0 g total fat, 0 mg cholesterol, 8 mg sodium, 38 g carbohydrate, 0 g protein.**

Mulled Wine

Because boiling wine makes it taste bitter (and preventing it from boiling on the stove top can be difficult), the slow, even heat of the slow cooker is the ideal way to make this classic drink.

Prep: 20 minutes **Cook:** 4 hours on low or 2 hours on high **Makes:** 12 (6-ounce) servings

1. For spice bag, cut a double thickness of 100-percent-cotton cheesecloth into a 5- or 6-inch square. Pinch cardamom pods to break open. Place cardamom, cloves, and cinnamon in center of cheesecloth square. Bring up corners of cheesecloth and tie with a clean string.

2. In a 3½-, 4-, or 5-quart slow cooker combine wine, water, and corn syrup. Add spice bag.

3. Cover; cook on low-heat setting for 4 to 5 hours or on high-heat setting for 2 to 2½ hours. (Do not let boil.) Add orange halves, if desired, the last ½ hour of cooking. Remove spice bag and orange halves and discard.

4. To serve, ladle beverage into cups. If desired, float a fresh orange slice on each serving and add a cinnamon stick.

Nutrition Facts per serving: **180 calories, 0 g total fat, 0 mg cholesterol, 102 mg sodium, 25 g carbohydrate, 1 g protein.**

 2 whole cardamom pods
16 whole cloves
 3 inches stick cinnamon, broken
 2 750-milliliter bottles dry red wine
 2 cups water
 1 cup light corn syrup
 2 oranges, halved
   Orange slices, halved (optional)
   Cinnamon sticks (optional)

Creamy Hot Cocoa

Serve a differently flavored cocoa each time you make this rich and warming drink by using a variety of flavored creamers and liqueurs. For a party, hold it up to one hour in the cooker.

Prep: 10 minutes **Cook:** 3 hours on low or 1½ hours on high **Makes:** 12 (6-ounce) servings

1 9.6-ounce package nonfat
   dry milk powder
   (about 3 ½ cups)
1 cup powdered sugar
1 cup plain powdered nondairy
   creamer
¾ cup unsweetened
   cocoa powder
8 cups water
½ cup crème de cacao
   (optional)
   Sweetened whipped cream

1. In a 3½-, 4-, or 5-quart slow cooker combine dry milk powder, powdered sugar, nondairy creamer, and cocoa powder. Gradually add water; stir well to dissolve.

2. Cover; cook on low-heat setting for 3 to 4 hours or on high-heat setting for 1½ to 2 hours. Hold on low for one hour, if desired.

3. Stir in the crème de cacao, if desired. Stir mixture before serving. Ladle into mugs; top with whipped cream.

Nutrition Facts per serving: **210 calories, 6 g total fat, 14 mg cholesterol, 132 mg sodium, 29 g carbohydrate, 9 g protein.**

White Hot Chocolate

The cinnamon scent and vanilla flavor of this elegant take on classic cocoa are as enticing as the creamy texture. Sprinkle a little ground cinnamon on each serving for color, if you like.

Prep: 10 minutes   **Cook:** 4 hours on low or 2 hours on high   **Makes:** 12 (6-ounce) servings

1. Place the cinnamon, cardamom, and vanilla bean, if using, on a square of 100-percent-cotton cheesecloth. Bring up corners of cheesecloth and tie with 100-percent-cotton string.

2. In a 3½- or 4-quart slow cooker stir together the cream, milk, and baking pieces. Add spice bag. Cover and cook on low-heat setting for 4 to 5 hours or on high-heat setting for 2 to 2½ hours, stirring halfway through cooking time. Remove spice bag and stir in vanilla, if using.

Nutrition Facts per serving: 403 calories, 24 g total fat, 40 mg cholesterol, 142 mg sodium, 35 g carbohydrate, 6 g protein.

6 inches stick cinnamon
8 cardamom pods
1 vanilla bean, split
  or 2 teaspoons vanilla
3 cups half-and-half
  or light cream
3 cups milk
1½ cups white baking pieces

soups and stews

From the lightest soup to enjoy as a starter or alongside
a sandwich to the heartiest stew, your slow cooker keeps food
warm and satisfying as it simmers all day.

Chicken & White Bean Soup, page 59

Beef and Noodle Soup

Buy the stew meat already cut and there's no chopping needed to make this hearty beef and vegetable soup. Use homemade-style egg noodles to make it especially toothsome.

Prep: 15 minutes **Cook:** 9 hours on low plus 30 minutes on high or 5 hours on high **Makes:** 8 servings

1 pound beef stew meat, cut into ½-inch cubes

1 16-ounce package frozen mixed vegetables

5 cups water

1 14½-ounce can diced tomatoes, undrained

1 8-ounce can tomato sauce

2 bay leaves

2 tablespoons instant beef bouillon granules

1½ teaspoons dried basil, crushed

½ teaspoon dried marjoram, crushed

¼ teaspoon ground black pepper

2 cups uncooked medium noodles

1. In a 4½-, 5- or 6-quart slow cooker combine meat, mixed vegetables, water, undrained tomatoes, tomato sauce, bay leaves, bouillon granules, basil, marjoram, and pepper.

2. Cover; cook on low-heat setting for 9 to 11 hours or on high-heat setting for 4½ to 5½ hours. If using low-heat setting, turn to high-heat setting. Stir in noodles. Cover and cook for 30 minutes more. Remove and discard bay leaves.

Nutrition Facts per serving: **179 calories, 4 g total fat, 36 mg cholesterol, 1,106 mg sodium, 19 g carbohydrate, 17 g protein.**

Beef and Spinach Soup with Rice

This soup is good made with lamb too. Simply substitute the beef with lamb stew meat and exchange the thyme and basil for ¾ teaspoon dried rosemary and ¾ teaspoon dried mint.

Prep: 25 minutes **Cook:** 8 hours on low or 4 hours on high **Makes:** 8 servings

---

1. Trim off fat from meat. In a large skillet brown meat, half at a time, in hot oil. Drain off the fat.

2. In a 3½-, 4-, or 5-quart slow cooker place carrots, squash, onion, garlic, thyme, and basil. Place meat atop vegetables. Pour broth and wine, if desired, over all.

3. Cover; cook on low-heat setting for 8 to 10 hours or on high-heat setting for 4 to 5 hours.

4. Stir in spinach and rice. Cover and let stand 5 to 10 minutes or until rice is tender.

Nutrition Facts per serving: **213 calories, 8 g total fat, 62 mg cholesterol, 693 mg sodium, 11 g carbohydrate, 25 g protein.**

1½ **pounds beef stew meat, cut into 1-inch cubes**
1 **tablespoon cooking oil**
2 **medium carrots, cut into ½-inch slices (1 cup)**
2 **medium yellow summer squash, halved lengthwise, and cut into ½-inch slices (2½ cups)**
1 **cup chopped onion**
1 **clove garlic, minced**
¾ **teaspoon dried thyme, crushed**
¾ **teaspoon dried basil, crushed**
6 **cups beef broth**
¼ **cup dry red or white wine (optional)**
2 **cups chopped fresh spinach**
½ **cup quick-cooking rice**

Beef-Barley Soup

Just a little bit of spaghetti sauce adds a nice tomato flavor and rosy hue to this homey soup.

Prep: 25 minutes **Cook:** 10 hours on low or 4½ hours on high **Makes:** 6 to 8 servings

1½ pounds beef stew meat

1 tablespoon cooking oil

1 cup thinly sliced carrots

1 cup sliced celery

1 medium onion, thinly sliced

½ cup coarsely chopped green
   sweet pepper

¼ cup snipped parsley

4 cups beef broth

1 14½-ounce can tomatoes,
   cut up

1 cup spaghetti sauce

⅔ cup pearl barley

1½ teaspoons dried basil,
   crushed

1 teaspoon salt

¼ teaspoon pepper

1. Cut meat into 1-inch cubes. In a large skillet brown meat, half at a time, in hot oil. Drain well. Meanwhile, in a 3½-, 4-, 5-, or 6-quart slow cooker combine carrots, celery, onion, green sweet pepper, and parsley. Add broth, undrained tomatoes, spaghetti sauce, barley, basil, salt, and pepper. Stir in browned meat.

2. Cover; cook on low-heat setting for 10 to 12 hours or on high-heat setting for 4½ to 5 hours. Skim off fat.

Nutrition Facts per serving: 395 calories, 18 g total fat, 73 mg cholesterol, 1,225 mg sodium, 30 g carbohydrate, 29 g protein.

Italian Wedding Soup

Italian wedding soup gets its name from the marriage of meat and greens. You can use ground beef, pork, or lamb—depending on your personal preferences.

Prep: 20 minutes **Cook:** 8 hours on low or 4 hours on high **Makes:** 6 servings

1. Finely chop three of the cipollini or boiling onions. Combine chopped cipollini or onion, ground beef, minced dried tomatoes, and half the Italian seasoning in a mixing bowl. Divide mixture and roll into 12 balls about an inch in diameter. Brown meatballs in a large, nonstick skillet brushed lightly with cooking oil. Transfer to a 4- or 5-quart slow cooker.

2. Trim fennel and cut into wedges, reserving several of the leafy fronds for garnish, if desired. Place remaining onions, fennel wedges, garlic, broth, remaining Italian seasoning, and pepper in the slow cooker.

3. Cover; cook on low-heat setting for 8 to 10 hours or on high-heat setting for 4 to 5 hours.

4. Gently stir in spinach and orzo; cover and cook 15 minutes more. Serve in deep bowls and top with reserved fennel fronds, if desired.

Nutrition Facts per serving: **172 calories, 6 g total fat, 27 mg cholesterol, 908 mg sodium, 17 g carbohydrate, 13 g protein.**

- **9 cipollini or boiling onions, peeled**
- **12 ounces lean ground beef**
- **2 oil-packed dried tomatoes, minced**
- **1 tablespoon dried Italian seasoning, crushed**
- **1 large fennel bulb**
- **4 cloves garlic, chopped**
- **3 14-ounce cans chicken broth**
- **¼ teaspoon coarsely ground white pepper**
- **5 cups shredded fresh spinach**
- **1½ cups cooked orzo pasta**

Zesty Beef and Vegetable Soup

Hot-style vegetable juice gives this soup a bit of zing. Round out the meal with some warm corn bread.

Prep: 25 minutes   **Cook:** 8 hours on low or 4 hours on high   **Makes:** 6 servings

1 pound ground beef

½ cup chopped onion

2 cloves garlic, minced

2 cups pre-shredded
   coleslaw mix

1 10-ounce package frozen
   whole kernel corn

1 9-ounce package frozen
   cut green beans

4 cups hot-style vegetable
   juice

1 14½-ounce can Italian-style
   stewed tomatoes

2 tablespoons Worcestershire
   sauce

1 teaspoon dried basil,
   crushed

¼ teaspoon pepper

1. In a large skillet cook ground beef, onion, and garlic until meat is brown and onion is tender. Drain off fat.

2. In a 3½-, 4-, or 5-quart slow cooker combine meat mixture, coleslaw mix, frozen corn, frozen beans, vegetable juice, undrained tomatoes, Worcestershire sauce, basil, and pepper.

3. Cover; cook on low-heat setting for 8 to 10 hours or on high-heat setting for 4 to 5 hours.

Nutrition Facts per serving: **269 calories, 10 g total fat, 48 mg cholesterol, 925 mg sodium, 29 g carbohydrate, 19 g protein.**

Beef 'n' Brew Vegetable Soup

A can of ale adds flavor to this beefy soup. Use a lighter beer for just a touch of beer taste; use a dark beer for a more intense taste.

Prep: 20 minutes **Cook:** 10 hours on low or 5 hours on high **Makes:** 6 servings

1. In a 5- or 6-quart slow cooker place onions, carrots, parsnips, garlic, bay leaves, dried thyme (if using), and pepper. Sprinkle with tapioca. Place meat on top of vegetables. Add beef broth and beer.

2. Cover; cook on low-heat setting for 10 to 12 hours or on high-heat setting for 5 to 6 hours. To serve, remove bay leaves; stir in fresh thyme if using.

Nutrition Facts per serving: 354 calories, 9 g total fat, 82 mg cholesterol, 336 mg sodium, 35 g carbohydrate, 31 g protein.

3 medium onions, sliced
1 pound carrots, cut into ½-inch slices
4 parsnips, cut into ½-inch slices
4 cloves garlic, minced
2 bay leaves
1 tablespoon snipped fresh thyme or 1 teaspoon dried thyme, crushed
½ teaspoon pepper
2 tablespoons quick-cooking tapioca
1½ pounds beef stew meat, cut into 1-inch cubes
1 14½-ounce can beef broth
1 12-ounce can beer

Ham and Black-Eyed Pea Soup

Ten minutes of boiling on the stove top gives the black-eyed peas a head start on the rest of the soup ingredients and ensures they'll be tender at serving time.

Prep: 20 minutes **Cook:** 11 hours on low or 4½ hours on high **Makes:** 6 servings

4 cups water

¾ pound dry black-eyed peas
   or navy beans (2 cups)

2 14½-ounce cans reduced-
   sodium chicken broth

1 cup reduced-sodium ham,
   cut into ½-inch pieces

4 medium carrots, sliced
   ½ inch thick (2 cups)

2 stalks celery, sliced (1 cup)

¼ cup dried minced onion

1 teaspoon dried sage,
   crushed

1 teaspoon dried thyme,
   crushed

¼ teaspoon ground red pepper

1½ cups water

1 tablespoon lemon juice

1. Bring 4 cups water and black-eyed peas or navy beans to boiling in a 3-quart saucepan. Boil, uncovered, for 10 minutes. Drain and rinse.

2. In a 4-quart slow cooker combine broth, ham, carrots, celery, onion, sage, thyme, red pepper, and 1½ cups water. Stir in peas or beans.

3. Cover and cook on low-heat setting for 11 to 12 hours or on high-heat setting for 4½ to 5½ hours. To serve, stir in lemon juice.

Nutrition Facts per serving: **251 calories, 3 g total fat, 12 mg cholesterol, 753 mg sodium, 41 g carbohydrate, 19 g protein.**

Calico Ham and Bean Soup

Use a pound of purchased bean mix or a pound of any one kind of bean to make this soup. It won't be "calico," but it will taste just as good. If you like a thicker soup, mash some of the beans before serving.

Prep: 20 minutes   **Cook:** 8 hours on low or 4 hours on high   **Makes:** 8 servings

1. Rinse beans; drain. In a large saucepan combine the beans, peas, and the 6 cups water. Bring to boiling; reduce heat. Simmer, uncovered, for 10 minutes. Drain and rinse beans.

2. Meanwhile, in a 3½-, 4-, or 5-quart slow cooker combine ham, onion, carrot, basil, oregano, ¾ teaspoon salt, ¼ teaspoon pepper, and bay leaves. Stir in drained beans and the remaining 6 cups fresh water.

3. Cover; cook on low-heat setting for 8 to 10 hours or on high-heat setting for 4 to 5 hours. Discard the bay leaves. Season to taste with additional salt and pepper.

Nutrition Facts per serving: **244 calories, 3 g total fat, 11 mg cholesterol, 696 mg sodium, 36 g carbohydrate, 19 g protein.**

½ cup dry navy or Great
    Northern beans
½ cup dry black beans
    or kidney beans
½ cup dry lima beans
½ cup dry garbanzo beans
½ cup dry split peas
6 cups water
2 cups fully cooked ham,
    cut into ½-inch pieces
    (about 10 ounces)
1 cup chopped onion
1 cup chopped carrot
1 teaspoon dried basil, crushed
1 teaspoon dried oregano,
    crushed
¾ teaspoon salt
¼ teaspoon pepper
2 bay leaves
6 cups water
    Salt
    Pepper

Autumn Harvest Soup

If you've only heard about parsnips in the tale "Peter Rabbit," taste what made Mr. MacGregor defend his garden so vigorously. Look for firm, small to medium parsnips that have smooth skin.

Prep: 25 minutes **Cook:** 7 hours on low or 3½ hours on high **Makes:** 4 servings

1 pound boneless pork
  shoulder
2 cups cubed, peeled sweet
  potatoes
2 medium parsnips, peeled
  and cut into ½-inch pieces
  (1¾ cups)
2 small cooking apples, cored
  and cut into ¼-inch slices
  (1¾ cups)
1 medium onion, chopped
¾ teaspoon dried thyme,
  crushed
½ teaspoon dried rosemary,
  crushed
½ teaspoon salt
¼ teaspoon pepper
2 cups apple cider
  or apple juice

1. Trim fat from meat. Cut pork into 1-inch cubes.

2. In a 3½- or 4-quart slow cooker layer potatoes, parsnips, apples, and onion. Sprinkle with thyme, rosemary, salt, and pepper. Add meat. Pour apple cider or juice over all.

3. Cover and cook on low-heat setting for 7 to 8 hours or on high-heat setting for 3½ to 4 hours or until meat and vegetables are tender. Ladle into bowls.

Nutrition Facts per serving: 365 calories, 8 g total fat, 76 mg cholesterol, 392 mg sodium, 37 g carbohydrate, 24 g protein.

Sausage-Sauerkraut Soup

For a garnish that adds both color and flavor to this hearty soup, sprinkle each bowl with a little bit of crumbled crisp-cooked bacon and chopped hard-cooked egg.

Prep: 15 minutes   **Cook:** 10 hours on low or 4½ hours on high   **Makes:** 4 servings

---

1. In a 3½-, 4-, 5-, or 6-quart slow cooker combine chicken, Polish sausage, potato, carrot, onion, and celery. Add mushroom soup, saucrkraut, undrained mushrooms, vinegar, dillweed, and pepper. Stir in chicken broth.

2. Cover; cook on low-heat setting for 10 to 12 hours or on high-heat setting for 4½ to 5½ hours.

Nutrition Facts per serving: **451 calories, 27 g total fat, 91 mg cholesterol, 2,070 mg sodium, 20 g carbohydrate, 31 g protein.**

1½ cups chopped cooked
   chicken
8 ounces smoked Polish
   sausage links, chopped
1 small potato, cut into
   ½-inch pieces (¾ cup)
1 medium carrot, cut into
   ½-inch pieces (½ cup)
½ cup chopped onion
½ cup sliced celery
1 10¾-ounce can condensed
   cream of mushroom soup
1 8-ounce can sauerkraut,
   rinsed and drained
1 4-ounce can mushroom
   stems and pieces
1 tablespoon vinegar
1 teaspoon dried dillweed
¼ teaspoon pepper
2½ cups chicken broth

Sausage-Escarole Soup

If you can't find escarole, substitute spinach, curly endive, or another mildly bitter green.

Prep: 30 minutes **Cook:** 8 hours on low or 4 hours on high **Makes:** 6 servings

1 beaten egg
2 tablespoons milk
¼ cup fine dry bread crumbs
1 pound bulk Italian sausage
 Nonstick spray coating
2 15-ounce cans Great
  Northern beans, drained
2 medium carrots, cut into
  ½-inch pieces
2 medium tomatoes, chopped
½ cup chopped onion
2 cloves garlic, minced
1 teaspoon dried Italian
  seasoning, crushed
½ teaspoon crushed
  red pepper
5 cups chicken broth
4 cups chopped escarole
 Grated Parmesan cheese

1. For meatballs, in a large bowl combine egg, milk, and bread crumbs. Add sausage and mix well. Shape into 1-inch meatballs. Spray a 12-inch skillet with nonstick coating. Add meatballs and brown on all sides over medium heat. Drain meatballs.

2. In a 3½-, 4-, or 5-quart slow cooker place beans, carrots, tomatoes, onion, garlic, Italian seasoning, and red pepper. Add meatballs to cooker. Pour broth over all.

3. Cover; cook on low-heat setting for 8 to 10 hours or on high-heat setting for 4 to 5 hours. Stir in escarole. Ladle into bowls. Sprinkle with grated Parmesan cheese.

Nutrition Facts per serving: 383 calories, 19 g total fat, 83 mg cholesterol, 1,531 mg sodium, 32 g carbohydrate, 28 g protein.

Split Pea and Ham Soup

A little rice gives this beautiful green soup body and texture in each hearty bite.

Prep: 15 minutes   **Cook:** 10 hours on high or 4 hours on low   **Stand:** 5 minutes   **Makes:** 6 servings

1. In a 3½-, 4-, or 5-quart slow cooker combine ham, peas, onion, celery, carrot, parsley, thyme, and pepper. Pour chicken broth and water over all.

2. Cover; cook on low-heat setting for 10 to 12 hours or on high-heat setting for 4 to 5 hours. Stir in rice. Cover; let stand 5 minutes or until rice is tender.

Nutrition Facts per serving: **256 calories, 4 g total fat, 15 mg cholesterol, 1,097 mg sodium, 35 g carbohydrate, 21 g protein.**

2 cups cubed fully cooked ham
1 cup dry split peas
1 cup chopped onion
1 cup chopped celery
  with leaves
1 cup shredded carrot
2 tablespoons snipped
  fresh parsley
½ teaspoon dried thyme,
  crushed
¼ teaspoon pepper
4 cups chicken broth
2 cups water
1 cup quick-cooking rice

Tuscan Sausage and Bean Soup

When you turn on the slow cooker, move the frozen spinach to the refrigerator to thaw.

All you have to do hours later is stir in the spinach and scoop up the soup.

Prep: 25 minutes   **Cook:** 11 hours on low   **Makes:** 4 to 5 servings

1¼ cups dry Great Northern
    beans
4 cups cold water
12 ounces fresh Italian sausage
    links, cut into ½-inch slices
4 cups water
1¾ cups beef broth
½ cup chopped onion
1 clove garlic, minced
½ teaspoon dried Italian
    seasoning, crushed
1 medium yellow summer
    squash or zucchini,
    sliced (2 cups)
1 14½-ounce can Italian-style
    tomatoes, cut up
⅓ cup dry red wine or water
½ of a 10-ounce package
    frozen chopped spinach,
    thawed and well drained
    Grated Parmesan cheese
    (optional)

1. Rinse beans. In a large saucepan or Dutch oven combine beans and 4 cups cold water. Boil, uncovered, for 10 minutes; drain.

2. Meanwhile, in a medium skillet cook Italian sausage until brown. Drain well on paper towels. In a 3½- or 4-quart slow cooker combine the drained beans, 4 cups fresh water, beef broth, onion, garlic, Italian seasoning, cooked and drained Italian sausage, squash or zucchini, undrained tomatoes, and red wine or water. Cook, covered, on low heat setting for 11 to 12 hours or until beans are tender.

3. Just before serving, stir spinach into soup. If desired, sprinkle each serving with Parmesan cheese.

Nutrition Facts per serving: **516 calories, 20 g total fat, 57 mg cholesterol, 1,104 mg sodium, 46 g carbohydrate, 28 g protein.**

Lamb and Barley Soup

Browning the lamb half at a time ensures that each piece will sear nicely and have good flavor. Trying to brown all of the meat at once would result in its stewing in its own juices.

Prep: 25 minutes **Cook:** 8 hours on low or 4 hours high **Makes:** 8 servings

1. In a large skillet brown lamb, half at a time, in hot oil. Drain fat.

2. In a 3½-, 4-, or 5 quart slow cooker place meat, mushrooms, barley, onion, carrot, parsnip, undrained tomatoes, garlic, marjoram, salt, pepper, and bay leaf. Pour beef broth over all.

3. Cover; cook on low-heat setting for 8 to 10 hours or on high-heat setting for 4 to 5 hours. Discard bay leaf.

Nutrition Facts per serving: 255 calories, 12 g total fat, 48 mg cholesterol, 854 mg sodium, 21 g carbohydrate, 17 g protein.

1½ pounds lamb stew meat,
  cut into 1-inch cubes
1 tablespoon cooking oil
2 cups sliced fresh mushrooms
½ cup pearl barley
1 cup chopped onion
1 medium carrot, cut into
  ½-inch pieces
1 large parsnip, peeled and
  cut into ½-inch pieces
1 14½-ounce can Italian-style
  stewed tomatoes
2 cloves garlic, minced
1 teaspoon dried marjoram,
  crushed
½ teaspoon salt
¼ teaspoon pepper
1 bay leaf
5 cups beef broth

Lamb, Lentil, and Onion Soup

Crushing dried herbs before adding them to a recipe releases their fragrance and flavor. Measure out the herb into the palm of your hand and rub it between your fingers as you add it to the cooker.

Prep: 25 minutes **Cook:** 7 hours on low or 3½ hours on high **Makes:** 4 to 5 servings

12 ounces lean boneless
   lamb or beef, cut into
   ½-inch cubes
1 tablespoon cooking oil
1 cup thinly sliced celery
1 cup coarsely chopped carrot
1 cup dry lentils, rinsed
   and drained
1 10½-ounce can condensed
   French onion soup
1 to 1½ teaspoons dried
   thyme, crushed
¼ teaspoon pepper
3¼ cups water

1. In a large skillet brown meat in hot oil. Meanwhile, in a 3½- or 4-quart slow cooker place celery, carrot, and lentils. Top with browned meat.

2. In a large bowl combine soup, thyme, and ¼ teaspoon pepper. Gradually stir in water; add soup mixture to slow cooker. Cover and cook on low-heat setting for 7 to 8 hours or 3½ to 4 hours on high-heat setting.

Nutrition Facts per serving: 376 calories, 10 g total fat, 57 mg cholesterol, 693 mg sodium, 38 g carbohydrate, 33 g protein.

Chicken and White Bean Soup

If you prefer a meatless variety, just omit the chicken from this Northern-Italian-style soup.

Garnish each bowl with a few sprinkles of minced fennel fronds (the leafy top of the bulb).

Prep: 20 minutes **Stand:** 1 hour **Cook:** 8 hours on low or 4 hours on high **Makes:** 4 to 6 servings

1. Rinse beans; drain. In a large saucepan combine beans and the 6 cups water. Bring to boiling; reduce heat. Simmer, uncovered, for 2 minutes. Remove from heat. Cover and let stand for 1 hour. (Or skip the boiling step and soak beans overnight in a covered pan.) Drain and rinse beans.

2. Meanwhile, in a 3½-, 4-, or 5-quart slow cooker combine onion, fennel, carrots, garlic, parsley, thyme, marjoram, and pepper. Place beans atop vegetables. Pour chicken broth over all.

3. Cover; cook on low-heat setting for 8 to 10 hours or on high-heat setting for 4 to 5 hours.

4. If using low-heat setting, turn to high-heat setting. Stir in chicken and undrained tomatoes. Cover and cook for 30 minutes longer or until heated through on high-heat setting.

Nutrition Facts per serving: 471 calories, 13 g total fat, 74 mg cholesterol, 1,250 mg sodium, 46 g carbohydrate, 44 g protein.

- 1 cup dry Great Northern beans
- 6 cups water
- 1 cup chopped onion
- 1 medium fennel bulb, trimmed and cut into ½-inch pieces
- 2 medium carrots, chopped
- 2 cloves garlic, minced
- 2 tablespoons snipped fresh parsley
- 1 teaspoon dried thyme, crushed
- 1 teaspoon dried marjoram, crushed
- ¼ teaspoon pepper
- 4½ cups chicken broth
- 2½ cups chopped cooked chicken
- 1 14½-ounce can stewed tomatoes

Wild Rice and Chicken Soup

To make pre-cooked chicken, place 12 ounces of chicken breasts in a skillet with 1½ cups water. Bring to boiling and reduce heat. Cover and simmer for 12 to 14 minutes or until chicken is no longer pink.

Prep: 15 minutes **Cook:** 6 hours on low or 3 hours on high **Makes:** 8 to 10 servings

1 10¾-ounce can condensed
   cream of mushroom soup
   or cream of chicken soup
2½ cups chopped
   cooked chicken
2 cups sliced fresh
   mushrooms
1 cup coarsely shredded
   carrot
1 cup sliced celery
1 6-ounce package long grain
   and wild rice mix
5 cups chicken broth
5 cups water

1. In a 5- or 6-quart slow cooker combine soup, chicken, mushrooms, carrot, celery, rice, and contents of seasoning packet from rice mix. Gradually stir in broth and water.

2. Cover; cook on low-heat setting for 6 hours or on high-heat setting for 3 hours.

Nutrition Facts per serving: 241 calories, 7 g total fat, 46 mg cholesterol, 1,237 mg sodium, 24 g carbohydrate, 21 g protein.

Deviled Chicken Soup

The word "deviled" refers to a food seasoned with fiery flavorings such as black pepper, hot pepper sauce, or, as in this soup, mustard. Add more or less to your liking.

Prep: 20 minutes **Cook:** 8 hours on low or 4 hours on high **Makes:** 6 servings

1. Cut chicken into bite-size pieces.

2. In a 3½- or 4-quart slow cooker combine the chicken, potato, corn, onion, celery, mustard, pepper, and garlic powder. Pour vegetable juice and chicken broth over all.

3. Cover; cook on low-heat setting for 8 to 10 hours or on high-heat setting for 4 to 5 hours.

Nutrition Facts per serving: **192 calories, 5 g total fat, 36 mg cholesterol, 800 mg sodium, 23 g carbohydrate, 15 g protein.**

1 pound skinless, boneless chicken thighs
1 large red potato, chopped
½ of a 16-ounce package frozen whole kernel corn (1½ cups)
1 medium onion, chopped
½ cup chopped celery
3 tablespoons Dijon-style mustard
¼ teaspoon pepper
⅛ teaspoon garlic powder
2½ cups vegetable juice
1 14½-ounce can reduced-sodium chicken broth

Chicken Tortilla Soup

If you like your soup steaming and spicy hot, top this south-of-the-border bowl with hot pepper cheese.

Prep: 20 minutes **Cook:** 8 hours on low plus 15 minutes on high or 4¼ hours on high **Makes:** 8 servings

1 14½-ounce can diced tomatoes, undrained
1 14-ounce can beef broth
2 cups water
1 8-ounce can tomato sauce
½ cup chopped onion
1 4-ounce can chopped green chile peppers
1 teaspoon ground cumin
1 teaspoon chili powder
1 teaspoon Worcestershire sauce
½ teaspoon garlic powder
1 9-ounce package frozen cooked Southwestern flavor chicken breast strips, thawed
8 to 10 corn tortillas, torn into 1- to 2-inch pieces
3 ounces cheddar cheese or Monterey Jack cheese with jalapeño peppers, shredded (¾ cup)

1. In a 3½- or 4-quart slow cooker combine undrained tomatoes, broth, water, tomato sauce, onion, chile peppers, cumin, chili powder, Worcestershire sauce, and garlic powder.

2. Cover; cook on low-heat setting for 8 to 10 hours or on high-heat setting for 4 to 5 hours. If using low-heat setting, turn to high-heat setting. Stir in chicken strips. Cover and cook for 15 minutes more. Stir in tortillas and serve immediately. Garnish each serving with shredded cheese.

Nutrition Facts per serving: 189 calories, 6 g total fat, 26 mg cholesterol, 615 mg sodium, 22 g carbohydrate, 13 g protein.

Thai Chicken Soup

Lemon grass gives this Asian soup a lemony flavor and fragrance. Look for it in the produce section with the other fresh herbs—it looks like a very large green onion. Use only the fibrous white bulb.

Prep: 20 minutes **Cook:** 6 hours on low or 3 hours on high **Stand:** 5 minutes **Makes:** 6 servings

---

1. In a 3½-, 4-, or 5-quart slow cooker combine the chicken, broth, carrots, onion, ginger, garlic, lemon grass or lemon peel, and crushed red pepper.

2. Cover; cook on low-heat setting for 6 to 7 hours or on high-heat setting for 3 to 3½ hours. If necessary, skim off fat. Stir coconut milk, pepper, mushrooms, and cilantro into chicken mixture. Cover; let stand 5 to 10 minutes. Remove and discard lemon grass (if using). Ladle soup into bowls. Sprinkle peanuts over each serving.

Nutrition Facts per serving: 328 calories, 20 g total fat, 40 mg cholesterol, 764 mg sodium, 15 g carbohydrate, 23 g protein.

1 pound skinless, boneless chicken breasts or thighs, rinsed and cut into ¾-inch pieces

4 cups chicken broth

2 cups bias-sliced carrots

1 large onion, chopped

2 tablespoons grated ginger

3 cloves garlic, minced

2 stalks lemon grass, cut into 1-inch pieces, or 1 teaspoon finely shredded lemon peel

½ teaspoon crushed red pepper

1 15-ounce can unsweetened coconut milk

1 pepper, cut into ½-inch pieces

2 4-ounce cans straw or button mushrooms, drained

¼ cup snipped cilantro

⅓ cup chopped roasted peanuts

Split Pea & Smoked Turkey Soup

Adding dry herbs to a soup as it cooks allows them to fully impart their flavor to the mix; adding fresh herbs right before serving prevents them from losing all of their flavor by getting overcooked.

Prep: 20 minutes   **Cook:** 6 hours on low or 3 hours on high   **Stand:** 10 minutes   **Makes:** 6 to 8 servings

2 cups dry yellow split peas
   (1 pound)
2 cups chopped cooked
   smoked turkey or sliced
   cooked turkey sausage
1½ cups coarsely shredded
   carrots
1 cup chopped chives
1 clove garlic, minced
1 tablespoon snipped fresh
   basil or 1 teaspoon
   dried basil, crushed
1 tablespoon snipped fresh
   oregano or 1 teaspoon
   dried oregano, crushed
5 cups chicken broth
2 cups water
½ cup snipped dried tomatoes
   (not oil-packed)

1. Rinse split peas; drain.

2. In a 3½- or 4-quart slow cooker combine the split peas, turkey or turkey sausage, carrots, chives, garlic, and dried basil and oregano (if using). Pour chicken broth and water over all.

3. Cover; cook on low-heat setting for 6 to 8 hours or on high-heat setting for 3 to 4 hours. Stir in dried tomatoes; cover and let stand for 10 minutes. If using, stir in fresh basil and oregano.

Nutrition Facts per serving: 204 calories, 2 g total fat, 22 mg cholesterol, 1,313 mg sodium, 26 g carbohydrate, 22 g protein.

Asian Turkey and Rice Soup

If your soup-making time will be short in the morning, cut up the turkey and vegetables the night before and store them in the refrigerator in separate plastic bags.

Prep: 25 minutes **Cook:** 8 hours on low or 4 hours on high **Stand:** 5 minutes **Makes:** 6 servings

1. In a 3½- or 4-quart slow cooker place mushrooms, bok choy, onion, and carrots. Add turkey or chicken to cooker. Combine chicken broth, soy sauce, sesame oil (if desired), garlic, and ginger. Pour over vegetables and turkey.

2. Cover and cook on low-heat setting for 8 to 10 hours or on high-heat setting for 4 to 5 hours. Stir in rice. Cover and let stand 5 to 10 minutes. Ladle into bowls.

Nutrition Facts per serving: **186 calories, 1 g total fat, 47 mg cholesterol, 584 mg sodium, 20 g carbohydrate, 24 g protein.**

2 cups sliced fresh mushrooms, such as shiitake or button

1½ cups sliced bok choy

1 medium onion, chopped

2 medium carrots, cut into bite-size strips (1 cup)

1 pound turkey breast tenderloins or skinless, boneless chicken breast halves, cut into 1-inch pieces

2 14½-ounce cans reduced-sodium chicken broth

2 tablespoons reduced-sodium soy sauce

1 tablespoon toasted sesame oil (optional)

4 cloves garlic, minced

2 teaspoons grated fresh ginger

1 cup instant rice

French Onion Soup

Pair this French bistro classic with a leafy green salad, some crusty bread, and a glass of wine.

Prep: 30 minutes **Cook:** 5 hours on low or 2½ hours on high **Makes:** 6 to 8 servings

4 to 6 onions, thinly sliced
    (4 to 6 cups)
1 clove garlic, minced
3 tablespoons margarine
    or butter
3 10½-ounce cans condensed
    beef broth
1 cup water
1½ teaspoons Worcestershire
    sauce
⅛ teaspoon pepper
6 to 8 1-inch slices
    French bread
6 to 8 ¾-ounce slices
    Swiss or Gruyère cheese

1. In a large skillet cook onions and garlic in hot margarine or butter, covered, over medium-low heat about 20 minutes or until tender, stirring occasionally.

2. Transfer onion mixture to a 3½- or 4-quart slow cooker. Add condensed beef broth, water, Worcestershire sauce, and pepper. Cover; cook on low-heat setting for 5 to 10 hours or on high-heat setting for 2½ to 3 hours.

3. Before serving soup, toast bread slices. Then arrange toast slices on a baking sheet and top each with a slice of cheese; broil 3 to 4 inches from the heat for 3 to 4 minutes or until cheese is light brown and bubbly. Ladle soup into bowls; top with toast.

For 5- or 6-quart slow cooker: Use 6 to 8 onions, thinly sliced; 1 clove garlic, minced; ¼ cup margarine or butter; four 10½-ounce cans condensed beef broth; 1½ cups water; 2 teaspoons Worcestershire sauce; ⅛ teaspoon pepper; 10 to 12 slices French bread; and 10 to 12 slices Swiss or Gruyère cheese. Prepare as above. Makes 10 to 12 servings.

Nutrition Facts per serving: **256 calories, 12 g total fat, 19 mg cholesterol, 1,064 mg sodium, 21 g carbohydrate, 15 g protein.**

Tomato-Rice Soup with Pesto

Look for prepared pesto on the grocery shelf or in the refrigerator section near the fresh pastas.

Prep: 15 minutes   **Cook:** 8 hours on low or 4 hours on high   **Stand:** 6 minutes   **Makes:** 6 servings

1. In a 3½- or 4-quart slow cooker combine onion, carrot, celery, undrained tomatoes, tomato paste, oregano, thyme, and pepper. Stir in water and chicken or vegetable broth.

2. Cover; cook on low-heat setting for 8 to 10 hours or on high-heat setting for 4 to 5 hours.

3. Stir in rice. Cover; let stand 6 to 7 minutes or until rice is tender. Stir in pesto. Ladle soup into bowls. Sprinkle with grated Parmesan cheese, if desired.

Nutrition Facts per serving: **229 calories, 8 g total fat, 2 mg cholesterol, 876 mg sodium, 33 g carbohydrate, 7 g protein.**

1 cup chopped onion
1 cup shredded carrot
3 stalks celery with leaves, chopped
1 14½-ounce can Italian-style stewed tomatoes
1 6-ounce can Italian-style tomato paste
½ teaspoon dried oregano, crushed
¼ teaspoon dried thyme, crushed
¼ teaspoon pepper
2 cups water
2 cups chicken broth or vegetable broth
1 cup quick-cooking rice
¼ cup pesto
Grated Parmesan cheese (optional)

Hot-and-Sour Soup

Use a whisk to stir the soup as you add the beaten egg to ensure it forms strands of cooked egg.

Prep: 20 minutes **Cook:** 9 hours 50 minutes on low or 3 hours 50 minutes on high **Makes:** 8 servings

4 cups chicken broth

1 8-ounce can bamboo shoots, drained

1 8-ounce can sliced water chestnuts, drained

1 6-ounce can sliced mushrooms, drained

3 tablespoons quick-cooking tapioca

3 tablespoons rice wine vinegar or vinegar

1 tablespoon soy sauce

1 teaspoon sugar

½ teaspoon pepper

1 8-ounce package frozen peeled and deveined shrimp

4 ounces firm tofu, (fresh bean curd), drained and cubed

1 beaten egg

2 tablespoons snipped parsley or fresh coriander

1. In a 3½- or 4-quart slow cooker combine broth, bamboo shoots, water chestnuts, mushrooms, tapioca, vinegar, soy sauce, sugar, and pepper. Cover; cook on low-heat setting for 9 to 11 hours or on high-heat setting for 3 to 4 hours. Add shrimp and tofu. Cover; cook on low- or high-heat setting for 50 minutes more.

2. Pour the beaten egg slowly into the soup in a thin stream. Stir the soup gently so the egg forms fine shreds instead of clumps. Top with parsley.

Nutrition Facts per serving: **114 calories, 2 g total fat, 83 mg cholesterol, 664 mg sodium, 9 g carbohydrate, 13 g protein.**

Black Bean Soup

If you soak the dry beans in water overnight, you can skip the pre-cooking step.

Prep: 25 minutes   **Stand:** 1 hour   **Cook:** 12 hours on low or 6 hours on high   **Makes:** 6 to 8 servings

---

1. Rinse beans; place in a large saucepan. Add 6 cups cold water. Bring to boiling; reduce heat. Simmer, uncovered, for 10 minutes. Remove from heat. Cover and let stand for 1 hour. Drain and rinse beans.

2. In a 4-, 5-, or 5½-quart slow cooker combine the beans, carrot, onion, celery, vegetable bouillon cubes, cumin, coriander, savory, chili powder, pepper, garlic, and 6 cups water. Stir to combine.

3. Cover; cook on low-heat setting for 12 to 14 hours or on high-heat setting for 6 to 7 hours. Mash beans slightly. Stir in half-and-half.

Nutrition Facts per serving: 346 calories, 6 g total fat, 15 mg cholesterol, 706 mg sodium, 56 g carbohydrate, 19 g protein.

1 pound dry black beans
    (about 2½ cups)
6 cups cold water
1 cup coarsely chopped carrot
1 cup coarsely chopped onion
1 cup coarsely chopped celery
2 large vegetable
    bouillon cubes
2 teaspoons ground cumin
2 teaspoons ground coriander
2 teaspoons dried savory,
    crushed
1 teaspoon chili powder
½ teaspoon pepper
2 cloves garlic, minced
6 cups water
1 cup half-and-half
    or light cream

Minestrone

Accompany this vegetable-rich soup with warm herbed bread sticks or focaccia.

Prep: 15 minutes   **Cook:** 10 hours on low or 5 hours on high   **Makes:** 8 servings

1 15-ounce can navy beans,
   drained
1 cup shredded cabbage
½ cup sliced carrot
½ cup sliced celery
½ cup chopped onion
2 tablespoons snipped parsley
1 clove garlic, minced
1 14½-ounce can tomatoes,
   cut up
1 10½-ounce can condensed
   beef broth
1½ teaspoons dried basil,
   crushed
¼ teaspoon dried oregano,
   crushed
3 cups water
¼ teaspoon pepper
1 9-ounce package frozen
   Italian green beans
2 ounces spaghetti, broken
   into 1-inch pieces (½ cup)
Grated Parmesan cheese

1. In a 3½-, 4-, 5-, or 6-quart slow cooker place navy beans, cabbage, carrot, celery, onion, parsley, and garlic. Stir in undrained tomatoes, beef broth, basil, oregano, 3 cups water, and ¼ teaspoon pepper. Cover; cook on low-heat setting for 9 to 11 hours or on high-heat setting for 4 to 5 hours.

2. Rinse green beans under running water to separate. Stir green beans and spaghetti into soup mixture. Cover; cook on low-heat or high-heat setting for 1 hour more. Ladle into soup bowls. Sprinkle each serving with Parmesan cheese.

Nutrition Facts per serving: **155 calories, 2 g total fat, 4 mg cholesterol, 630 mg sodium, 25 g carbohydrate, 10 g protein.**

Winter Minestrone

Give this classic a pronounced Italian accent by using fresh escarole, a slightly bitter green that is much beloved by Southern Italians and widely available during the cold months.

Prep: 25 minutes **Cook:** 8 hours on low or 4 hours on high **Makes:** 8 servings

1. In a large skillet cook the sausage until brown; drain well.

2. In a 5- to 6-quart slow cooker place squash, potatoes, fennel, onion, garlic, beans, and sage. Top with sausage. Pour broth and wine over all.

3. Cover and cook on low-heat setting for 8 to 10 hours or on high-heat setting for 4 to 5 hours. Stir in kale or spinach. Cover and cook 5 minutes more.

Nutrition Facts per serving: 315 calories, 14 g total fat, 38 mg cholesterol, 933 mg sodium, 27 g carbohydrate, 16 g protein.

1 pound uncooked Italian
  or pork sausage links,
  cut into ¾-inch slices
2½ cups peeled winter squash,
  such as butternut squash,
  cut into 1-inch cubes
1½ cups cubed potatoes
2 medium fennel bulbs,
  trimmed and cut into
  1-inch pieces
1 large onion, chopped
2 cloves garlic, minced
1 15-ounce can red kidney
  beans, rinsed and drained
½ teaspoon dried sage, crushed
4 cups chicken broth
  or vegetable broth
1 cup dry white wine
4 cups chopped kale
  or fresh spinach
  or fresh escarole

Five-Bean Soup

With only one onion to chop, a hearty, delicious homemade soup doesn't get any easier than this one.

Prep: 15 minutes **Cook:** 10 hours on low or 5 hours on high **Makes:** 8 servings

1 15½-ounce can red kidney
    beans
1 15-ounce can garbanzo
    beans
1 15-ounce can navy beans
1 8½-ounce can lima beans
1 9-ounce package frozen
    cut green beans
1 cup chopped onion
1 4-ounce can diced green
    chile peppers, drained
4 teaspoons chili powder
1½ teaspoons dried basil,
    crushed
½ teaspoon dried oregano,
    crushed
¼ teaspoon bottled hot
    pepper sauce
2½ cups beef broth
1 12-ounce can beer
1 cup shredded cheddar
    cheese (4 ounces)

1. Drain kidney beans, garbanzo beans, navy beans, and lima beans. In a 3½-, 4-, 5-, or 6-quart slow cooker combine drained beans, frozen green beans, chopped onion, chile peppers, chili powder, basil, oregano, and hot pepper sauce. Stir in beef broth and beer.

2. Cover; cook on low-heat setting for 10 to 12 hours or on high-heat setting for 5 to 6 hours. Ladle into soup bowls. Top each serving with shredded cheese.

Nutrition Facts per serving: **301 calories, 6 g total fat, 15 mg cholesterol, 930 mg sodium, 44 g carbohydrate, 19 g protein.**

Potato and Leek Soup

A package of frozen hash browns makes this creamy potato soup a no-peel proposition.

Prep: 15 minutes   **Cook:** 7 hours on low plus 15 minutes on high or 3¾ hours on high   **Makes:** 10 to 12 servings

1. In a 3½- or 4-quart slow cooker stir water into white sauce mix until mixture is smooth. Stir in frozen potatoes, the 3 leeks, Canadian-style bacon or ham, evaporated milk, and dillweed.

2. Cover and cook on low-heat setting for 7 to 9 hours or on high-heat setting for 3½ to 4½ hours.

3. If using low-heat setting, turn to high-heat setting. In a medium bowl stir about 2 cups of the hot potato mixture into the sour cream. Return sour cream mixture to cooker. Cover and cook about 15 minutes more on high-heat setting or until heated through. Ladle into bowls. Sprinkle with parsley or additional sliced leek, if desired.

Nutrition Facts per serving: **212 calories, 10 g total fat, 28 mg cholesterol, 476 mg sodium, 23 g carbohydrate, 8 g protein.**

3 cups water
1 1.8-ounce envelope white sauce mix
1 28-ounce package frozen loose-pack diced hash brown potatoes with onion and peppers
3 medium leeks, sliced (about 1 cup total)
1 cup diced Canadian-style bacon or cooked ham
1 12-ounce can evaporated milk
½ teaspoon dried dillweed
1 8-ounce carton dairy sour cream
Snipped fresh parsley or sliced leek (optional)

Southwest Vegetable Soup

Pump up the flavor of this soup with Mexican-style stewed tomatoes. Serve it with warm flour tortillas.

Prep: 15 minutes **Cook:** 7 hours on low or 3½ hours on high **Makes:** 6 to 8 servings

2 14½-ounce cans stewed tomatoes

1 15-ounce can black beans, rinsed and drained

1 cup chopped celery

1 cup water

1 8-ounce can whole kernel corn, drained

½ large green sweet pepper, chopped (¾ cup)

½ large onion, chopped (½ cup)

¼ cup vegetable soup mix

½ fresh jalapeño pepper, seeded and finely chopped

½ teaspoon dried cilantro, crushed

½ teaspoon garlic powder

½ teaspoon pepper

¼ teaspoon dried basil, crushed

¼ teaspoon chili powder

1. In a 3½- or 4-quart slow cooker combine all ingredients. Cover and cook on low-heat setting for 7 to 8 hours or on high-heat setting for 3½ to 4 hours.

Nutrition Facts per serving: 209 calories, 2 g total fat, 0 mg cholesterol, 1,288 mg sodium, 44 g carbohydrate, 11 g protein.

Velvety Pumpkin Bisque

Creamy and elegant, this beautiful golden soup is just the thing to start off a holiday dinner in style.

Prep: 15 minutes **Cook:** 7 hours on low or 3½ hours on high **Makes:** 12 to 14 servings

1. In a 3½-, 4-, or 5-quart slow cooker combine pumpkin, chicken broth, onion, celery, brown sugar, pumpkin pie spice, salt, and pepper.

2. Cover; cook on low-heat setting for 7 to 8 hours or on high-heat setting for 3½ to 4 hours. Stir in half-and-half and butter. Ladle into bowls.

Nutrition Facts per serving: **128** calories, 7 g total fat, 20 mg cholesterol, 402 mg sodium, 13 g carbohydrate, 4 g protein.

3 15-ounce cans pumpkin
2 14-ounce cans chicken broth
½ cup finely chopped onion
½ cup finely chopped celery
2 tablespoons brown sugar
1 tablespoon pumpkin
   pie spice
¾ teaspoon salt
¼ teaspoon pepper
2 cups half-and-half
   or light cream
2 tablespoons butter

Double-Bean Soup with Cornmeal Dumplings

You won't miss the meat in this chunky vegetable-bean soup that's topped with a crown of puffy, tender cornmeal dumplings.

Prep: 15 minutes   **Cook:** 10½ hours on low   **Makes:** 6 servings

3 cups water
1 15-ounce can red kidney beans, rinsed and drained
1 15-ounce can black beans, pinto beans, or Great Northern beans, rinsed and drained
1 14½-ounce can Mexican-style stewed tomatoes
1 10-ounce package frozen whole kernel corn
1 cup sliced carrot
1 cup chopped onion
1 4-ounce can diced green chile peppers
2 tablespoons instant beef or chicken bouillon granules
1 to 2 teaspoons chili powder
2 cloves garlic, minced
⅓ cup all-purpose flour
¼ cup yellow cornmeal
1 teaspoon baking powder
Dash salt
Dash pepper
1 beaten egg white
2 tablespoons milk
1 tablespoon cooking oil

1. In a 3½- or 4-quart slow cooker combine water, beans, undrained tomatoes, corn, carrot, onion, undrained chile peppers, bouillon granules, chili powder, and garlic. Cover and cook on low-heat setting for 10 to 12 hours.

2. In a medium mixing bowl stir together flour, cornmeal, baking powder, salt, and pepper. In a small mixing bowl combine egg white, milk, and oil. Add to flour mixture; stir with a fork just until combined. Drop dumpling mixture into 6 mounds atop the bubbling soup. Cover and cook for 30 minutes more. (Do not lift lid while dumplings are cooking.)

Nutrition Facts per serving: 270 calories, 3 g total fat, 1 mg cholesterol, 1,593 mg sodium, 54 g carbohydrate, 15 g protein.

Potato-Cheese Soup

Mashing a few of the potatoes right before serving gives this popular spud soup great body.

Prep: 15 minutes **Cook:** 10 hours on low or 4½ hours on high **Makes:** 6 to 8 servings

1. In a 3½- or 4-quart slow cooker combine potatoes, water, onion, bouillon granules, and pepper. Cover; cook on low-heat setting for 9 to 11 hours or on high-heat setting 4 to 4½ hours.

2. Stir cheese and milk into soup. Cover; cook on low-heat setting for 1 hour more or on high-heat setting for 30 minutes more. Mash potatoes slightly.

For 5- or 6-quart slow cooker: Use 8 medium potatoes, peeled and chopped; 4 cups water; ¾ cup chopped onion; 1 tablespoon instant chicken bouillon granules; ¼ teaspoon pepper; 2 cups shredded American cheese (8 ounces); and one 12-ounce can evaporated milk plus one 5-ounce can evaporated milk. Prepare as above. Makes 9 to 12 servings.

Nutrition Facts per serving: **308 calories, 13 g total fat, 43 mg cholesterol, 765 mg sodium, 35 g carbohydrate, 14 g protein.**

6 medium potatoes, peeled and chopped (6 cups)

2½ cups water

½ cup chopped onion

2 teaspoons instant chicken bouillon granules

¼ teaspoon pepper

1½ cups shredded American cheese (6 ounces)

1 12-ounce can evaporated milk (1½ cups)

Vegetarian Lentil Soup

Lentils are one of the few legumes that don't require long cooking times. Here, they simply benefit from it when combined with a medley of vegetables and seasonings.

Prep: 15 minutes **Cook:** 12 hours on low or 5 hours on high **Makes:** 6 servings

1 cup dry lentils
1 cup chopped carrot
1 cup chopped celery
1 cup chopped onion
2 cloves garlic, minced
½ teaspoon dried basil, crushed
½ teaspoon dried oregano, crushed
¼ teaspoon dried thyme, crushed
1 bay leaf
2 14½-ounce cans vegetable broth or chicken broth (3½ cups)
1½ cups water
1 14½-ounce can Italian-style stewed tomatoes
¼ cup snipped fresh parsley
2 tablespoons cider vinegar (optional)

1. Rinse lentils. In a 3½-, 4-, or 5-quart slow cooker place lentils, carrot, celery, onion, garlic, basil, oregano, thyme, and bay leaf. Stir in vegetable or chicken broth, water, and tomatoes.

2. Cover; cook on low-heat setting for 12 hours or on high-heat setting for 5 to 6 hours. Discard bay leaf. Stir in parsley and vinegar (if desired).

Nutrition Facts per serving: **185 calories, 1 g total fat, 1 mg cholesterol, 725 mg sodium, 32 g carbohydrate, 13 g protein.**

Cheesy Vegetable Soup

Even kids will eat their veggies when they come cloaked in a creamy, cheesy bowlful of soup.

Serve it with fresh fruit and corn bread.

Prep: 15 minutes **Cook:** 10½ hours on low plus 30 minutes on high or 4½ hours on high **Makes:** 4 servings

1. In a 3½-, 4-, or 5-quart slow cooker combine corn, potatoes, carrot, onion, celery seeds, and pepper. Add vegetable or chicken broth.

2. Cover; cook on low-heat setting for 10 to 11 hours or on high-heat setting for 4 to 4½ hours.

3. If using low-heat setting, turn to high-heat setting. Stir cheese into hot soup. Cover and cook on high-heat setting 30 to 60 minutes longer or until cheese is melted.

Nutrition Facts per serving: 291 calories, 11 g total fat, 25 mg cholesterol, 1,575 mg sodium, 38 g carbohydrate, 14 g protein.

1 16½-ounce can
    cream-style corn
1 cup chopped, peeled
    potatoes
½ cup shredded carrot
½ cup chopped onion
½ teaspoon celery seeds
¼ teaspoon pepper
2 14½-ounce cans vegetable
    broth or chicken broth
    (3½ cups)
1½ cups shredded American
    cheese (6 ounces)

Vegetable Barley Soup

Light and fresh, this soup is terrific when paired with a sandwich for a healthful and satisfying lunch.

Prep: 20 minutes **Cook:** 9 hours on low or 4½ hours on high **Makes:** 5 servings

3 cups water

1 14½-ounce can diced
    tomatoes

1 10-oz. package frozen mixed
    vegetables

1 medium zucchini, quartered
    lengthwise and sliced

2 stalks celery, chopped
    (1 cup)

2 medium carrots, chopped
    (1 cup)

1 medium onion, chopped
    (½ cup)

½ of an 8-ounce can tomato
    sauce (about ½ cup)

⅓ cup regular barley

2 vegetable bouillon cubes
    or 4 teaspoons instant
    chicken bouillon granules

½ teaspoon dried basil,
    crushed

¼ teaspoon dried oregano,
    crushed

    Dash ground red pepper

1. In a 3½- or 4-quart slow cooker combine all ingredients. Cover; cook on low-heat setting for 9 to 11 hours or cook on high-heat setting for 4½ to 5½ hours.

Nutrition Facts per serving: **134 calories, 1 g total fat, 0 mg cholesterol, 702 mg sodium, 29 g carbohydrate, 5 g protein.**

Savory Spinach Soup

Stirring the fresh spinach in right before serving ensures that it will be tender, flavorful, and a beautiful bright green color that's enticing to eat.

Prep: 15 minutes **Cook:** 5 hours on low or 2½ hours on high **Makes:** 6 servings

1. In a 3½- or 4-quart slow cooker place onion, garlic, tomato puree, drained beans, rice, vegetable broth, basil, salt, and pepper.

2. Cover; cook on low-heat setting for 5 to 7 hours or on high-heat setting for 2½ to 3½ hours. Stir in spinach or kale. To serve, ladle into bowls and top with Parmesan.

Nutrition Facts per serving: 150 calories, 3 g total fat, 4 mg cholesterol, 1,137 mg sodium, 31 g carbohydrate, 9 g protein.

½ cup finely chopped onion

2 cloves garlic, minced

1 15-ounce can tomato puree

1 15-ounce can white or
   Great Northern beans,
   rinsed and drained

½ cup dry converted rice

3 14-ounce cans vegetable
   broth

1 teaspoon dried basil, crushed

¼ teaspoon salt

¼ teaspoon pepper

8 cups coarsely chopped fresh
   spinach or kale leaves
   (about ½ pound)
   Finely shredded Parmesan
   cheese

Spicy Pumpkin Soup

Put this warming soup on to simmer on a chilly autumn day. Top it with crunchy pumpkin seeds (pepitas), which can be found in large supermarkets, health foods stores, or Hispanic markets.

Prep: 10 minutes **Cook:** 6 hours on low or 3 hours on high **Makes:** 6 to 8 servings

1 16-ounce can pumpkin
1 cup chopped celery
½ cup chopped carrot
½ cup chopped onion
½ teaspoon salt
½ teaspoon dried oregano, crushed
½ teaspoon dried rosemary, crushed
¼ teaspoon ground red pepper
4 cups vegetable broth or chicken broth
2 medium tomatoes, peeled and chopped, or one 8-ounce can tomatoes, cut up
Dairy sour cream or plain yogurt (optional)
Shelled pumpkin or sunflower seeds (optional)

1. In a 3½- or 4-quart slow cooker place pumpkin, celery, carrot, onion, salt, oregano, rosemary, and ground red pepper. Gradually stir in vegetable or chicken broth.

2. Cover; cook on low-heat setting for 6 to 8 hours or on high-heat setting for 3 to 4 hours. Stir in chopped tomatoes or undrained canned tomatoes. Ladle into bowls. Add a tablespoon of sour cream and sprinkle with seeds, if desired.

Nutrition Facts per serving: **56 calories, 1 g total fat, 0 mg cholesterol, 918 mg sodium, 15 g carbohydrate, 2 g protein.**

Dilled Barley Vegetable Soup

Dill gives this soup a taste of summer. Serve it with drop biscuits, and for dessert serve frozen yogurt.

Prep: 10 minutes **Cook:** 8 hours on low or 4 hours on high **Makes:** 6 servings

1. In a 3½-, 4-, or 5-quart slow cooker place beans, corn, barley, undrained tomatoes, mushrooms, onion, carrot, celery, garlic, dillweed, pepper, and bay leaf. Pour broth over all.

2. Cover; cook on low-heat setting for 8 to 10 hours or on high-heat setting for 4 to 5 hours.

3. Discard bay leaf.

Nutrition Facts per serving: **191** calories, **2** g total fat, **0** mg cholesterol, **1,111** mg sodium, **45** g carbohydrate, **10** g protein.

1 15-ounce can red beans, drained
1 10-ounce package frozen whole kernel corn
½ cup medium pearl barley
1 14½-ounce can stewed tomatoes
2 cups sliced fresh mushrooms
1 cup chopped onion
1 medium carrot, coarsely chopped
1 stalk celery, coarsely chopped
3 cloves garlic, minced
2 teaspoons dried dillweed
¼ teaspoon pepper
1 bay leaf
5 cups vegetable broth or chicken broth

Creamy Clam Chowder

Can't keep your chowders straight? This creamy bacon-topped version is the one that's usually referred to as New-England style.

Prep: 20 minutes **Cook:** 8 hours on low plus 15 minutes on high or 4¼ hours on high **Makes:** 6 to 8 servings

2 6½-ounce cans minced
  clams
2 cups peeled potatoes,
  cut into ½-inch cubes
1 cup finely chopped onion
1 cup chopped celery
½ cup shredded carrot
1 teaspoon sugar
¼ teaspoon salt
¼ teaspoon pepper
2 10¾-ounce cans condensed
  cream of potato soup
2 cups water
1 cup nonfat dry milk powder
⅓ cup all-purpose flour
1 cup cold water
4 slices bacon, crisp-cooked,
  drained, and crumbled
  Paprika

1. Drain clams, reserving liquid. Cover clams; chill.

2. In a 3½-, 4-, or 5-quart slow cooker combine reserved clam liquid, potatoes, onion, celery, carrot, sugar, salt, and pepper. Stir in potato soup and 2 cups water.

3. Cover; cook on low-heat setting for 8 to 10 hours or on high-heat setting for 4 to 5 hours.

4. If using low-heat setting, turn to high-heat setting. In a medium bowl combine nonfat dry milk powder and flour. Gradually whisk in 1 cup cold water; stir into soup. Cover; cook on high-heat setting 10 to 15 minutes or until thickened.

5. Stir in clams. Cover; cook 5 minutes more. Ladle soup into bowls. Sprinkle each serving with crumbled bacon and paprika.

Nutrition Facts per serving: **268 calories, 5 g total fat, 49 mg cholesterol, 735 mg sodium, 43 g carbohydrate, 14 g protein.**

Manhattan Clam Chowder

It turns out saving time is good for you: Don't peel the nutrient-rich potatoes.

Simply scrub the skins well, then cut the potatoes into cubes.

Prep: 15 minutes **Cook:** 8 hours on low plus 5 minutes on high or 4 hours on high **Makes:** 6 servings

---

1. Drain clams, reserving liquid. Cover clams; chill.

2. In a 3½- or 4-quart slow cooker combine reserved clam liquid, potatoes, onion, celery, green sweet pepper, undrained tomatoes, tomato juice or vegetable juice, salt, thyme, and bay leaf.

3. Cover; cook on low-heat setting for 8 to 10 hours or on high-heat setting for 4 to 5 hours.

4. If using low-heat setting, turn to high-heat setting. Stir in clams. Cover and cook on high-heat setting 5 minutes. Discard bay leaf. Ladle soup into bowls. Sprinkle each serving with crumbled bacon.

Nutrition Facts per serving: **146 calories, 3 g total fat, 42 mg cholesterol, 761 mg sodium, 24 g carbohydrate, 9 g protein.**

2 6½-ounce cans minced clams
2 cups potatoes, cut into
  ½-inch cubes
1 cup chopped onion
1 cup chopped celery
  with leaves
½ cup chopped green sweet
  pepper
1 14½-ounce can Italian-style
  stewed tomatoes
1½ cups hot-style tomato juice
  or hot-style vegetable juice
½ teaspoon salt
½ teaspoon dried thyme,
  crushed
1 bay leaf
4 slices bacon, crisp-cooked,
  drained, and crumbled

Corn and Sausage Chowder

A fresh chive garnish adds color and a little something extra to this sunny golden soup.

Prep: 10 minutes **Cook:** 8 hours on low or 4 hours on high **Makes:** 6 servings

1 pound fully cooked smoked
   turkey sausage, halved
   lengthwise and cut into
   ½-inch-thick slices
3 cups loose-pack frozen hash
   brown potatoes with onions
   and peppers
1 medium carrot, coarsely
   chopped
1 stalk celery, coarsely
   chopped
2 10¾-ounce cans condensed
   golden corn soup
2½ cups water
   Snipped fresh chives
   or parsley

1. In a 3½-, 4-, or 5-quart slow cooker place sausage, frozen hash brown potatoes, carrot, and celery. In a bowl combine soup and water. Add to cooker.

2. Cover; cook on low-heat setting for 8 to 10 hours or on high-heat setting for 4 to 5 hours. Ladle into bowls. Sprinkle with chives or parsley.

Nutrition Facts per serving: **275 calories, 8 g total fat, 52 mg cholesterol, 668 mg sodium, 32 g carbohydrate, 16 g protein.**

Brunswick Fish Chowder

Although it's not recommended that frozen meat or poultry be used in the slow cooker, using partially frozen fish keeps the delicate flesh from overcooking.

Prep: 20 minutes **Cook:** 7 hours on low or 3½ hours on high **Makes:** 6 servings

1. Let fish stand at room temperature while preparing all of the other ingredients.

2. In a 3½-, 4-, or 5-quart slow cooker combine potatoes, onion, garlic, soup, frozen corn, frozen lima beans, chicken broth, white wine or water, lemon-pepper seasoning, and bay leaf. Halve the fillets crosswise; place frozen fish fillet halves in the cooker.

3. Cover; cook on low-heat setting for 7 to 8 hours or on high-heat setting for 3½ to 4 hours.

4. Discard bay leaf. Break fish into bite-size chunks with a fork. Stir in undrained tomatoes and dry milk powder.

Nutrition Facts per serving: 300 calories, 4 g total fat, 37 mg cholesterol, 1,058 mg sodium, 44 g carbohydrate, 23 g protein.

1 pound frozen cod
  or whiting fillets
2 medium potatoes,
  finely chopped
1 cup chopped onion
2 cloves garlic, minced
1 10¾-ounce can condensed
  cream of celery soup
1 10-ounce package frozen
  whole kernel corn
1 10-ounce package frozen
  baby lima beans
1½ cups chicken broth
⅓ cup dry white wine or water
1 teaspoon lemon-pepper
  seasoning
1 bay leaf
1 14½-ounce can stewed
  tomatoes
⅓ cup nonfat dry milk powder

Mexican Chicken Chowder

Stirring a little hot soup into the sour cream before adding it to the big pot keeps it from curdling.

Prep: 15 minutes **Cook:** 8 hours on low or 4 hours on high **Stand:** 5 minutes **Makes:** 6 servings

2½ cups chopped cooked chicken

1 11-ounce can whole kernel corn with sweet peppers, drained

1 10¾-ounce can condensed cream of potato soup

1 4-ounce can diced green chile peppers

2 tablespoons snipped fresh cilantro

1 1¼-ounce envelope taco seasoning mix

3 cups chicken broth

1 8-ounce carton dairy sour cream

½ of an 8-ounce package cheese spread with jalapeño peppers

1. In a 3½- or 4-quart slow cooker combine chicken, corn, soup, undrained chile peppers, cilantro, and taco seasoning mix. Stir in chicken broth.

2. Cover; cook on low-heat setting for 8 to 10 hours or on high-heat setting for 4 to 5 hours.

3. Stir about 1 cup of the hot soup into sour cream. Stir sour cream mixture and cheese into the mixture in slow cooker; cover and let stand 5 minutes. Stir until combined.

Nutrition Facts per serving: **351 calories, 20 g total fat, 80 mg cholesterol, 1,986 mg sodium, 20 g carbohydrate, 26 g protein.**

Classic Chili

Have some friends over to watch the big game—and enjoy a hearty bowl of chili slowly simmered in an unwatched pot, allowing you to play host rather than kitchen crew.

Prep: 20 minutes **Cook:** 8 hours on low or 4 hours on high **Makes:** 4 servings

1. In a large saucepan cook ground beef, onion, sweet pepper, and garlic until meat is brown and onion is tender. Drain fat.

2. In a 3½- or 4-quart slow cooker combine meat mixture, undrained tomatoes, beans, tomato sauce, chili powder, basil, and pepper. Cover; cook on low-heat setting for 8 to 10 hours on high-heat setting for 4 to 5 hours.

Nutrition Facts per serving: 308 calories, 11 g total fat, 53 mg cholesterol, 755 mg sodium, 31 g carbohydrate, 26 g protein.

12 ounces ground beef

 1 cup chopped onion (1 large)

½ cup chopped green
    sweet pepper

 2 cloves garlic, minced

 1 14½-ounce can tomatoes,
    cut up

 1 15-ounce can dark red kidney
    beans, rinsed and drained

 1 8-ounce can tomato sauce

 2 to 3 teaspoons chili powder

½ teaspoon dried basil, crushed

¼ teaspoon pepper

Old-Fashioned Beef Stew

Beef and vegetables in a rich broth make this a perennial favorite.

Prep: 25 minutes **Cook:** 10 hours on low or 5 hours on high **Makes:** 4 to 6 servings

   2 tablespoons all-purpose flour
   1 pound beef or pork
       stew meat, cut into
       ¾-inch cubes
   2 tablespoons cooking oil
2½ cups cubed potatoes
   1 cup frozen cut green beans
   1 cup frozen whole kernel corn
   1 cup sliced carrot
   1 medium onion, cut into
       thin wedges
   2 teaspoons instant beef
       bouillon granules
   2 teaspoons Worcestershire
       sauce
   1 teaspoon dried oregano,
       crushed
   ½ teaspoon dried marjoram
       or basil, crushed
   ¼ teaspoon pepper
   1 bay leaf
2½ cups vegetable juice or
       hot-style vegetable juice

1. Place flour in a plastic bag. Add meat cubes and shake until meat is coated with flour. In a large skillet brown half of the meat in 1 tablespoon of the hot oil, turning to brown evenly. Brown remaining meat in remaining oil. Drain off fat.

2. In a 3½- or 4-quart slow cooker layer potatoes, green beans, corn, carrot, and onion. Add meat. Add bouillon granules, Worcestershire sauce, oregano, marjoram, pepper, and bay leaf. Pour vegetable juice over all.

3. Cover and cook on low-heat setting for 10 to 12 hours or on high-heat setting for 5 to 6 hours or until meat and vegetables are tender. Discard bay leaf. Ladle into bowls.

Nutrition Facts per serving: **525 calories, 28 g total fat, 77 mg cholesterol, 953 mg sodium, 42 g carbohydrate, 27 g protein.**

Beef and Fresh Mushroom Stew

A mushroom medley makes this sherried soup extra-special. Be sure to remove and discard the tough stems before slicing the caps of shiitake mushrooms.

Prep: 20 minutes **Cook:** 8 hours on low or 4 hours on high **Makes:** 6 servings

---

1. In a 4-, 5-, or 6-quart slow cooker place mushrooms, carrots, celery, and rice mix with seasoning packet. Place meat on top of vegetables. Pour broth and sherry over all.

2. Cover and cook on low-heat setting for 8 to 10 hours or on high-heat setting for 4 to 5 hours.

Nutrition Facts per serving: **279 calories, 5 g total fat, 43 mg cholesterol, 1,394 mg sodium, 30 g carbohydrate, 24 g protein.**

4 cups sliced assorted fresh
  mushrooms, such as button,
  crimini, and shiitake
3 medium carrots, cut into
  ½-inch slices (1½ cups)
1 cup sliced celery
1 6-ounce package long grain
  and wild rice mix
1 pound beef stew meat,
  cut into 1-inch cubes
6 cups beef broth
½ cup dry sherry

Tex-Mex Chili

If you like your chili hot, add a minced jalapeño or two and use hot-style vegetable juice.

Prep: 15 minutes   **Cook:** 8 hours on low or 4 hours on high   **Makes:** 4 to 6 servings

1 pound ground beef
  or bulk pork sausage
2 cloves garlic, minced
3 to 4 teaspoons chili powder
½ teaspoon ground cumin
1 15½-ounce can red kidney
  beans, drained
1 cup chopped celery
1 cup chopped onion
½ cup chopped green
  sweet pepper
1 16-ounce can tomatoes,
  cut up
1 10-ounce can tomatoes
  with green chile peppers
1 cup vegetable juice
  or tomato juice
1 6-ounce can tomato paste
¼ teaspoon salt
  Shredded cheddar cheese
  Dairy sour cream

1. In a large skillet cook the beef or sausage and garlic until meat is brown. Drain off fat. Stir in chili powder and cumin; cook 2 minutes more.

2. Meanwhile, in a 3½-, 4-, or 5-quart slow cooker combine beans, celery, onion, and green sweet pepper. Add undrained tomatoes, undrained tomatoes with chile peppers, vegetable juice or tomato juice, tomato paste, and salt. Stir in meat mixture.

3. Cover; cook on low-heat setting for 8 to 10 hours or on high-heat setting for 4 to 5 hours. Ladle chili into soup bowls. Pass shredded cheese and sour cream with chili.

Nutrition Facts per serving: 477 calories, 25 g total fat, 66 mg cholesterol, 2,012 mg sodium, 44 g carbohydrate, 26 g protein.

Salsa Verde Beef Stew

A salad of romaine, orange sections, and avocado slices drizzled with a cumin vinaigrette would be a fresh accompaniment to this hearty stew.

Prep: 30 minutes **Cook:** 8 hours on low or 5 hours on high **Makes:** 6 servings

1. Trim fat from meat. Cut beef into 1-inch pieces. In a large skillet brown half of the beef at a time in hot oil over medium-high heat.

2. In a 3½-, 4-, or 5-quart slow cooker combine beef, potatoes, onion, sweet pepper, undrained tomatoes, beans, salsa, garlic and cumin. Cover and cook on low-heat setting for 8 to 9 hours or on high-heat setting for 5 to 6 hours. Serve with warmed tortillas.

Nutrition Facts per serving: **465 calories, 12 g total fat, 72 mg cholesterol, 709 mg sodium, 56 g carbohydrate, 33 g protein.**

1½ pounds boneless beef
    chuck pot roast
1 tablespoon cooking oil
4 medium unpeeled potatoes,
    cut into 1-inch pieces
1 large onion, coarsely
    chopped
1 green sweet pepper,
    cut into ½-inch pieces
1 14½-ounce can Mexican-
    style stewed tomatoes
1 15- or 16-ounce can pinto
    beans, rinsed and drained
1 cup bottled mild or medium
    green salsa
2 cloves garlic, minced
1 teaspoon ground cumin
6 flour tortillas

Meatball and Vegetable Stew

Keep the ingredients for this easy stew on hand. Even as late as 4 p.m. you'll never need to ask yourself what you're having for dinner!

Prep: 10 minutes **Cook:** 6 hours on low or 3 hours on high **Makes:** 4 servings

1 16- to 18-ounce package
   frozen cooked meatballs
½ of a 16-ounce package
   frozen mixed vegetables
   (about 2 cups)
1 14½-ounce can diced
   tomatoes with onion and
   garlic, or stewed tomatoes
1 12-ounce jar mushroom
   gravy
1½ teaspoons dried basil,
   crushed
⅓ cup water

1. In a 3½- or 4-quart slow cooker place meatballs and mixed vegetables. In a bowl stir together tomatoes, gravy, basil, and ⅓ cup water; pour over meatballs and vegetables.

2. Cover and cook on low-heat setting for 6 to 8 hours or on high-heat setting for 3 to 4 hours.

Nutrition Facts per serving: 472 calories, 32 g total fat, 87 mg cholesterol, 1,883 mg sodium, 26 g carbohydrate, 21 g protein.

Provençal Beef Stew

Herbes de Provence (a blend of basil, fennel, lavender, marjoram, rosemary, sage, savory, and thyme), red wine, and olives add a French touch to this dish.

Prep: 20 minutes   **Cook:** 10 hours on low or 4 hours on high   **Makes:** 6 servings

1. Peel a strip from the center of each potato. Place potatoes, carrots, shallots or onion, and olives in a 4-quart slow cooker; top with beef. Combine broth, garlic, herbes de Provence, salt, pepper, and tapioca; pour over beef.

2. Cover; cook on low-heat setting for 10 to 12 hours or on high-heat setting for 4 to 5 hours. Stir in wine during last 30 minutes of cooking. Serve sprinkled with parsley and garnished with capers, if desired.

Nutrition Facts per serving: **198 calories, 5 g total fat, 54 mg cholesterol, 308 mg sodium, 16 g carbohydrate, 20 g protein.**

8 small new potatoes
1 pound small carrots with tops, peeled and trimmed, or one 16-ounce package peeled baby carrots
1 cup cut-up, peeled shallots or coarsely chopped onion
½ cup green and/or black European-style olives, pitted
1½ pounds lean boneless beef chuck roast, cut into 2-inch pieces
1 cup beef broth
4 to 6 cloves garlic, minced
1 teaspoon herbes de Provence
¼ teaspoon salt
¼ teaspoon whole black pepper or cracked black pepper
1 tablespoon quick-cooking tapioca
¼ cup dry red wine
Snipped fresh parsley (optional)
Capers (optional)

Santa Fe Beef Stew

If you can't find jalapeño pinto beans, add one finely chopped jalapeño pepper to the mix.

Prep: 25 minutes **Cook:** 10 hours on low plus 30 minutes on high or 5½ hours on high **Makes:** 6 servings

1 pound beef chuck pot roast

1 tablespoon cooking oil

2 14½-ounce cans Mexican-style stewed tomatoes

1½ cups coarsely chopped onion

1 15-ounce can pinto beans or jalapeño pinto beans

3½ cups beef broth

1 6-ounce can tomato paste

4 teaspoons chili powder

1 tablespoon dried Italian seasoning, crushed

½ teaspoon crushed red pepper

¼ teaspoon ground cloves

¼ teaspoon ground allspice

¼ teaspoon ground cinnamon

1 medium zucchini, halved lengthwise, and cut into ½-inch pieces

1 medium yellow or green sweet pepper, cut into 1-inch pieces

1. Trim fat from meat. Cut meat into 1-inch cubes. In a large skillet brown meat, half at a time, in hot oil. Drain off fat.

2. Transfer meat to a 3½-, 4-, or 5-quart slow cooker. Add undrained tomatoes, onion, and beans.

3. In a bowl combine beef broth, tomato paste, chili powder, Italian seasoning, crushed red pepper, cloves, allspice, and cinnamon. Add to cooker.

4. Cover; cook on low-heat setting for 10 to 12 hours or on high-heat setting for 5 to 6 hours.

5. If using low-heat setting, turn to high-heat setting. Add zucchini and sweet peppers. Cover and cook 30 minutes longer on high-heat setting.

Nutrition Facts per serving: **360 calories, 10 g total fat, 76 mg cholesterol, 1,258 mg sodium, 35 g carbohydrate, 35 g protein.**

Kielbasa Stew

Try to use reduced-sodium chicken broth, if you can; the sausage adds plenty of salt to this stew.

Prep: 20 minutes **Cook:** 7 hours on low or 3½ hours on high **Makes:** 4 or 5 servings

1. In a 4- or 5-quart slow cooker combine cabbage, potato, and carrots. Top with kielbasa. Sprinkle basil, thyme, and pepper over kielbasa. Pour chicken broth over all.

2. Cover; cook on low-heat setting for 7 to 9 hours or on high-heat setting for 3½ to 4½ hours.

Nutrition Facts per serving: **522 calories, 34 g total fat, 76 mg cholesterol, 1,658 mg sodium, 34 g carbohydrate, 23 g protein.**

4 cups coarsely chopped cabbage

3 cups peeled, cubed potato

1½ cups sliced carrots

1 pound cooked kielbasa (Polska Kielbasa), sliced

½ teaspoon dried basil, crushed

½ teaspoon dried thyme, crushed

½ teaspoon ground black pepper

2 14-ounce cans reduced-sodium chicken broth

Pork and Hominy Stew

In Mexico, the combination of pork, hominy, and chili powder in a savory broth has a special name—posole—and people have been known to close shop early on the day it's the special at the local cafe.

Prep: 25 minutes **Cook:** 8 hours on low or 4 hours on high **Makes:** 6 servings

1 pound boneless
  pork shoulder
1 tablespoon cooking oil
1 medium red or green
  sweet pepper, cut into
  ½-inch pieces
1 medium tomato, chopped
½ cup chopped onion
4 cloves garlic, minced
2 16-ounce cans golden
  hominy, drained
1 4-ounce can diced green
  chile peppers, drained
1 tablespoon chili powder
½ teaspoon dried oregano,
  crushed
2 14½-ounce cans
  chicken broth
  Tortilla chips (optional)

1. Trim fat from meat; cut pork into 1-inch cubes. In a large skillet brown pork, half at a time, in hot oil. Drain off fat.

2. Transfer pork to a 3½-, 4-, or 5-quart slow cooker. Add sweet pepper, tomato, onion, garlic, hominy, chile peppers, chili powder, and oregano. Pour broth over all.

3. Cover; cook on low-heat setting for 8 to 10 hours or on high-heat setting for 4 to 5 hours. Serve with tortilla chips, if desired.

Nutrition Facts per serving: **289 calories, 11 g total fat, 50 mg cholesterol, 897 mg sodium, 27 g carbohydrate, 19 g protein.**

Italian Pork and Bean Stew

A little bit of pork sausage gives this stew great flavor. You can also use ground turkey that's spiced to taste like Italian pork sausage.

Prep: 30 minutes **Stand:** 1 hour **Cook:** 7 hours on low plus 15 minutes on high or 3¾ hours on high **Makes:** 6 servings

---

1. Rinse beans; drain. In a large saucepan combine beans and the 6 cups water. Bring to boiling; reduce heat. Simmer, uncovered, for 10 minutes. Remove from heat. Cover and let stand for 1 hour. Drain and rinse beans. Transfer beans to a 3½-, 4-, or 5-quart slow cooker; add carrot.

2. In a large skillet cook sausage, onion, and garlic over medium heat until sausage is no longer pink, breaking up sausage as it cooks. Drain off fat. Transfer mixture to slow cooker. Add cubed pork.

3. Stir in the 3 cups water, bouillon granules, thyme, and oregano. Cover; cook on low-heat setting for 7 to 8 hours or on high-heat setting for 3½ to 4 hours.

4. If using low-heat setting, turn to high-heat setting. Stir wine into tomato paste. Add to mixture in cooker along with parsley. Cover and cook for 15 minutes more.

Nutrition Facts per serving: 473 calories, 13 g total fat, 73 mg cholesterol, 566 mg sodium, 49 g carbohydrate, 37 g protein.

2 cups dry Great Northern beans
6 cups cold water
1½ cups carrot, cut into ½-inch pieces
8 ounces bulk Italian sausage
1½ cups coarsely chopped onion
3 cloves garlic, minced
1 pound lean boneless pork, cut into cubes
3 cups water
1 teaspoon instant beef bouillon granules
½ teaspoon dried thyme, crushed
½ teaspoon dried oregano, crushed
¼ cup dry red wine
⅓ cup tomato paste (½ of a 6-ounce can)
¼ cup snipped fresh parsley

Sweet Potato and Sausage Stew

Tapioca added to slow-cooked stews such as this one thickens them without making them pasty.

Prep: 15 minutes **Cook:** 10 hours on low or 4½ hours on high **Makes:** 4 servings

1 pound smoked turkey
   sausage links

2 small sweet potatoes,
   peeled and cut into
   ½-inch pieces (2 cups)

1 medium green pepper,
   cut into 1-inch thick pieces
   (¾ cup)

1 stalk celery, cut into
   ½-inch pieces (½ cup)

½ cup chopped onion

2 tablespoons quick cooking
   tapioca

1 14½-ounce can tomatoes,
   cut up

1 15-ounce can garbanzo
   beans, drained

1 cup beef broth

1. Cut sausage in half lengthwise; cut into 1-inch thick slices. In a 3½, 4-, 5-, or 6-quart slow cooker combine sausage pieces, sweet potatoes, green pepper, celery, onion, and tapioca. Add undrained tomatoes, garbanzo beans, and beef broth.

2. Cover; cook on low-heat setting for 10 to 12 hours or on high-heat setting for 4½ to 5 hours.

Nutrition Facts per serving: **438 calories, 11 g total fat, 76 mg cholesterol, 1,800 mg sodium, 57 g carbohydrate, 29 g protein.**

Lone Star Stew

All over the South, black-eyed peas are standard good-luck fare for New Year's Day.

Revel in the tradition with this Southwest-style take on the dish.

Prep: 20 minutes **Cook:** 8 hours on low plus 30 minutes on high or 4½ hours on high **Makes:** 6 servings

1. Sort through peas to remove any pebbles or other foreign matter. Rinse peas; combine with 5 cups water in a large saucepan. Bring to boiling. Reduce heat. Cook, uncovered, over low heat for 10 minutes. Drain and rinse.

2. In a 4- or 4½-quart slow cooker combine peas, the quartered peppers, sage, salt, and the 3 cups water. Add turkey or pork.

3. Cover; cook on low-heat setting for 8 to 10 hours or on high-heat setting for 4 to 5 hours. If using low-heat setting, turn to high-heat setting.

4. Stir in squash; cover and cook 30 minutes more. Serve topped with red onion, cilantro, and, if desired, Lime Sour Cream and chopped jalapeño pepper.

Nutrition Facts per serving: **144 calories, 1 g total fat, 47 mg cholesterol, 423 mg sodium, 13 g carbohydrate, 21 g protein.**

Lime Sour Cream: Combine ½ cup light dairy sour cream, ½ teaspoon finely shredded lime peel, and 1 teaspoon lime juice in a small bowl. Cover and chill before serving.

- 2 cups dry black-eyed peas
- 5 cups water
- 1 to 3 whole jalapeño peppers, quartered lengthwise
- 1½ teaspoons dried leaf sage, crushed
- 1 teaspoon salt
- 3 cups water
- 1 pound turkey or pork tenderloin, cut into 1½-inch pieces
- 2 medium yellow summer squashes, cut into wedges (about 2½ cups)
- ½ cup finely chopped red onion
  Snipped fresh cilantro
  Lime Sour Cream (optional)
  Finely chopped jalapeño pepper (optional)

Pork Stew with Cornmeal Dumplings

If you're rushed and don't have time to make the cornmeal dumplings, serve the stew with cornmeal muffins or corn bread.

Prep: 25 minutes **Cook:** 9 hours on low plus 50 minutes on high or 4 hours 50 minutes on high **Makes:** 4 servings

1 1-pound boneless pork shoulder roast

1 clove garlic, minced

1 tablespoon cooking oil

4 medium carrots, cut into ½-inch pieces (2 cups)

2 medium potatoes, peeled and cubed (2 cups)

1 12-ounce can beer (1½ cups)

¼ cup quick-cooking tapioca

1 tablespoon sugar

1 tablespoon Worcestershire sauce

2 bay leaves

1 teaspoon dried thyme, crushed

½ teaspoon salt

¼ teaspoon ground nutmeg

¼ teaspoon pepper

1 28-ounce can tomatoes, cut up

Cornmeal Dumplings

2 tablespoons shredded cheddar cheese

1. Cut pork into 1-inch cubes. In a large skillet brown pork and garlic in hot oil. Drain well.

2. Meanwhile, in a 3½- or 4-quart slow cooker combine carrots, potatoes, beer, tapioca, sugar, Worcestershire sauce, bay leaves, thyme, salt, nutmeg, and pepper. Stir in browned meat and undrained tomatoes. Cover; cook on low-heat setting for 9 to 11 hours or on high-heat setting for 4 to 5 hours.

3. If using low-heat setting, turn to high-heat setting. Prepare Cornmeal Dumplings. Remove bay leaves. Stir stew; drop dumplings by tablespoonfuls onto stew. Cover; cook for 50 minutes more (do not lift cover). Sprinkle dumplings with cheese.

Cornmeal Dumplings

½ cup all-purpose flour

½ cup shredded cheddar cheese

⅓ cup yellow cornmeal

1 teaspoon baking powder

Dash pepper

1 beaten egg

2 tablespoons milk

2 tablespoons cooking oil

In a medium mixing bowl stir together flour, cheddar cheese, cornmeal, baking powder, and pepper. Combine beaten egg, milk, and oil. Add to flour mixture; stir with a fork just until combined.

For 5- or 6-quart slow cooker: Use one 1½-pound boneless pork shoulder roast, 5 medium carrots, and 3 medium potatoes. Leave remaining ingredient amounts the same. Makes 6 servings.

Nutrition Facts per serving: 649 calories, 25 g total fat, 146 mg cholesterol, 980 mg sodium, 65 g carbohydrate, 36 g protein.

Green Chile Stew

Hominy—dried white or yellow corn from which the hull has been removed—
adds a pleasantly chewy texture to this Tex-Mex-style stew.

Prep: 25 minutes **Cook:** 7 hours on low or 4 hours on high **Makes:** 5 to 6 servings

1. Trim fat from pork. Cut pork into ½-inch cubes. In a large skillet brown half of the pork in hot oil. Transfer meat to a 3½- or 4 ½-quart slow cooker. Brown remaining meat with onion. Drain off the fat and transfer meat and onion to the slow cooker.

2. Add water, potatoes, hominy, chile peppers, tapioca, garlic salt, salt, black pepper, cumin, and oregano. Cover; cook on low-heat setting for 7 to 8 hours or on high-heat setting for 4 to 5 hours. Garnish with snipped cilantro, if desired.

Nutrition Facts per serving: 414 calories, 11 g total fat, 102 mg cholesterol, 980 mg sodium, 40 g carbohydrate, 39 g protein.

2 pounds boneless pork sirloin
  or shoulder roast
1 tablespoon cooking oil
½ cup chopped onion
3 cups water
4 medium potatoes, peeled
  and cut into ½-inch cubes
1 15-ounce can hominy or
  whole kernel corn, drained
2 4-ounce cans chopped
  green chile peppers
2 tablespoons quick-cooking
  tapioca
1 teaspoon garlic salt
½ teaspoon salt
½ teaspoon ground
  black pepper
½ teaspoon ground cumin
⅛ teaspoon dried oregano,
  crushed
  Snipped fresh cilantro
  (optional)

Persian-Style Stew

As the yellow split peas simmer, they fall apart and give the stew a thick, hearty consistency. The small amount of raisins provides a slight sweetness.

Prep: 25 minutes **Cook:** 8 hours on low plus 15 minutes on high or 4¼ hours on high **Makes:** 6 to 8 servings

1½ to 2 pounds lamb or beef
    stew meat, cut into
    1-inch cubes
1 tablespoon cooking oil
3 leeks, cut into 1-inch pieces
1 large onion, chopped
½ cup dry yellow split peas
4 cloves garlic, sliced
2 bay leaves
1 tablespoon snipped fresh
    oregano or 1 teaspoon
    dried oregano, crushed
1½ teaspoons ground cumin
¼ teaspoon pepper
3 cups chicken broth
⅓ cup raisins
2 tablespoons lemon juice
3 cups hot cooked bulgur
    or rice

1. In a large skillet brown meat, half at a time, in hot oil. Drain off fat. Transfer meat to a 3½-, 4-, or 5-quart slow cooker. Stir in leeks, onion, split peas, garlic, bay leaves, dried oregano (if using), cumin, and pepper. Pour chicken broth over all.

2. Cover; cook on low-heat setting for 8 to 10 hours or on high-heat setting for 4 to 5 hours. If using low-heat setting, turn to high-heat setting. Stir raisins into stew. Cover; cook for 15 minutes more. Remove the bay leaves and discard. Stir in lemon juice and, if using, the fresh oregano. Serve with hot bulgur or rice.

Nutrition Facts per serving: **357 calories, 9 g total fat, 58 mg cholesterol, 449 mg sodium, 42 g carbohydrate, 29 g protein.**

Brunswick Stew

Early 19th-century settlers in Brunswick County, Virginia, created this classic stew that's loaded with vegetables associated with the South: okra, lima beans, and corn.

Prep: 20 minutes **Cook:** 8 hours on low plus 45 minutes on high or 4¾ hours on high **Makes:** 6 servings

1. In a 3½- or 4-quart slow cooker place onion. Top with chicken and ham. In a small bowl combine undrained tomatoes, broth, garlic, Worcestershire sauce, mustard, thyme, pepper, and hot pepper sauce; pour over chicken and ham.

2. Cover and cook on low-heat setting for 8 to 10 hours or on high-heat setting for 4 to 5 hours.

3. If desired, remove chicken; cool slightly. (Keep lid on the slow cooker.) Remove meat from chicken bones; cut meat into bite-size pieces. Return chicken to slow cooker; discard bones.

4. Add okra, lima beans, and corn to crockery cooker. If using low-heat setting, turn to high-heat setting. Cover and cook 45 minutes more or until vegetables are tender.

Nutrition Facts per serving: 322 calories, 9 g total fat, 84 mg cholesterol, 990 mg sodium, 24 g carbohydrate, 34 g protein.

3 medium onions, cut into
   thin wedges
2 pounds meaty chicken
   pieces, skinned
1½ cups diced cooked ham
   (8 ounces)
1 14½-ounce can diced
   tomatoes
1 14-ounce can chicken broth
4 cloves garlic, minced
1 tablespoon Worcestershire
   sauce
1 teaspoon dry mustard
1 teaspoon dried thyme,
   crushed
¼ teaspoon pepper
¼ teaspoon bottled hot
   pepper sauce
1 10-ounce package frozen
   sliced okra (2 cups)
1 cup frozen baby lima beans
1 cup frozen whole kernel corn

Chicken and Sausage Gumbo

You can make the roux the night before and keep it in the refrigerator, covered. When cooked, the roux should be a coppery color, similar to a tarnished penny.

Prep: 30 minutes **Cook:** 6 hours on low or 3 hours on high **Makes:** 5 servings

⅓ cup all-purpose flour

⅓ cup cooking oil

3 cups water

12 ounces fully cooked smoked sausage links, quartered lengthwise and sliced

1½ cups chopped cooked chicken or 12 ounces skinless, boneless chicken breasts or thighs, cut into ¾-inch pieces

2 cups sliced okra or one 10-ounce package frozen whole okra, partially thawed and cut into ½-inch slices

1 cup chopped onion

½ cup chopped green sweet pepper

½ cup chopped celery

4 cloves garlic, minced

½ teaspoon salt

½ teaspoon pepper

¼ teaspoon ground red pepper

3 cups hot cooked rice

1. For the roux, in a heavy 2-quart saucepan stir together the flour and oil until smooth. Cook over medium-high heat for 5 minutes, stirring constantly. Reduce heat to medium. Cook and stir constantly about 15 minutes more or until a dark, reddish-brown roux forms. Cool.

2. In a 3-½-, 4-, or 5-quart slow cooker place water. Stir in roux. Add sausage, chicken, okra, onion, sweet pepper, celery, garlic, salt, pepper, and ground red pepper.

3. Cover; cook on low-heat setting for 6 to 7 hours or on high-heat setting for 3 to 3½ hours. Skim off fat. Serve over the hot cooked rice.

Nutrition Facts per serving: **637 calories, 39 g total fat, 83 mg cholesterol, 952 mg sodium, 45 g carbohydrate, 28 g protein.**

Chicken and Wild Rice Stew

With two kinds of rice, mushrooms, and leeks, this hearty chicken stew makes for earthy and elegant autumn fare. Serve it with a salad of field greens and whole wheat rolls.

Prep: 20 minutes **Cook:** 7 hours on low or 3½ hours on high **Makes:** 6 servings

1. In a 3½-, 4-, 5-, or 6-quart slow cooker place mushrooms, carrots, leeks, and rices. Place chicken on vegetables and rices. Top with thyme, rosemary, and pepper. Pour broth over all.

2. Cover and cook on low-heat setting for 7 to 8 hours or on high-heat setting for 3½ to 4 hours. Stir in mushroom soup.

Nutrition Facts per serving: **264 calories, 6 g total fat, 33 mg cholesterol, 908 mg sodium, 32 g carbohydrate, 22 g protein.**

3 cups quartered button mushrooms (8 ounces)

2 medium carrots, sliced (1 cup)

2 medium leeks, sliced (⅔ cup)

½ cup uncooked brown rice

½ cup uncooked wild rice, rinsed and drained

12 ounces skinless, boneless chicken breasts, cut into ¾-inch pieces

1 teaspoon dried thyme, crushed

½ teaspoon dried rosemary, crushed

¼ teaspoon coarse ground pepper

3 14-ounce cans reduced-sodium chicken broth (5¼ cups)

1 10¾-ounce can condensed cream of mushroom soup

Shrimp Creole

Creole cooking is a fusion of Spanish, French, and African cuisines that came together in New Orleans. It makes great use of tomatoes, such as those in this sophisticated seafood stew.

Prep: 20 minutes **Cook:** 5 hours on low or 2½ hours on high **Makes:** 6 to 8 servings

1½ cups chopped onion

1 cup chopped green
   sweet pepper

2 stalks celery, cut into
   ½-inch slices (1 cup)

⅓ cup thinly sliced green onion

2 cloves garlic, minced

1 14½-ounce can diced
   tomatoes

1 14-ounce can chicken broth

1 6-ounce can tomato paste

1½ teaspoons paprika

½ teaspoon pepper

¼ teaspoon salt

1 bay leaf
   Several dashes bottled
   hot pepper sauce

1½ pounds peeled, deveined,
   cooked medium shrimp

3 cups hot cooked rice

1. In a 3½-quart slow cooker place onion, green sweet pepper, celery, green onion, garlic, undrained tomatoes, chicken broth, tomato paste, paprika, pepper, salt, bay leaf, and hot pepper sauce. Stir to combine.

2. Cover; cook on low-heat setting for 5 to 6 hours or on high-heat setting for 2½ to 3 hours. Remove bay leaf. Stir in shrimp. Serve over cooked rice.

Nutrition Facts per serving: 344 calories, 3 g total fat, 227 mg cholesterol, 673 mg sodium, 39 g carbohydrate, 37 g protein.

Vegetarian Chili

Between the kidney beans, chunky tomatoes, green pepper and celery, you won't miss the meat in this highly textured bowl o' red.

Prep: 15 minutes **Cook:** 9 hours on low or 4½ hours on high **Makes:** 6 servings

1. In a 4- or 4½-quart slow cooker place all ingredients. Stir to combine.

2. Cover; cook on low-heat setting for 9 to 10 hours or on high-heat setting for 4½ to 5 hours.

Nutrition Facts per serving: **229 calories, 1 g total fat, 0 mg cholesterol, 1,271 mg sodium, 51 g carbohydrate, 14 g protein.**

3 cups hot-style tomato juice
  or hot-style vegetable juice
2 15-ounce cans red kidney
  beans, rinsed and drained
1 15½-ounce can whole kernel
  corn, drained
1 14½-ounce can chunky
  chili-style tomatoes or one
  14½-ounce can Mexican-
  style stewed tomatoes,
  undrained
1 cup chopped onion
1 cup chopped green
  sweet pepper
1 cup chopped celery
1 clove garlic, minced
1 to 2 teaspoons chili powder
¼ teaspoon salt
¼ teaspoon ground
  black pepper

Hearty Vegetarian Stew

Savory steak sauce (but no steak) gives great flavor to this meatless one-dish meal.

Prep: 15 minutes **Cook:** 9 hours on low or 4½ hours on high **Makes:** 5 servings

1 pound potatoes, cut into
 1-inch cubes

1 large onion, chopped

2 medium carrots, sliced

1 15-ounce can red kidney
 beans, rinsed and drained

1 15-ounce can tomato sauce

1 14½-ounce can diced
 tomatoes with basil, garlic,
 and oregano

1 10-ounce package frozen
 whole kernel corn

2 teaspoons steak sauce

⅔ cup shredded cheddar
 cheese

1. In a 3½- or 4-quart slow cooker combine potatoes, onion, carrots, beans, tomato sauce, undrained tomatoes, corn, and steak sauce.

2. Cover and cook on low-heat setting for 9 to 11 hours or on high-heat setting for 4½ to 5½ hours. To serve, sprinkle cheese over stew.

Nutrition Facts per serving: **325 calories, 6 g total fat, 16 mg cholesterol, 1,219 mg sodium, 60 g carbohydrate, 16 g protein.**

Vegetable-Patch Chili

Some like it hot—some don't. If you're in the latter group, use regular stewed tomatoes and a mild salsa in this meatless chili. Serve it with warm cornmeal biscuits.

Prep: 15 minutes **Cook:** 8 hours on low or 4 hours on high **Makes:** 4 servings

1. In a 3½- or 4-quart slow cooker combine zucchini, green sweet pepper, onion, celery, garlic, chili powder, oregano, and cumin. Stir in undrained tomatoes, undrained corn, drained beans, and salsa.

2. Cover; cook on low-heat setting for 8 to 10 hours or on high-heat setting for 4 to 5 hours. To serve, ladle the chili into bowls and top with a small amount of sour cream.

Nutrition Facts per serving: **277 calories, 7 g total fat, 6 mg cholesterol, 1,599 mg sodium, 54 g carbohydrate, 13 g protein.**

1 medium zucchini, cut into ½-inch pieces (1½ cups)

1 medium green sweet pepper, coarsely chopped (1 cup)

½ cup coarsely chopped onion

½ cup coarsely chopped celery

2 cloves garlic, minced

2 to 3 teaspoons chili powder

1 teaspoon dried oregano, crushed

½ teaspoon ground cumin

2 14½-ounce cans Mexican-style stewed tomatoes

1 17-ounce can whole kernel corn

1 15-ounce can black beans, rinsed and drained

1 8-ounce jar salsa

Dairy sour cream

meats

Enjoy family favorites such as melt-in-your-mouth pot roast, homestyle meat loaf, or falling-off-the-bone barbecued ribs—or put on a company-special meal of lamb or veal—any day of the week.

Tangy Barbecue Beef, page 122

Pot Roast with Basil Mashed Potatoes

Melt-in-your-mouth pot roast and basil-infused mashed potatoes are just the thing for a comfort-food-to-the-max dinner after a long, hard day.

Prep: 25 minutes   **Cook:** 8 hours on low or 4 hours on high   **Stand:** 10 minutes   **Makes:** 6 servings

---

2 carrots, cut into ½-inch pieces

1 medium turnip, peeled and cubed (1 cup)

1 small onion, chopped

½ cup snipped dried tomatoes (not oil-packed)

1 clove garlic, minced

1 teaspoon instant beef bouillon granules

½ teaspoon dried basil, crushed

½ teaspoon dried oregano, crushed

⅛ teaspoon pepper

1 1½-to 2-pound boneless beef chuck pot roast

1 cup water

1 10-ounce package frozen lima beans or whole kernel corn

1 cup frozen peas

1 20-ounce package refrigerated mashed potatoes

1 tablespoon finely snipped fresh basil

1. In a 3½- or 4-quart slow cooker combine the carrots, turnip, onion, dried tomatoes, garlic, bouillon granules, dried basil, dried oregano, and pepper. Trim fat from meat. If necessary, cut roast to fit into cooker. Place meat on vegetables. Pour water over all.

2. Cover; cook on low-heat setting for 8 to 10 hours or on high-heat setting for 4 to 5 hours. Stir in lima beans or corn and peas. Let stand, covered, for 10 minutes.

3. Meanwhile, prepare mashed potatoes according to package directions, except stir the 1 tablespoon fresh basil into potatoes just before serving. Remove meat and vegetables from cooker with a slotted spoon. If desired, reserve cooking juices. Serve meat and vegetables over hot mashed potatoes. Serve cooking juices over meat if desired.

Nutrition Facts per serving: 436 calories, 12 g total fat, 87 mg cholesterol, 497 mg sodium, 46 g carbohydrate, 35 g protein.

Beef Stroganoff

Considered classic company fare in the 1960s, time hasn't changed the elegance of this stew that features tender chunks of beef in a rich herbed sauce on a bed of egg noodles.

Prep: 25 minutes **Cook:** 8 hours on low plus 30 minutes on high or 4½ hours on high **Makes:** 6 servings

---

1. In a large skillet brown beef, half at a time, in hot oil. Drain off fat.

2. In a 3½-quart slow cooker combine beef, mushrooms, onions, garlic, oregano, salt, thyme, pepper, and bay leaf. Pour beef broth and sherry over all.

3. Cover; cook on low-heat setting for 8 to 10 hours or on high-heat setting for 4 to 5 hours. Discard bay leaf.

4. If using low-heat setting, turn to high-heat setting. Mix together sour cream, flour, and water. Stir about 1 cup of the hot liquid into sour cream mixture. Return all to cooker; stir to combine. Cover and cook on high-heat setting for 30 minutes or until thickened and bubbly.

5. Serve over hot cooked noodles or rice. Sprinkle with snipped fresh parsley, if desired.

Nutrition Facts per serving: 497 calories, 20 g total fat, 135 mg cholesterol, 368 mg sodium, 38 g carbohydrate, 36 g protein.

1½ pounds beef stew meat,
    cut into 1-inch cubes
1 tablespoon cooking oil
2 cups sliced fresh mushrooms
½ cup sliced green onions
2 cloves garlic, minced
½ teaspoon dried oregano,
    crushed
¼ teaspoon salt
¼ teaspoon dried thyme,
    crushed
¼ teaspoon pepper
1 bay leaf
1½ cups beef broth
⅓ cup dry sherry
1 8-ounce carton dairy
    sour cream
½ cup all-purpose flour
¼ cup water
4 cups hot cooked noodles
    or rice
    Snipped fresh parsley
    (optional)

Cajun Pot Roast

If you can't find Cajun seasoning, mix together 1 to 1½ teaspoons seasoned salt, ½ to ¾ teaspoon ground red pepper, and ½ to ¾ teaspoon ground black pepper.

Prep: 25 minutes **Cook:** 10 hours on low or 5 hours on high **Makes:** 6 servings

1 2- to 2½-pound boneless beef chuck pot roast

2 to 3 teaspoons Cajun seasoning

1 tablespoon cooking oil

1 14½-ounce can Cajun-style or Mexican-style stewed tomatoes

1 cup chopped onion

1 cup chopped celery

¼ cup quick-cooking tapioca

1 teaspoon bottled minced garlic or 2 cloves garlic, minced

Hot cooked rice

1. Trim fat from roast. Cut roast to fit in slow cooker, if necessary. Rub Cajun seasoning all over meat. In a large skillet brown meat on all sides in hot oil.

2. In a 3½- to 4-quart slow cooker combine undrained tomatoes, onion, celery, tapioca, and garlic. Place meat on top of vegetable mixture.

3. Cover and cook on low-heat setting for 10 to 12 hours or on high-heat setting for 5 to 6 hours.

4. Slice meat; serve with sauce over rice.

5. *Make-Ahead Tip:* This mildly spiced meat and sauce also make a delicious hot sandwich. Using two forks, shred any leftover meat. Combine the shredded beef and remaining sauce in a storage container; cover and freeze for up to 3 months. Thaw mixture overnight in the refrigerator. Pour into a saucepan and heat through. Serve on hard rolls with sliced tomato and sliced green onion.

Nutrition Facts per serving: **273 calories, 7 g total fat, 55 mg cholesterol, 366 mg sodium, 31 g carbohydrate, 21 g protein.**

Beef Brisket in Beer

Slow cooking is the key to tenderizing tougher cuts of meat, such as brisket. After simmering in a slow cooker all day, you won't even need a butter knife to dig into this beef-and-onions dish.

Prep: 15 minutes   **Cook:** 10 hours on low or 5 hours on high   **Makes:** 10 servings

---

1. Trim fat from brisket. If necessary, cut brisket to fit into cooker. In a 3½-, 4-, 5-, or 6-quart slow cooker place onions, bay leaf, and brisket. Combine beer, chili sauce, sugar, thyme, salt, pepper, and garlic; pour over brisket. Cover; cook on low-heat setting for 10 to 12 hours or high-heat setting 5 to 6 hours.

2. Transfer brisket and onions to a platter; keep warm. Discard bay leaf. For gravy, skim fat from cooking juices. Measure 2½ cups juices and place in a saucepan. Combine cornstarch and water; add to saucepan. Cook and stir until thick and bubbly; cook and stir 2 minutes more. Pass gravy with meat.

Nutrition Facts per serving: 227 calories, 7 g total fat, 78 mg cholesterol, 242 mg sodium, 8 g carbohydrate, 30 g protein.

1 3 to 4-pound fresh
   beef brisket
2 onions, thinly sliced and
   separated into rings
1 bay leaf
1 cup beer
¼ cup chili sauce
2 tablespoons brown sugar
½ teaspoon dried thyme,
   crushed
¼ teaspoon salt
¼ teaspoon pepper
1 clove garlic, minced
2 tablespoons cornstarch
2 tablespoons water

Chinese Black Bean Pot Roast

Whole green beans, black bean garlic sauce, and rice turn everyday pot roast into a Chinese feast.

Look for the bean sauce in the Asian section of your supermarket or at an Asian market.

Prep: 30 minutes **Cook:** 10 hours on low plus 15 minutes on high or 5¼ hours on high **Makes:** 6 servings

1 2-pound boneless beef
   chuck pot roast
1 tablespoon cooking oil
1½ cups hot water
¼ cup black bean garlic sauce
1 teaspoon instant beef
   bouillon granules
1 tablespoon sugar
1 medium red sweet pepper,
   cut into thin strips
½ medium white onion,
   sliced into thin strips
8 ounces green beans,
   trimmed
3 tablespoons cornstarch
3 tablespoons cold water
3 cups hot cooked white or
   brown rice

1. Trim fat from roast. If necessary, cut roast to fit into a 4- or 5½-quart slow cooker. In a large skillet brown roast on all sides in hot oil. Drain off fat.

2. In the cooker stir together the 1½ cups water, bean sauce, bouillon granules, and sugar. Add sweet pepper, onion, and green beans. Place meat on top of vegetables.

3. Cover and cook on low-heat setting for 10 to 12 hours or on high-heat setting for 5 to 6 hours or until beef is tender.

4. Transfer meat and vegetables to a serving platter, reserving juices; cover meat and keep warm. If using low-heat setting, turn to high-heat setting. For sauce, combine cornstarch and cold water; stir into cooking juices in cooker. Cover and cook 15 minutes more on high-heat setting or until sauce is slightly thickened.

5. Using two forks, separate beef into serving pieces. Serve meat over rice with the sauce and vegetables.

Nutrition Facts per serving: 382 calories, 11 g total fat, 79 mg cholesterol, 513 mg sodium, 34 g carbohydrate, 35 g protein.

Beef Burgundy

Using the reduced-fat versions of the cream soups cuts down on fat grams, but not on flavor.

Prep: 25 minutes **Cook:** 8 hours on low or 4 hours on high **Makes:** 6 servings

1. In a large skillet brown the meat, half at a time, in hot oil. Drain off fat.

2. In a 3½-, 4-, or 5-quart slow cooker combine celery soup, mushroom soup, Burgundy, onion soup mix, and mushrooms. Stir in browned meat. Cover and cook on low-heat setting for 8 to 10 hours or on high-heat setting for 4 to 5 hours. Serve over noodles or rice.

Nutrition Facts per serving: 435 calories, 18 g total fat, 60 mg cholesterol, 985 mg sodium, 33 g carbohydrate, 30 g protein.

1½ pounds beef stew meat, trimmed and cut into 1-inch cubes

2 tablespoons cooking oil

1 10¾-ounce can condensed cream of celery soup or reduced-fat and reduced-sodium condensed cream of celery soup

1 10¾-ounce can condensed cream of mushroom soup or reduced-fat and reduced-sodium condensed cream of mushroom soup

¾ cup Burgundy wine

1 envelope onion soup mix (½ of a 2.2-ounce package)

8 ounces fresh mushrooms, sliced (3 cups)

Hot cooked noodles or rice

French Dips with Portobellos

Meaty portobello mushrooms add a new dimension to classic French dip sandwiches. Serve the seasoned broth in bowls just large enough to dunk a corner of the sandwich.

Prep: 25 minutes **Cook:** 8 hours on low or 4 hours on high **Stand:** 10 minutes **Makes:** 8 sandwiches

1 3- to 3½-pound beef bottom
  round or rump roast
1 tablespoon cooking oil
4 portobello mushrooms
  (3 to 4 inches in diameter)
1 14½-ounce can beef broth
  seasoned with onion
8 hoagie buns, split and
  toasted
1 large red onion, cut into
  ½ inch slices

1. Trim fat from roast. If necessary, cut roast to fit into a 3½-, 4-, 5-, or 6-quart slow cooker. In a large skillet brown meat on all sides in hot oil. Drain off fat. Transfer meat to cooker.

2. Clean mushrooms; remove and discard stems. Cut mushrooms into ¼-inch slices. Add to cooker. Pour broth over meat and mushrooms.

3. Cover and cook on low-heat setting for 8 to 9 hours or on high-heat setting for 4 to 4½ hours. Remove meat from cooker; cover and let stand for 10 minutes.

4. Meanwhile, using a slotted spoon, remove mushrooms and set aside. Thinly slice meat. Arrange meat and mushroom and onion slices on toasted buns. Pour cooking juices into a measuring cup; skim off fat. Drizzle a little of the juices onto each sandwich and pour the remaining juices into individual bowls; serve with sandwiches for dipping.

Nutrition Facts per serving: 780 calories, 33 g total fat, 106 mg cholesterol, 955 mg sodium, 73 g carbohydrate, 47 g protein.

Dilled Pot Roast

Many cooks prefer kosher salt to regular salt for both its texture and flavor. Kosher salt has tiny flakes rather than grains and has a fresher flavor than standard table salt.

Prep: 20 minutes **Cook:** 10 hours on low or 5 hours on high **Makes:** 6 to 8 servings

1. In a large skillet brown roast in hot oil. Place roast in a 3½- or 4-quart slow cooker, cutting the meat to fit, if necessary. Add the water to cooker. Sprinkle roast with 2 teaspoons of the fresh dillweed or ¾ teaspoon of the dried dillweed, salt, and pepper. Cover and cook on low-heat setting for 10 to 12 hours or on high-heat setting for 5 to 6 hours until meat is tender. Remove roast from cooker, reserving liquid; cover roast and keep warm. Measure liquid from cooker; skim fat. Reserve 1 cup of the juices.

2. Meanwhile, in a small saucepan stir together yogurt and flour until well combined. Stir in the 1 cup reserved cooking liquid and remaining dillweed. Cook and stir until thickened and bubbly. Cook and stir 1 minute more. Serve meat with sauce and noodles.

Nutrition Facts per serving: **373 calories, 12 g total fat, 136 mg cholesterol, 443 mg sodium, 22 g carbohydrate, 41 g protein.**

- **1 2- to 2½-pound boneless beef chuck roast**
- **2 tablespoons cooking oil**
- **½ cup water**
- **1 tablespoon snipped fresh dillweed or 1 teaspoon dried dillweed**
- **1 teaspoon coarse salt (kosher) or ¾ teaspoon regular salt**
- **½ teaspoon pepper**
- **½ cup plain yogurt**
- **2 tablespoons all-purpose flour**
- **3 cups hot cooked noodles**

Tangy Barbecue Beef

Sweet slices of mango add a fresh touch to these barbecued beef sandwiches. To save time, look for pre-peeled and sliced mango in the refrigerator case of the grocery produce section.

Prep: 25 minutes **Cook:** 10 hours on low **Stand:** 15 minutes **Makes:** 8 servings

2 tablespoons chili powder

1 teaspoon celery seeds

½ teaspoon salt

½ teaspoon freshly
  ground pepper

1 3-pound fresh beef brisket,
  trimmed of fat

2 onions, thinly sliced

1 cup bottled smoke-flavored
  barbecue sauce

½ cup beer or ginger ale

8 large sandwich buns
  or Portuguese rolls,
  split and toasted
  Bottled hot pepper sauce
  (optional)
  Mango slices

1. In a small bowl combine the chili powder, celery seeds, salt, and pepper. Rub the spice mixture onto all sides of the brisket. Scatter half of the sliced onions in the bottom of a 3½-, 4-, 5-, or 6-quart slow cooker. Place the brisket on the onions, cutting the meat to fit, if necessary. Scatter the remaining onions on top of the brisket. In a small bowl stir together the barbecue sauce and beer or ginger ale. Pour over the brisket and onions.

2. Cover and cook on low-heat setting for 10 to 12 hours or until meat is fork-tender. Transfer meat to a cutting board and let stand for 15 minutes. Halve meat crosswise. Using 2 forks, pull meat apart into shreds. Return meat to sauce mixture in slow cooker. Heat through using the high-heat setting.

3. To serve, use a slotted spoon to transfer beef and onion mixture into the buns. If desired, season to taste with bottled hot pepper sauce. Top with mango slices. (Freeze any remaining beef mixture in a freezer container for up to 3 months.)

Nutrition Facts per serving: 442 calories, 11 g total fat, 98 mg cholesterol, 971 mg sodium, 41 g carbohydrate, 41 g protein.

Sunday Dinner Pot Roast

If you're looking for a pot roast like Mom used to make, this is it: potatoes, mushrooms, carrots, and herbs in a creamy mushroom sauce.

Prep: 15 minutes **Cook:** 10 hours on low **Makes:** 5 servings

1. Trim fat from meat. Spray an unheated large skillet with nonstick cooking spray. Add meat and brown on all sides.

2. Place unpeeled potatoes, mushrooms, carrots, and tarragon or basil in a 3½- or 4-quart electric slow cooker. Place browned meat on top of vegetables. Sprinkle with salt. Pour condensed soup over meat. Cover and cook on low-heat setting for 10 to 12 hours.

3. To serve, transfer meat and vegetables to a serving platter. Serve the sauce over meat and vegetables.

Nutrition Facts per serving: 437 calories, 17 g total fat, 102 mg cholesterol, 780 mg sodium, 37 g carbohydrate, 35 g protein.

1 1½-pound boneless beef
   chuck eye roast,
   eye of round roast,
   or round rump roast
   Nonstick cooking spray
4 medium potatoes, quartered
1 4-ounce can mushroom
   stems and pieces, drained
2 cups packaged, peeled
   baby carrots
½ teaspoon dried tarragon
   or basil, crushed
¼ teaspoon salt
1 10¾-ounce can condensed
   mushroom soup
   Nonstick cooking spray

Vegetable-Stuffed Meat Loaf

Serve this family-pleasing meat loaf with steamed green beans, boiled new potatoes, and tall glasses of cold milk.

Prep: 30 minutes **Cook:** 10 hours on low or 4 hours on high **Makes:** 8 servings

½ cup shredded carrot

½ cup shredded potato

1 tablespoon cooking oil

1 beaten egg

2 tablespoons milk

⅓ cup fine dry bread crumbs

3 tablespoons snipped parsley

½ teaspoon onion salt

¼ teaspoon garlic powder

¼ teaspoon pepper

1½ pounds lean ground beef

3 tablespoons catsup

1 teaspoon yellow mustard

1. In a small skillet cook carrot and potato in hot oil until tender, stirring occasionally. In a medium mixing bowl combine egg and milk. Stir in bread crumbs, parsley, onion salt, garlic powder, and pepper. Add ground meat and mix well.

2. Crisscross three 18x2-inch foil strips atop a sheet of waxed paper. In the center of the foil strips pat half of the meat mixture into a 5-inch circle. Spread carrot mixture on meat circle to within ½ inch of edges. On another sheet of waxed paper pat remaining meat mixture into a 6-inch circle. Invert atop the first circle. Remove paper. Press edges of meat to seal well. Bringing up foil strips, transfer meat to a 3½-, 4-, 5-, or 6-quart slow cooker. Press meat away from sides of the cooker.

3. Cover; cook on low-heat setting for 9½ to 11½ hours or on high-heat setting for 3½ to 4 hours. In a bowl combine catsup and mustard. Spread over meat. Cover; cook on low-heat or high-heat setting for 30 minutes more. Using the foil strips, transfer meat loaf to a platter; discard the foil strips.

Nutrition Facts per serving: **194 calories, 11 g total fat, 80 mg cholesterol, 306 mg sodium, 7 g carbohydrate, 17 g protein.**

Short Ribs with Leeks

The best way to clean leeks—which can be gritty—is to cut off the tops and bottoms then cut them lengthwise down the middle. Run each half under cold water, fanning the layers.

Prep: 30 minutes **Cook:** 7 hours on low or 3½ hours on high **Makes:** 6 servings

1. Place mushrooms, carrots, and leeks in a 3½- or 4-quart slow cooker. Place beef over vegetables. Sprinkle with lemon peel, pepper, rosemary, thyme, and salt. Add broth. Cover; cook on low-heat setting for 7 to 8 hours or on high-heat setting for 3½ to 4 hours.

2. Use a slotted spoon to transfer meat and vegetables to serving dish. Cover and keep warm.

3. Skim fat from remaining cooking liquid. Measure 1 cup cooking liquid. Place in a small saucepan. In a small bowl stir together sour cream and flour. Stir into cooking liquid using a whisk. Cook and stir over medium heat until slightly thickened and bubbly; cook and stir for 1 minute more. Ladle sauce over meat and vegetables.

Nutrition Facts per serving: **173** calories, **8** g total fat, **33** mg cholesterol, **252** mg sodium, **10** g carbohydrate, **15** g protein.

- 8 ounces fresh mushrooms, halved
- 4 medium carrots, cut into 1-inch pieces
- 4 medium leeks, cut into 1-inch slices
- 2 pounds boneless beef short ribs
- 2 teaspoons finely shredded lemon peel
- ½ teaspoon pepper
- ½ teaspoon dried rosemary, crushed
- ½ teaspoon dried thyme, crushed
- ¼ teaspoon salt
- ¾ cup beef broth
- ⅓ cup dairy sour cream
- 1 tablespoon all-purpose flour

Asian Beef and Broccoli

To make very thin slices of beef, slice the steak against the grain when it is partially frozen.

Prep: 10 minutes **Cook:** 7 hours on low plus 15 minutes on high or 3¾ hours on high **Makes:** 8 servings

3 pounds boneless beef round steak, cut into strips

1 14½-ounce can tomatoes, cut up

1 8-ounce can tomato sauce

⅓ cup soy sauce

⅓ cup cider vinegar

4 cloves garlic, minced

¼ teaspoon pepper

6 cups broccoli florets

Hot cooked rice or linguine

1. In a 3½-, 4-, or 5-quart slow cooker place beef strips. In a small bowl combine tomatoes, tomato sauce, soy sauce, vinegar, garlic, and pepper; add to the cooker.

2. Cover; cook on low-heat setting for 7 to 8 hours or on high-heat setting for 3½ to 4 hours.

3. If using low-heat setting, turn to high-heat setting. Stir in broccoli. Cover and cook for 15 minutes or until broccoli is tender-crisp. Serve over rice or linguine.

Nutrition Facts per serving: 376 calories, 8 g total fat, 98 mg cholesterol, 915 mg sodium, 30 g carbohydrate, 44 g protein.

Beef and Peppers Sandwiches

Just serve cut-up, fresh vegetables and a light dip as a sidecar to these Italian-style beef sandwiches, and dinner is on the table.

Prep: 10 minutes **Cook:** 10 hours on low plus 30 minutes on high or 5½ hours on high **Broil:** 1 minute **Makes:** 8 servings

1. In a 3½- or 4-quart slow cooker combine meat, onion, Worcestershire sauce, bouillon granules, oregano, basil, thyme, and garlic.

2. Cover; cook on low-heat setting for 10 hours or on high-heat setting for 5 to 6 hours. Stir to break up meat cubes. Stir in chopped pepperoncini or other pickled peppers. Cook, uncovered, on high-heat setting for 30 minutes more, stirring often to break up meat.

3. Using a slotted spoon, place meat mixture on the bottom halves of buns. Top each sandwich with cheese. Broil sandwiches 4 inches from heat about 1 minute or until cheese melts. Add top halves of buns.

Nutrition Facts per serving: 493 calories, 18 g total fat, 122 mg cholesterol, 1,009 mg sodium, 35 g carbohydrate, 46 g protein.

1 2½- to 3-pound boneless beef chuck pot roast, cut into 1-inch cubes
1 large onion, chopped
¼ cup Worcestershire sauce
1 tablespoon instant beef bouillon granules
1 teaspoon dried oregano, crushed
½ teaspoon dried basil, crushed
½ teaspoon dried thyme, crushed
2 cloves garlic, minced
½ cup chopped pepperoncini (Italian pickled peppers) or other pickled peppers
8 hoagie buns or kaiser rolls, split and toasted
6 ounces sliced Swiss cheese

Beef and Vegetables in Red Wine Sauce

Use a hearty red wine, such as a Cabernet Sauvignon or Merlot, to make this delicious dish—and enjoy it with a glass of the same.

Prep: 25 minutes **Cook:** 8 hours on low or 4 hours on high **Makes:** 6 to 8 servings

1½ pounds boneless beef
   bottom round steak,
   cut into 1-inch cubes
1 tablespoon cooking oil
2 medium carrots, cut into
   ½-inch pieces
2 stalks celery, cut into
   ½-inch pieces
1 cup quartered fresh
   mushrooms
½ cup sliced green onions
3 tablespoons quick-cooking
   tapioca
1 14½-ounce can Italian-style
   stewed tomatoes
1 cup beef broth
½ cup dry red wine, white
   wine, or beef broth
1 teaspoon dried Italian
   seasoning, crushed
½ teaspoon salt
¼ teaspoon pepper
1 bay leaf
3 cups hot cooked noodles

1. In a large skillet brown beef, half at a time, in hot oil. Drain off fat.

2. Transfer beef to a 3½- or 4-quart slow cooker. Add carrots, celery, mushrooms, and green onions. Sprinkle with tapioca.

3. Combine undrained tomatoes, beef broth, wine or broth, Italian seasoning, salt, pepper, and bay leaf. Pour over vegetables and meat.

4. Cover; cook on low-heat setting for 8 to 10 hours or on high-heat setting for 4 to 5 hours. Discard bay leaf. Serve over hot cooked noodles.

Nutrition Facts per serving: 365 calories, 9 g total fat, 98 mg cholesterol, 662 mg sodium, 34 g carbohydrate, 33 g protein.

Beef Fajitas

Chile peppers contain volatile oils that can burn skin and eyes. Wear plastic or rubber gloves when working with them. If your bare hands touch chile peppers, wash your hands well with soap and water.

Prep: 15 minutes **Bake:** 10 minutes **Cook:** 8 hours on low or 4 hours on high **Makes:** 6 servings

1. Trim fat from meat. Cut flank steak into 6 portions. In a 3½-quart slow cooker combine meat, onion, green sweet pepper, jalapeño pepper(s), cilantro, garlic, chili powder, cumin, coriander, and salt. Add undrained tomatoes.

2. Cover; cook on low-heat setting for 8 to 10 hours or on high-heat setting for 4 to 5 hours.

3. To heat tortillas wrap them in foil and heat in a 350° oven for 10 to 15 minutes or until softened. Remove meat from cooker and shred. Return meat to cooker. Stir in lime juice, if desired. To serve fajitas, use a slotted spoon and fill the warmed tortillas with the beef mixture. If desired, add shredded cheese, guacamole, sour cream, and salsa. Roll up tortillas.

Nutrition Facts per serving: **426 calories, 13 g total fat, 53 mg cholesterol, 592 mg sodium, 46 g carbohydrate, 29 g protein.**

1½ pounds beef flank steak
1 cup chopped onion
1 green sweet pepper, cut into ½-inch pieces
1 or 2 jalapeño peppers, chopped
1 tablespoon snipped fresh cilantro
2 cloves garlic, minced
1 teaspoon chili powder
1 teaspoon ground cumin
1 teaspoon ground coriander
¼ teaspoon salt
1 8-ounce can stewed tomatoes
12 7-inch flour tortillas
2 to 3 teaspoons lime juice (optional)
  Shredded co-jack cheese (optional)
  Guacamole (optional)
  Dairy sour cream (optional)
  Salsa (optional)

Beef Brisket with Smoky Barbecue Sauce

Serve this smoky, saucy beef on buns or rolls. Round out the meal with baked beans and coleslaw.

Prep: 15 minutes **Cook:** 8 hours on low or 4 hours on high **Makes:** 6 to 8 servings

1 2- to 3-pound fresh
   beef brisket
1 teaspoon chili powder
½ teaspoon garlic powder
¼ teaspoon celery seeds
⅛ teaspoon pepper
½ cup catsup
½ cup chili sauce
¼ cup packed brown sugar
2 tablespoons vinegar
2 tablespoons Worcestershire
   sauce
1½ teaspoons liquid smoke
½ teaspoon dry mustard

1. Trim fat from brisket. If necessary, cut brisket to fit into slow cooker.

2. Combine chili powder, garlic powder, celery seeds, and pepper; rub evenly over meat. Place meat in a 3½-, 4-, or 5-quart slow cooker.

3. For sauce, combine catsup, chili sauce, brown sugar, vinegar, Worcestershire sauce, liquid smoke, and dry mustard. Pour sauce over brisket.

4. Cover; cook on low-heat setting for 8 to 10 hours or on high-heat setting for 4 to 5 hours. Remove meat from cooker. Cut the brisket into thin slices across the grain. Skim fat off juices in cooker; serve juices with meat.

Nutrition Facts per serving: 358 calories, 15 g total fat, 104 mg cholesterol, 676 mg sodium, 22 g carbohydrate, 34 g protein.

Herbed Mushroom Round Steak

Bottom round steak—which is more economical than tip round steak—is a great choice for a slow cooker because the moist heat tenderizes the meat.

Prep: 20 minutes   **Cook:** 8 hours on low or 4 hours on high   **Makes:** 6 servings

1. Trim fat from meat. Cut meat into serving-size portions. In a large skillet brown beef on both sides in hot oil.

2. In a 3½- or 4-quart slow cooker place onion slices and mushrooms. Place beef on top of vegetables.

3. In a small bowl combine soup, wine (if desired), oregano, thyme, and pepper; pour over meat.

4. Cover; cook on low-heat setting for 8 to 10 hours or on high-heat setting for 4 to 5 hours. Serve over hot cooked noodles.

Nutrition Facts per serving: 414 calories, 15 g total fat, 123 mg cholesterol, 488 mg sodium, 27 g carbohydrate, 42 g protein.

2 pounds beef round steak, cut ¾ inch thick

1 tablespoon cooking oil

1 medium onion, sliced

2 cups sliced fresh mushrooms or two 4-ounce jars canned mushrooms

1 10¾-ounce can condensed cream of mushroom soup

¼ cup dry white wine (optional)

½ teaspoon dried oregano, crushed

¼ teaspoon dried thyme, crushed

¼ teaspoon pepper

3 cups hot cooked noodles

Rump Roast and Vegetables

No stirring needed: A delicious gravy forms as the roast and vegetables slowly simmer.

Serve them with mashed potatoes or soft rolls to sop up every last bite of the delicious stuff.

Prep: 20 minutes **Cook:** 10 hours on low or 5 hours on high **Makes:** 6 servings

1 2- to 2½-pound boneless
   beef round rump, round tip,
   or chuck pot roast

2 tablespoons cooking oil

1½ pounds small potatoes
   (about 10) or medium
   potatoes (about 4), halved

2 medium carrots, cut into
   ½-inch pieces (1 cup)

1 small onion, sliced

1 10-ounce package frozen
   lima beans

1 bay leaf

2 tablespoons quick-cooking
   tapioca

1 10¾-ounce can condensed
   vegetable beef soup

¼ cup water

¼ teaspoon pepper

1. If necessary, cut roast to fit into the slow cooker. In a large skillet brown roast on all sides in hot oil. Meanwhile, in a 3½-, 4-, 5-, or 6-quart slow cooker place potatoes, carrots, and onion. Add frozen beans and bay leaf. Sprinkle tapioca over vegetables. Place roast atop vegetables.

2. In a medium bowl combine condensed soup, water, and pepper; pour over roast. Cover; cook on low-heat setting for 10 to 12 hours or on high-heat setting for 5 to 6 hours.

3. To serve, discard bay leaf and remove any strings from roast. Arrange roast and vegetables on a warm serving platter. Skim fat from gravy. Spoon some of the gravy over roast; pass remaining gravy with roast and vegetables.

Nutrition Facts per serving: 432 calories, 12 g total fat, 82 mg cholesterol, 460 mg sodium, 38 g carbohydrate, 43 g protein.

Hungarian Goulash

Hungarian paprika is considered superior to paprikas produced in other parts of the world. Either sweet or hot paprika can be used in this classic dish.

Prep: 25 minutes   **Cook:** 9½ hours on low plus 30 minutes on high or 4 hours on high   **Makes:** 6 servings

1. In a large skillet brown beef, half at a time, in hot oil. Drain fat.

2. Transfer meat to a 3½- or 4-quart slow cooker. Add carrots, onions, and garlic. In a small bowl combine beef broth, tomato paste, paprika, lemon peel, salt, caraway seeds, black pepper, and bay leaf. Stir into vegetable-meat mixture.

3. Cover; cook on low-heat setting for 9½ to 11½ hours or on high-heat setting for 3½ to 4½ hours.

4. If using low-heat setting, turn to high-heat setting. Stir in sweet pepper strips. Cover and cook 30 minutes longer on high-heat setting. Discard bay leaf. Serve with hot cooked noodles and a small amount of sour cream or yogurt.

Nutrition Facts per serving: 391 calories, 13 g total fat, 115 mg cholesterol, 442 mg sodium, 34 g carbohydrate, 34 g protein.

1½ pounds beef stew meat, cut into 1-inch cubes
1 tablespoon cooking oil
2 medium carrots, bias-sliced into ½-inch pieces
2 medium onions, thinly sliced
3 cloves garlic, minced
1¼ cups beef broth
1 6-ounce can tomato paste
1 tablespoon Hungarian paprika
1 teaspoon finely shredded lemon peel
½ teaspoon salt
½ teaspoon caraway seeds
¼ teaspoon ground black pepper
1 bay leaf
1 green sweet pepper, cut into strips
1 red or green sweet pepper, cut into strips
3 cups hot cooked noodles
Dairy sour cream or yogurt

Country Swiss Steak

"Swissing" is a term that refers to the process of smoothing cloth between rollers. In this recipe, the phrase likely refers to the pounding and flattening of the meat in traditional Swiss steak.

Prep: 15 minutes **Cook:** 10 hours on low or 5 hours on high **Makes:** 4 servings

1 pound boneless beef round
   steak, cut 1 inch thick
4 ounces spicy fresh
   bratwurst or other sausage,
   cut into
   ¾-inch slices
1 tablespoon cooking oil
1 small onion, sliced and
   separated into rings
1 teaspoon dried thyme,
   crushed
2 tablespoons quick-cooking
   tapioca
½ teaspoon salt
¼ teaspoon pepper
1 14½-ounce can chunky
   tomatoes with olive oil,
   garlic, and spices
2 cups hot cooked noodles
   or rice
   Fresh thyme sprigs
   (optional)

1. Trim fat from meat. Cut meat into 4 serving-size pieces. Brown meat and sausage in hot oil in a skillet. In a 3½- or 4-quart slow cooker place onion. Sprinkle with thyme, tapioca, salt, and pepper. Pour undrained tomatoes over vegetables. Add meat.

2. Cover and cook on low-heat setting for 10 to 12 hours or 4 to 5 hours on high-heat setting. Serve with hot cooked noodles or rice. Sprinkle with thyme sprigs, if desired.

Nutrition Facts per serving: **412 calories, 15 g total fat, 110 mg cholesterol, 755 mg sodium, 32 g carbohydrate, 35 g protein.**

Philadelphia Cheesesteak Wraps

A favorite street food is just as good eaten at the table for a quick dinner.

Serve these hearty wraps with a fresh fruit salad.

Prep: 20 minutes **Cook:** 10 hours on low or 5 hours on high **Makes:** 6 servings

1. In a large skillet, heat oil over medium-high heat. Add flank steak and brown well on both sides. Place pepper strips, onion wedges, and Italian seasoning in a 4 or 5-quart slow cooker. Top with flank steak. Pour beef broth over all.

2. Cover; cook on low-heat setting for 10 to 12 hours or on high-heat setting for 5 to 6 hours.

3. Remove flank steak from slow cooker and shred the meat. Combine mayonnaise and prepared horseradish; spread on each flour tortilla. Place sliced meat along the center of each tortilla. Remove pepper and onion mixture from slow cooker with a slotted spoon and place on top of beef. Place a half slice of Provolone on top. Roll tightly.

Nutrition Facts per serving: 484 calories, 30 g total fat, 48 mg cholesterol, 627 mg sodium, 27 g carbohydrate, 25 g protein.

1 tablespoon cooking oil
1 pound beef flank steak
1 cup red sweet pepper strips
1 cup thin onion wedges
1½ teaspoons dried Italian
  seasoning, crushed
1 14-ounce can beef broth
½ cup mayonnaise
4 teaspoons prepared
  horseradish
6 10-inch flour tortillas
3 slices Provolone cheese
  slices, halved

Port-Wine Pot Roast

The rich, seasoned gravy is terrific over hot cooked noodles or mashed potatoes. Just add a crisp lettuce salad or steamed green beans to complete the meal.

Prep: 15 minutes **Cook:** 8 hours on low or 4 hours on high **Makes:** 8 to 10 servings

1 2½- to 3-pound beef chuck pot roast

½ cup chopped onion

½ cup port wine or apple juice

1 8-ounce can tomato sauce

3 tablespoons quick-cooking tapioca

1 tablespoon Worcestershire sauce

1 teaspoon dried thyme, crushed

1 teaspoon dried oregano, crushed

2 cloves garlic, minced

4 cups hot cooked noodles

1. Trim fat from pot roast. If necessary, cut roast to fit into a 3½- or 4-quart slow cooker. Place meat in cooker.

2. In a small bowl combine onion, port or apple juice, tomato sauce, tapioca, Worcestershire, thyme, oregano, and garlic. Pour over pot roast.

3. Cover; cook on low-heat setting for 8 to 10 hours or on high-heat setting for 4 to 5 hours. Transfer roast to a serving platter. Skim fat from gravy. Pass gravy with meat. Serve with hot cooked noodles.

Nutrition Facts per serving: **426 calories, 20 g total fat, 104 mg cholesterol, 229 mg sodium, 29 g carbohydrate, 27 g protein.**

Ginger Beef with Broccoli

Bursting with the flavors and fixings of a traditional stir-fry, this easy beef and veggie combo is cloaked in a sauce that begins with an envelope of gravy mix.

Prep: 20 minutes   **Cook:** 8 hours on low plus 15 minutes on high or 4¼ hours on high   **Makes:** 6 servings

1. In a 3½- or 4-quart slow cooker place carrots, onions, beef strips, ginger, and garlic. Stir together water, soy sauce, and beef gravy mix. Pour over meat and vegetables in cooker.

2. Cover and cook on low-heat setting for 8 to 10 hours or on high-heat setting for 4 to 5 hours.

3. If using low-heat setting, turn to high-heat setting. Stir in broccoli. Cover and cook 15 minutes more on high-heat setting or until broccoli is crisp-tender. Serve over hot cooked rice.

Nutrition Facts per serving: 327 calories, 6 g total fat, 54 mg cholesterol, 476 mg sodium, 37 g carbohydrate, 31 g protein.

6 medium carrots,
   cut into 1-inch pieces
2 medium onions,
   cut into wedges
1½ pounds beef round steak,
   cut into ½-inch bias-sliced
   strips
1 tablespoon minced
   fresh ginger
2 cloves garlic, minced
½ cup water
2 tablespoons reduced-sodium
   soy sauce
1 ¾-ounce envelope
   beef gravy mix
4 cups broccoli florets
3 cups hot cooked rice

Beef-and-Bean Medley

Served over corn chips and topped with shredded cheddar, this zesty three-bean and beef combo is sure to please even the pickiest eaters.

Prep: 25 minutes **Cook:** 4 hours on low or 2 hours on high **Makes:** 8 to 10 servings

---

1 pound ground beef

1 cup chopped onion (1 large)

6 slices bacon, crisp-cooked, drained, and crumbled

2 16-ounce cans baked beans

1 15-ounce can butter beans, rinsed and drained

1 15-ounce can red kidney beans, rinsed and drained

1 cup catsup

½ cup water

¼ cup packed brown sugar

3 tablespoons vinegar

⅛ teaspoon pepper

1 8- to 10-ounce bag corn chips or tortilla chips

2 cups shredded cheddar cheese (8 ounces)

½ cup sliced green onions

1. In a large skillet cook ground beef and onion until beef is brown. Drain off fat. Transfer beef mixture to a 3½- or 4-quart slow cooker. Add crumbled bacon, baked beans, butter beans, and kidney beans. In a small bowl combine catsup, water, brown sugar, vinegar, and pepper. Add catsup mixture to slow cooker. Stir to combine. Cover and cook on low-heat setting for 4 to 6 hours or on high-heat setting for 2 to 3 hours.

2. Serve over or with corn or tortilla chips. Sprinkle with shredded cheese and green onions.

Nutrition Facts per serving: 664 calories, 32 g total fat, 74 mg cholesterol, 1,505 mg sodium, 65 g carbohydrate, 31 g protein.

Nacho-Style Casserole

Refrigerated sliced potatoes and condensed cheese soup make quick work of preparing this fun layered casserole. Top each serving with sour cream, salsa, and green onions.

Prep: 20 minutes **Cook:** 4 hours on low or 2½ hours on high **Makes:** 4 servings

1. In a large skillet cook ground beef and onion until meat is brown. Drain fat. In a medium bowl, stir together the soup, undrained chile peppers, and milk.

2. In a 3½-, 4-, or 5-quart slow cooker layer half of the potatoes, half of the ground beef mixture, and half of the soup mixture. Repeat layers.

3. Cover and cook on low-heat setting for 4 hours or on high-heat setting for 2½ hours or until potatoes are tender. Gently stir before serving. If desired, serve with sour cream, salsa, and sliced green onion.

Nutrition Facts per serving: **368 calories, 16 g total fat, 66 mg cholesterol, 866 mg sodium, 31 g carbohydrate, 23 g protein.**

- 12 ounces lean ground beef
- ½ cup chopped onion
- 1 11-ounce can condensed fiesta nacho cheese soup
- 1 4-ounce can diced green chile peppers
- ½ cup milk
- 1 20-ounce package refrigerated sliced potatoes
- Dairy sour cream (optional)
- Salsa (optional)
- Sliced green onions (optional)

Italian Steak Rolls

Pretty to look at and delicious to eat, these veggie-stuffed steak spirals are perfect for casual entertaining. Just add a salad and some good bread.

Prep: 30 minutes **Cook:** 7 hours on low or 3½ hours on high **Makes:** 6 servings

1½ to 2 pounds boneless
    beef round steak
½ cup grated carrot
⅓ cup chopped zucchini
⅓ cup chopped red
    or green sweet pepper
¼ cup sliced green onion
2 tablespoons grated
    Parmesan cheese
1 tablespoon snipped
    fresh parsley
1 clove garlic, minced
¼ teaspoon pepper
1 tablespoon cooking oil
1 14-ounce jar meatless
    spaghetti sauce
6 ounces pasta, cooked
    and drained

1. Trim fat from meat. Cut meat into 6 portions. Place the meat between 2 pieces of plastic wrap and, with a meat mallet, pound steak to a ⅛ to ¼ inch thickness.

2. In a small bowl combine carrot, zucchini, red or green sweet pepper, green onion, Parmesan cheese, parsley, garlic, and pepper. Spoon ⅙ of the vegetable filling on each piece of meat. Roll up meat around the filling and tie each roll with string or secure with wooden toothpicks.

3. Brown meat rolls on all sides in hot oil. Transfer meat rolls to a 3½- or 4-quart slow cooker. Pour spaghetti sauce over the meat rolls.

4. Cover; cook on low-heat setting for 7 to 8 hours or on high-heat setting for 3½ to 4 hours. Discard string or toothpicks. Serve meat rolls with hot cooked pasta.

Nutrition Facts per serving: **358 calories, 10 g total fat, 74 mg cholesterol, 341 mg sodium, 32 g carbohydrate, 33 g protein.**

Deviled Steak Strips

If you don't like the tiny granules of tapioca in the finished dish, grind the tapioca with a mortar and pestle, in a coffee grinder, or blender container for a smoother sauce.

Prep: 15 minutes   **Cook:** 7 hours on low or 3½ hours on high   **Makes:** 6 to 8 servings

1. Cut steak across the grain into bite-size strips. In a 3½- or 4-quart slow cooker place steak strips, onion, garlic, water, tomato sauce, mustard, pepper, bouillon granules, and tapioca. Stir to combine.

2. Cover and cook on low-heat setting for 7 to 9 hours or on high-heat setting for 3½ to 4½ hours. Serve over hot cooked noodles, rice, or mashed potatoes.

Nutrition Facts per serving: 324 calories, 4 g total fat, 86 mg cholesterol, 754 mg sodium, 32 g carbohydrate, 38 g protein.

2 pounds boneless beef
   round steak
1 cup chopped onion
3 cloves garlic, minced
1 cup water
1 16-ounce can tomato sauce
3 tablespoons horseradish
   mustard
¼ teaspoon pepper
2 teaspoons instant beef
   bouillon granules
3 tablespoons quick-cooking
   tapioca
   Hot cooked noodles, rice,
   or mashed potatoes

Italian-Style Meat Loaf

To make your morning go more smoothly, shape the meat loaf the night before, then cover it well and refrigerate it. The next morning, just set the loaf in the cooker and turn on the heat.

Prep: 25 minutes **Cook:** 7 hours on low or 3½ hours on high **Stand:** 5 minutes **Makes:** 8 servings

---

1 **8-ounce can pizza sauce**
1 **beaten egg**
½ cup chopped onion
½ cup chopped green
  sweet pepper
⅓ cup fine dry seasoned
  bread crumbs
½ teaspoon garlic salt
¼ teaspoon pepper
¼ teaspoon fennel seeds,
  crushed (optional)
1½ pounds lean ground beef
½ cup shredded mozzarella
  cheese (2 ounces)

1. Reserve ⅓ cup pizza sauce; cover and chill. In a medium mixing bowl combine remaining pizza sauce and egg. Stir in onion, green sweet pepper, bread crumbs, garlic salt, pepper, and fennel, if desired. Add ground beef and mix well.

2. Crisscross three 18x2-inch foil strips (layered on a sheet of waxed paper to keep counter clean). In center of the foil strips shape a 6-inch-round meat loaf. Bringing up foil strips, lift and transfer meat and foil to a 3½-, 4-, or 5-quart slow cooker. Press meat away from sides of the cooker to avoid burning.

3. Cover; cook on low-heat setting for 7 to 9 hours or on high-heat setting for 3½ to 4½ hours (or to 170°F internal temperature).

4. Spread meat with reserved ⅓ cup pizza sauce. Sprinkle with mozzarella cheese. Cover cooker and let stand 5 to 10 minutes.

5. Using foil strips, carefully lift meat loaf and transfer to a serving plate; discard the foil strips.

Nutrition Facts per serving: **228 calories, 13 g total fat, 83 mg cholesterol, 510 mg sodium, 8 g carbohydrate, 20 g protein.**

Beefy Mexican Macaroni with Cheese

Kids will love this fun take on macaroni and cheese.

Prep: 20 minutes   **Cook:** 8¼ hours on low or 4¼ hours on high   **Makes:** 4 to 6 servings

1. In a large skillet cook ground beef and onion until meat is brown and onion is tender. Drain off fat.

2. Meanwhile, in a 3½- or 4-quart slow cooker combine cheese sauce, stewed tomatoes, drained mushrooms, and chili powder. Stir in meat mixture.

3. Cover; cook on low-heat setting for 8 to 10 hours or on high-heat setting for 4 to 5 hours. Stir in macaroni. Cover and cook 15 minutes more.

Nutrition Facts per serving: **335 calories, 20 g total fat, 69 mg cholesterol, 1,179 mg sodium, 20 g carbohydrate, 19 g protein.**

- 1 pound ground beef
- ½ cup chopped onion
- 1 16-ounce jar process cheese sauce
- 1 14½-ounce can Mexican-style stewed tomatoes
- 1 2½-ounce jar sliced mushrooms, drained
- 2 teaspoons chili powder
- 2 cups cooked wagon wheel or elbow macaroni

Sloppy Joes

It may be messy eating, but it sure does taste good! Make this classic sandwich with ground pork or ground turkey rather than beef for a change of pace.

Prep: 20 minutes **Cook:** 6 hours on low or 3 hours on high **Makes:** 8 servings

1½ **pounds ground beef**
1 **cup chopped onion**
2 **cloves garlic, minced**
¾ **cup catsup**
½ **cup chopped green sweet pepper**
½ **cup chopped celery**
¼ **cup water**
1 **to 2 tablespoons brown sugar**
2 **tablespoon prepared mustard**
2 **tablespoons vinegar**
2 **tablespoons Worcestershire sauce**
1½ **teaspoons chili powder**
8 **hamburger buns, split and toasted**

1. In a large skillet cook ground beef, onion, and garlic until meat is brown and onion is tender. Drain off fat.

2. Meanwhile, in a 3½- or 4-quart slow cooker combine catsup, green sweet pepper, celery, water, brown sugar, mustard, vinegar, Worcestershire sauce, and chili powder. Stir in meat.

3. Cover; cook on low-heat setting for 6 to 8 hours or on high-heat setting for 3 to 4 hours. Spoon into toasted buns.

Nutrition Facts per serving: 340 calories, 13 g total fat, 53 mg cholesterol, 690 mg sodium, 35 g carbohydrate, 21 g protein.

Hot-and-Spicy Sloppy Joes

Hot-style tomato juice and jalapeño peppers give new life to these saucy sandwiches.

Prep: 20 minutes **Cook:** 10 hours on low or 3 hours on high **Makes:** 8 servings

1. In a large skillet cook ground beef, onion, and garlic until meat is brown and onion is tender. Drain off fat.

2. Meanwhile, in a 3 ½- or 4-quart slow cooker combine tomato juice; catsup; water; brown sugar; jalapeño peppers, if desired; mustard; chili powder; and Worcestershire sauce. Stir in meat mixture. Cover; cook on low-heat setting for 10 to 12 hours or high-heat setting for 3 to 5 hours. Toast buns; spoon meat mixture into buns and sprinkle with cheese.

For 5- or 6-quart slow cooker: Double all ingredients; prepare as above. Makes 16 servings.

Nutrition Facts per serving: 361 calories, 16 g total fat, 60 mg cholesterol, 606 mg sodium, 33 g carbohydrate, 21 g protein.

1½ pounds ground beef
1 large onion, chopped (1 cup)
1 clove garlic, minced
1 6-ounce can hot-style tomato juice or vegetable juice cocktail
½ cup catsup
½ cup water
2 tablespoons packed brown sugar
2 tablespoons chopped canned jalapeño peppers (optional)
1 tablespoon yellow mustard
2 teaspoons chili powder
1 teaspoon Worcestershire sauce
8 hamburger buns
Shredded cheddar cheese

New England Boiled Dinner

A creamy horseradish-sour cream sauce freshens up this hearty American classic.

Prep: 20 minutes **Cook:** 11 hours on low plus 30 minutes on high or 6 hours on high **Makes:** 8 servings

½ cup mayonnaise
    or salad dressing
½ cup dairy sour cream
2 tablespoons horseradish
    mustard
2 teaspoons snipped
    fresh chives
6 medium potatoes, peeled
    and quartered (about
    2 pounds)
6 medium carrots,
    cut in 2-inch lengths
1 large onion, quartered
3 cloves garlic, minced
1 3- to 3½-pound
    corned beef brisket
2 teaspoons dill seeds
1 teaspoon dried rosemary,
    crushed
½ teaspoon salt
2 14-ounce cans beef broth
1 small head cabbage,
    cut into 8 wedges

1. In a small bowl stir together mayonnaise, sour cream, horseradish mustard, and chives. Cover and chill until serving time or up to 24 hours.

2. In a 5- or 6-quart slow cooker place potatoes, carrots, onion, and garlic. Top with corned beef brisket; discard seasoning packet if present. Sprinkle with dill seeds, rosemary, and salt. Pour beef broth over meat.

3. Cover; cook on low-heat setting for 11 to 12 hours or on high-heat setting for 5½ to 6 hours.

4. If using low-heat setting, turn to high-heat setting. Add cabbage wedges. Cover and cook for 30 minutes more. Remove meat from cooker. Thinly slice meat across the grain. Remove vegetables with a slotted spoon and serve with meat. Serve mayonnaise mixture with meat and vegetables.

Nutrition Facts per serving: 540 calories, 35 g total fat, 100 mg cholesterol, 767 mg sodium, 27 g carbohydrate, 30 g protein.

Corned Beef Hash

A warming dinner for those red-flannel days in the fall and winter.

Prep: 10 minutes **Cook:** 4 hours on low or 2 hours on high **Makes:** 6 to 8 servings

1. In a 3½-, 4-, or 5-quart slow cooker combine hash brown potatoes, corned beef, onion, broth, and pepper.

2. Cover; cook on low-heat setting for 4 to 6 hours or on high-heat setting for 2 to 3 hours.

Nutrition Facts per serving: **393 calories, 20 g total fat, 98 mg cholesterol, 1,303 mg sodium, 30 g carbohydrate, 23 g protein.**

Roast Beef Hash: Substitute cooked roast beef for the corned beef, beef broth for the chicken broth, and add ¼ teaspoon salt.

1 32-ounce package
  frozen hash brown potatoes
4 cups finely chopped
  cooked corned beef
1 cup chopped onion
1 cup chicken broth
½ teaspoon pepper

Wheelies and Franks

Wagon wheel pasta and cocktail wieners make this whimsical dish perfect for kids' parties. A fruit salad and brownies (or birthday cake!) complete the menu.

Prep: 15 minutes **Cook:** 7 hours on low or 3 hours on high **Makes:** 6 servings

2 15-ounce cans tomato
   sauce with chunky
   tomatoes
1 14½-ounce can Mexican-
   style stewed tomatoes
1 15-ounce can red kidney
   beans, drained and rinsed
½ cup water
1 medium onion, chopped
½ cup chopped green
   sweet pepper
2 teaspoons chili powder
1 clove garlic, minced
1 5.3-ounce package
   cocktail wieners (16),
   or sausage links
8 ounces dried wagon
   wheel pasta
   Shredded cheddar
   or Monterey Jack cheese
   (optional)
   Dairy sour cream (optional)

1. In a 3½- or 4-quart slow cooker combine tomato sauce, undrained stewed tomatoes, beans, water, onion, sweet pepper, chili powder, and garlic. Stir in wieners or sausage links.

2. Cover; cook on low-heat setting for 7 to 9 hours or on high-heat setting for 3 to 4 hours.

3. Just before serving, cook pasta according to package directions; drain. Stir cooked pasta into wiener mixture. Spoon into bowls. If desired, serve with cheese and sour cream.

Nutrition Facts per serving: 350 calories, 8 g total fat, 13 mg cholesterol, 1,489 mg sodium, 57 g carbohydrate, 15 g protein.

Cheesy Scalloped Potatoes and Ham

This old-fashioned favorite used to require lots of potato-peeling and a stint in the oven. This easy version takes advantage of prepared potatoes and the convenience of a slow cooker.

Prep: 10 minutes **Cook:** 7 hours on low or 3½ hours on high **Makes:** 4 servings

1. In a 3½-, 4-, or 5-quart slow cooker combine frozen hash brown potatoes, ham, pimiento, parsley, and pepper.

2. In a medium bowl combine the soup and milk; pour over the potato mixture in the slow cooker.

3. Cover; cook on low-heat setting for 7 to 9 hours or on high-heat setting for 3½ to 4 hours. Stir before serving.

Nutrition Facts per serving: 470 calories, 24 g total fat, 43 mg cholesterol, 1,454 mg sodium, 42 g carbohydrate, 24 g protein.

1 24-ounce package loose-pack
  frozen hash brown potatoes
  with onion and peppers
2 cups diced fully cooked ham
  (10-ounces)
1 2-ounce jar diced pimiento,
  drained
1 tablespoon snipped
  fresh parsley
¼ teaspoon pepper
1 11-ounce can condensed
  cheddar cheese soup
¾ cup milk

Bavarian Pork Roast

For a truly German-style meal, serve this well-seasoned pork and tangy gravy with Bavarian-style sauerkraut, dark rye bread, and a mug of cold beer.

Prep: 25 minutes   **Cook:** 8 hours on low or 4 hours on high   **Makes:** 6 servings

1 1½- to 2-pound boneless
   pork shoulder roast
2 teaspoons caraway seeds
1 teaspoon dried marjoram,
   crushed
¾ teaspoon salt
½ teaspoon pepper
1 tablespoon olive oil
   or cooking oil
½ cup water
2 tablespoons white
   wine vinegar
1 8-ounce carton dairy
   sour cream or plain yogurt
4 teaspoons cornstarch

1. Trim fat from roast. If necessary, cut roast to fit into a 3½-, 4-, 5-, or 6-quart slow cooker. Combine caraway seeds, marjoram, salt, and pepper. Rub all over roast.

2. In a large skillet brown pork roast on all sides in hot oil. Drain off fat. Place meat in slow cooker. Add the water to skillet; bring to a gentle boil over medium heat, stirring to loosen brown bits in bottom of skillet. Pour skillet juices and vinegar into slow cooker.

3. Cover and cook on low-heat setting for 8 to 10 hours or on high-heat setting for 4 to 5 hours. Remove meat from cooker; keep warm.

4. For gravy, skim fat from juices; measure 1¼ cups juices (add water, if necessary). Pour juices into a saucepan; bring to boiling. Combine sour cream or yogurt and cornstarch. Stir into juices. Cook and stir over medium heat until thickened and bubbly. Cook and stir 2 minutes more. Slice meat and serve with gravy.

Nutrition Facts per serving: **262 calories, 15 g total fat, 73 mg cholesterol, 365 mg sodium, 4 g carbohydrate, 26 g protein.**

Apple Pork Roast and Vegetables

Apple juice and cinnamon give this autumnal dish a little sweetness and a little spice.

Prep: 15 minutes **Cook:** 10 hours on low or 5 hours on high **Makes:** 6 servings

1. Trim fat from roast. If necessary, cut roast to fit into slow cooker. Brown roast in a large skillet on all sides in hot oil.

2. Meanwhile, in a 3½-, 4-, 5-, or 6-quart slow cooker place parsnips, carrots, green sweet pepper, and celery. Sprinkle with tapioca. Add apple juice concentrate, water, beef bouillon granules, pepper, and cinnamon. Place roast atop vegetables.

3. Cover; cook on low-heat setting for 10 to 12 hours or on high-heat setting for 5 to 6 hours.

4. To serve, transfer the meat and vegetables to a serving platter. Strain cooking liquid and skim off fat. Drizzle some of the cooking liquid over the sliced meat and pass the remaining liquid.

Nutrition Facts per serving : 344 calories, 14 g total fat, 74 mg cholesterol, 266 mg sodium, 33 g carbohydrate, 21 g protein.

1 1½- to 2-pound boneless
  pork shoulder roast
1 tablespoon cooking oil
3 medium parsnips, cut into
  ½-inch pieces (2 cups)
3 medium carrots, cut into
  1-inch pieces (1½ cups)
1 large green sweet pepper,
  cut into 1-inch wide strips
2 stalks celery, cut into
  ½-inch pieces (1 cup)
3 tablespoons quick-cooking
  tapioca
1 6-ounce can frozen apple
  juice concentrate, thawed
¼ cup water
1 teaspoon instant beef
  bouillon granules
¼ teaspoon pepper
¼ teaspoon ground cinnamon

Cranberry Pork Roast

In this slow-simmered pork dish, a ruby-color fruit sauce provides good nutrition and great taste.

Prep: 20 minutes **Cook:** 5½ hours on low **Makes:** 12 servings

4 medium potatoes,
   peeled and cubed
1 3-pound boneless pork
   top loin roast (single loin)
1 16-ounce can whole
   cranberry sauce
1 15-ounce can apricot
   halves, drained
1 medium onion, chopped
½ cup snipped dried apricots
2 tablespoons sugar
1 teaspoon dry mustard
¼ teaspoon ground red pepper
1 tablespoon cornstarch
1 tablespoon cold water

1. Place potatoes in bottom of a 5- or 6-quart slow cooker. Place meat on potatoes; set aside. In a blender container or food processor bowl combine cranberry sauce, drained apricots, onion, dried apricots, sugar, mustard, and red pepper. Cover and blend or process until nearly smooth.

2. Pour fruit mixture over pork. Cover and cook on low-heat setting for 5½ to 6½ hours. Remove roast and potatoes to platter. Cover and keep warm.

3. For sauce, transfer cooking juices from cooker to a 4-cup glass measure. Skim off fat. Measure 2 cups juices; discard remaining juices. Pour juices into a medium saucepan. Stir together cornstarch and the water. Add to saucepan, stirring to combine. Cook and stir over medium heat until thickened and bubbly; cook and stir 2 minutes more. Slice roast. Serve sauce with potatoes and roast.

Nutrition Facts per serving : 307 calories, 6 g total fat, 67 mg cholesterol, 75 mg sodium, 36 g carbohydrate, 26 g protein.

Cuban Pork

Serve these spice-and-citrus-sauced wraps with a tropical fruit salad.

Prep: 25 minutes **Marinate:** 6 hours **Cook:** 10 hours on low or 5 hours on high **Makes:** 8 to 10 servings

1. For the marinade, in a small bowl combine fruit juices, water, garlic, oregano, cumin, salt, pepper, and the bay leaves. Trim fat from meat*. Pierce pork roast in several places with a large fork. Place in a plastic bag set in a deep bowl or a baking dish; add marinade. Close bag and turn to coat. Marinate, covered, in the refrigerator for 6 to 24 hours, turning occasionally.

2. In a 3½-, 4, or 5-quart slow cooker, place onion. Top with meat and marinade mixture.

3. Cover; cook on low-heat setting for 10 to 12 hours or on high-heat setting for 5 to 6 hours.

4. To serve, remove meat from cooker; cool slightly. Skim fat from juices. Shred meat; remove onions from juices with a slotted spoon and add to meat. Discard bay leaves. Serve meat in flour tortillas with small bowls of the hot juices.

***Trimming meat:** If meat has netting, peel back netting to trim.

Nutrition Facts per serving: **385 calories, 13 g total fat, 110 mg cholesterol, 465 mg sodium, 27 g carbohydrate, 37 g protein.**

- ½ cup lime juice
- ¼ cup grapefruit juice
- ¼ cup water
- 3 cloves garlic, minced
- 1 teaspoon dried oregano, crushed
- ½ teaspoon ground cumin
- ½ teaspoon salt
- ¼ teaspoon pepper
- 2 bay leaves
- 1 3- to 4-pound boneless pork shoulder roast
- 1 cup sliced onion
   flour tortillas

Pork Roast with Cherries

Cherries pair perfectly with pork, but you also can use coarsely chopped cranberries, apricots, golden raisins, or dried mixed fruit.

Prep: 20 minutes **Cook:** 7 hours on low or 3½ hours on high **Makes:** 6 to 8 servings

---

1 2- to 2½-pound boneless
    pork shoulder roast
2 tablespoons cooking oil
1 tablespoon quick-cooking
    tapioca
1 tablespoon snipped fresh
    thyme or 1 teaspoon dried
    thyme, crushed
½ teaspoon pepper
1 medium onion, sliced
1 cup dried cherries
½ cup apple juice
    or apple cider
3 to 4 cups hot cooked rice
    or noodles

1. Trim fat from meat. If necessary, cut roast to fit into a 3½-, 4-, 5-, or 6-quart slow cooker. In a large skillet brown meat on all sides in hot oil. Drain off fat.

2. Transfer meat to cooker. Sprinkle tapioca, dried thyme (if using), and pepper over meat. Add onion and dried cherries. Pour apple juice or cider over all.

3. Cover; cook on low-heat setting for 7 to 9 hours or on high-heat setting for 3½ to 4½ hours. Transfer meat to serving platter; cover to keep warm.

4. For sauce, skim fat from cooking juices. If using, stir fresh thyme into juices. Serve meat and cooking juices with hot cooked rice or noodles.

Nutrition Facts per serving: 460 calories, 18 g total fat, 99 mg cholesterol, 80 mg sodium, 43 g carbohydrate, 29 g protein.

Pork Hocks and Black-Eyed Peas

Southerners swear by a feast of black-eyed peas on New Year's Day to give them good luck throughout the year. Serve 'em up with warm corn bread.

Prep: 25 minutes **Stand:** 1 hour **Cook:** 8 hours on low or 4 hours on high **Stand:** 10 minutes **Makes:** 6 servings

1. Rinse black-eyed peas; place in a large saucepan. Add enough water to cover peas by 2 inches. Bring to boiling; reduce heat. Simmer, uncovered, for 10 minutes. Remove from heat. Cover and let stand for 1 hour. Drain and rinse peas.

2. In a 3½-, 4-, or 5-quart slow cooker combine the black-eyed peas, pork hocks, broth, sweet pepper, onion, celery, bay leaves, and red pepper.

3. Cover; cook on low-heat setting for 8 to 10 hours or on high-heat setting for 4 to 5 hours. Add okra. Cover; let stand for 10 minutes or until okra is tender. Remove pork hocks. When cool enough to handle, cut meat off bones; cut meat into bite-size pieces. Discard bones and bay leaves. To serve, stir meat into black-eyed pea mixture.

Nutrition Facts per serving: **191 calories, 3 g total fat, 14 mg cholesterol, 763 mg sodium, 28 g carbohydrate, 15 g protein.**

- 1½ cups dry black-eyed peas
- 4 small smoked pork hocks (1½ pounds)
- 4 cups reduced-sodium chicken broth
- 1 medium green sweet pepper, chopped
- 1 medium onion, chopped
- 1 stalk celery, chopped
- 2 bay leaves
- ¼ teaspoon ground red pepper
- 2 cups sliced okra or one 10-ounce package frozen whole okra, thawed and cut into ½-inch slices

Barbecue-Style Pork Sandwiches

Coleslaw is a great condiment for these zippy barbecued sandwiches—piled right on top of the meat—or served alongside as an accompaniment.

Prep: 15 minutes **Cook:** 10 hours on low or 5 hours on high **Makes:** 6 servings

2 large green sweet peppers, cut into strips (2½ cups)

1 large onion, thinly sliced and separated into rings (1 cup)

2 tablespoons quick-cooking tapioca

1 2½- to 3-pound pork shoulder roast

1 10¾-ounce can condensed tomato soup

2 tablespoons steak sauce

3 to 4 teaspoons chili powder

½ teaspoon sugar

¼ teaspoon garlic powder

¼ teaspoon pepper

Several dashes bottled hot pepper sauce

6 kaiser rolls, split

Coleslaw, drained (optional)

1. In a 3½-, 4-, 5-, or 6-quart slow cooker combine sweet pepper strips and onion rings. Sprinkle tapioca over vegetables. Trim fat from roast. If necessary, cut roast to fit into cooker. Place roast atop vegetables.

2. For barbecue sauce, in a medium bowl combine tomato soup, steak sauce, chili powder, sugar, garlic powder, pepper, and hot pepper sauce. Pour over roast.

3. Cover; cook on low-heat setting for 10 to 12 hours or on high-heat setting for 5 to 6 hours. Remove roast from cooker and thinly slice or shred meat. Skim fat from sauce.

4. Serve meat on kaiser rolls; top with barbecue sauce and coleslaw, if desired.

Nutrition Facts per serving: **511 calories, 14 g total fat, 122 mg cholesterol, 867 mg sodium, 49 g carbohydrate, 45 g protein.**

Curried Pork and Apples

Tart Granny Smith apples are a great choice to make this aromatic curry.

Prep: 25 minutes **Cook:** 10 hours on low or 5 hours on high **Makes:** 6 servings

1. Trim fat from roast; cut pork into 1-inch cubes. In a large skillet brown pork, half at a time, in hot oil. Transfer pork to a 3½- or 4-quart slow cooker; sprinkle with tapioca. Add water, apples, onion, raisins, curry, bouillon granules, and paprika.

2. Cover; cook on low-heat setting for 10 to 12 hours or on high-heat setting for 5 to 6 hours. Serve over rice.

For 5- or 6-quart slow cooker: Use one 3-pound boneless pork shoulder roast; 3 tablespoons cooking oil; ⅓ cup quick-cooking tapioca; 3 cups water; 3 medium cooking apples, cored and quartered; 1⅓ cups chopped onion; ⅔ cup raisins; 3 tablespoons curry powder; 4 teaspoons instant chicken bouillon granules; ½ teaspoon paprika; and hot cooked rice. Prepare as above. Makes 8 to 10 servings.

Nutrition Facts per serving: 461 calories, 14 g total fat, 98 mg cholesterol, 562 mg sodium, 49 g carbohydrate, 34 g protein.

1 2-pound boneless pork
   shoulder roast
2 tablespoons cooking oil
¼ cup quick-cooking tapioca
2 cups water
2 medium cooking apples,
   cored and cut into quarters
1 cup chopped onion
½ cup raisins
2 tablespoons curry powder
1 tablespoon instant chicken
   bouillon granules
½ teaspoon paprika
   Hot cooked rice

Fennel Pork Roast and Vegetables

Fresh fennel is at its peak from September through April. Look for firm, smooth bulbs without cracks and brown spots. Use the bright green fennel leaves as a garnish.

Prep: 25 minutes **Cook:** 8 hours on low or 4 hours on high **Makes:** 6 to 8 servings

1 2- to 2½-pound boneless
   pork shoulder roast
1 teaspoon fennel seeds,
   crushed
½ teaspoon garlic powder
½ teaspoon dried oregano,
   crushed
¼ teaspoon pepper
2 tablespoons cooking oil
1½ pounds small red potatoes,
   halved
1 large fennel bulb, trimmed
   and cut into 1-inch pieces
1½ cups water
2 teaspoons instant chicken
   bouillon granules
½ cup cold water
¼ cup all-purpose flour
   Salt and pepper

1. Trim fat from meat. In a small bowl combine crushed fennel seeds, garlic powder, oregano, and pepper. Rub about 1 teaspoon of the seasoning mixture evenly over roast. In a Dutch oven brown meat on all sides in hot oil. Drain off fat.

2. Place potatoes and fennel in bottom of a 3½- or 4-quart slow cooker. Sprinkle with remaining seasoning mixture. Stir together the 1½ cups water and bouillon granules; add to cooker. Cut meat, if necessary, to fit into the slow cooker. Place roast atop vegetable mixture.

3. Cover; cook on low-heat setting for 8 to 10 hours or on high-heat setting for 4 to 5 hours.

4. For gravy, skim fat from juices. Measure 1½ cups juices into a medium saucepan. Stir the ½ cup cold water into the flour; stir into reserved juices in saucepan. Cook and stir until thickened and bubbly. Cook and stir 1 minute more. Season to taste with salt and pepper. Pass gravy with meat.

Nutrition Facts per serving: **439 calories, 20 g total fat, 99 mg cholesterol, 451 mg sodium, 33 g carbohydrate, 30 g protein.**

Orange-Herbed Pork Roast

This orange-sauced pork roast goes great with parslied new potatoes and steamed baby carrots and sugar snap peas.

Prep: 25 minutes **Cook:** 8 hours on low or 4 hours on high **Makes:** 8 servings

1. Trim fat from pork roast. If necessary, cut roast to fit into slow cooker. In a small bowl combine garlic powder, ginger, thyme, and pepper. Rub spice mixture over entire surface of meat with fingers. In a large skillet brown roast on all sides in hot oil. Drain.

2. Transfer meat to a 3½-, 4-, or 5-quart slow cooker. Combine chicken broth, sugar, lemon juice, soy sauce, and orange peel; pour over roast.

3. Cover; cook on low-heat setting for 8 to 10 hours or on high-heat setting for 4 to 5 hours.

4. Transfer roast to a serving platter; keep warm. For sauce, pour juices into glass measure. Skim fat. If necessary, add water to equal 2 cups. Transfer to saucepan. Combine cornstarch and orange juice; stir into juices in saucepan. Cook and stir until thickened and bubbly. Cook and stir 2 minutes more. If desired, season to taste. Pass sauce with meat.

Nutrition Facts per serving: **197 calories, 6 g total fat, 78 mg cholesterol, 224 mg sodium, 8 g carbohydrate, 29 g protein.**

- 1 2½- to 3-pound pork sirloin roast
- ½ teaspoon garlic powder
- ½ teaspoon ground ginger
- ½ teaspoon dried thyme, crushed
- ¼ teaspoon pepper
- 1 tablespoon cooking oil
- 1 cup chicken broth
- 2 tablespoons sugar
- 2 tablespoons lemon juice
- 2 teaspoons soy sauce
- 1½ teaspoons finely shredded orange peel
- 3 tablespoons cornstarch
- ½ cup orange juice

Apricot-Glazed Pork Roast

Cook some rice to serve as a side and to soak up the sweet and savory mustard-spiked apricot sauce.

Prep: 15 minutes   **Cook:** 10 hours on low or 5 hours on high   **Makes:** 6 to 8 servings

1   3- to 3½-pound boneless pork shoulder roast
1   18-ounce jar apricot preserves
¼   cup chicken broth
2   tablespoons Dijon-style mustard
1   large onion, chopped

1. Trim fat from roast. If necessary, cut roast to fit into a 3½-, 4-, 5-, or 6-quart slow cooker. Place meat in cooker. Combine preserves, broth, mustard, and onion; pour over meat.

2. Cover and cook on low-heat setting for 10 to 12 hours or on high-heat setting for 5 to 6 hours. Transfer meat to a serving plate. Skim off fat from sauce. Spoon some of the sauce over meat; discard any remaining sauce.

Nutrition Facts per serving: 456 calories, 10 g total fat, 93 mg cholesterol, 184 mg sodium, 61 g carbohydrate, 29 g protein.

Lemon Pork and Couscous

Flavored with fresh basil and shallots, this one-dish dinner is well-suited to weeknight entertaining or for weekend celebrations when you want to be part of the party instead of stuck in the kitchen.

Prep: 30 minutes **Cook:** 7 hours on low or 3½ hours on high **Makes:** 6 servings

1. Trim fat from pork. Cut pork into 1-inch pieces. Combine flour and pepper in a plastic bag. Add pork, close bag, and shake until pork is coated with flour. In a large skillet brown half of the meat in 1 tablespoon of the oil about 5 minutes, turning to brown evenly. Remove from skillet. Brown remaining pork in remaining 1 tablespoon oil about 5 minutes, turning to brown evenly.

2. In a 3½-, 4-, 5-, or 6-quart slow cooker place carrots, parsnips, shallots, lemon, and basil. Place pork on top of vegetables. Pour broth over all.

3. Cover and cook on low-heat setting for 7 to 8 hours or on high-heat setting for 3½ to 4 hours. Discard lemon pieces.

4. Use a slotted spoon to remove pork and vegetables to a serving dish, reserving juices; cover meat and keep warm. Measure 1¾ cups of the cooking juices and return to slow cooker. Discard remaining cooking liquid. If using low-heat setting, turn to high-heat setting. Stir in couscous. Cover and cook for 5 minutes more on high-heat setting. Fluff couscous with a fork. Serve pork and vegetables over couscous.

Nutrition Facts per serving: 511 calories, 16 g total fat, 101 mg cholesterol, 368 mg sodium, 53 g carbohydrate, 38 g protein.

2 pounds boneless
   pork shoulder
¼ cup all-purpose flour
½ teaspoon pepper
2 tablespoons cooking oil
1 16-ounce package peeled
   baby carrots
8 ounces parsnips, cut into
   ½-inch slices
2 medium shallots, sliced
1 lemon, quartered
¼ cup thinly sliced fresh basil
1 14½-ounce can
   chicken broth
1⅓ cups quick-cooking couscous

Pineapple-Ginger Pork

You have to stand over a stir-fry and, well, stir. This Chinese-inspired dish cooks without watching or stirring and costs a lot less than take-out.

Prep: 30 minutes **Cook:** 6 hours on low plus 10 minutes on high or 3 hours and 10 minutes on high **Makes:** 6 to 8 servings

2 pounds boneless
    pork shoulder
2 tablespoons cooking oil
¾ cup chicken broth
3 tablespoons quick-cooking
    tapioca
3 tablespoons low-sodium
    soy sauce
3 tablespoons oyster sauce
    (optional)
1 teaspoon grated
    fresh ginger
1 15¼-ounce can pineapple
    chunks (juice pack)
4 medium carrots, cut into
    ½-inch slices (2 cups)
1 large onion, cut into
    1-inch pieces
1 8-ounce can sliced water
    chestnuts, drained
1½ cups fresh snow pea pods
    or one 6-ounce package
    frozen pea pods
3 cups hot cooked rice

1. Trim fat from pork. Cut pork into 1-inch pieces. In a large skillet brown half of the pork at a time in hot oil. Drain off fat.

2. In a 3½- or 4-quart slow cooker combine chicken broth, tapioca, soy sauce, oyster sauce (if using), and ginger. Drain pineapple, reserving juice. Stir juice into broth mixture; cover and chill pineapple chunks. Add carrots, onion, and water chestnuts to cooker. Add pork.

3. Cover and cook on low-heat setting for 6 to 8 hours or on high-heat setting for 3 to 4 hours.

4. If using low-heat setting, turn to high-heat setting. Stir pineapple chunks and the fresh or frozen snow peas into cooker. Cover and cook 10 to 15 minutes more on high-heat setting or until peas are crisp-tender. Serve over rice.

For a 5- to 6-quart cooker: Recipe may be doubled.

Nutrition Facts per serving: 402 calories, 11 g total fat, 62 mg cholesterol, 477 mg sodium, 51 g carbohydrate, 23 g protein.

North Carolina Pork Barbecue

Barbecue styles vary greatly from region to region. Some—like this spicy North Carolina-style pork—don't call for even a smidgen of catsup or molasses.

Prep: 10 minutes **Cook:** 10 hours on low or 5 hours on high **Makes:** 16 servings

1. In a 4-, 5-, or 6-quart slow cooker place the meat, vinegar, water, sugar, salt, and peppers.

2. Cover; cook on low-heat setting 10 to 12 hours or high-heat setting 5 to 6 hours. Remove meat from cooker; cool slightly. Remove meat from bone. Shred or chop the meat. Stir in as much of the cooking liquid as desired to moisten meat. Serve on rolls.

Nutrition Facts per serving: **183** calories, **5** g total fat, **44** mg cholesterol, **284** mg sodium, **17** g carbohydrate, **16** g protein.

1 4- to 5-pound pork shoulder roast or Boston butt
1 cup white vinegar
½ cup water
2 tablespoons sugar
½ teaspoon salt
½ teaspoon crushed red pepper
¼ teaspoon black pepper
8 kaiser rolls, split and toasted, if desired

Plum-Sauced Pork Wraps

Make your own moo-shu! Crisp Chinese cabbage is a great companion for the sweet, spicy meat.

Prep: 15 minutes **Cook:** 8 hours on low or 4 hours on high **Makes:** 8 servings

1 2½- to 3-pound boneless pork shoulder roast
1 teaspoon ground ginger
½ teaspoon garlic powder
1 16-ounce package frozen stir-fry vegetables
1 8½-ounce jar plum or hoisin sauce
½ cup chicken broth
2 cups shredded chinese cabbage (Napa or Bok Choy)
8 10-inch flour tortillas, warmed

1. Remove string from meat, if present. Trim fat from pork roast. If necessary, cut roast to fit into slow cooker. Sprinkle meat with ginger and garlic powder and rub into meat with fingers.

2. Transfer meat to a 3½- or 4-quart slow cooker. Add vegetables, half of the plum or hoisin sauce, and the broth.

3. Cover; cook on low-heat setting for 8 to 10 hours or on high-heat setting for 4 to 5 hours.

4. Remove meat from cooker. Using forks, shred meat and place in a large bowl. Remove vegetables with a slotted spoon and add to pork in bowl (discard liquid). Add remaining plum or hoisin sauce and stir to combine. Place shredded cabbage and pork and vegetable mixture on centers of tortillas. Fold bottom edges of warmed tortillas up and over filling. Fold opposite sides in, just until they meet. Roll up from the bottom. Secure with wooden toothpicks.

Nutrition Facts per serving: 393 calories, 13 g total fat, 92 mg cholesterol, 377 mg sodium, 35 g carbohydrate, 34 g protein.

Jamaican Jerk Pork Sandwiches

Jerk seasoning—a savory blend of chiles, thyme, cinnamon, ginger, allspice, and cloves—flavors these sandwiches. Serve them with sweet potato chips.

Prep: 30 minutes **Cook:** 8 hours on low or 4 hours on high **Makes:** 6 to 8 servings

1. Trim fat from meat. Rub jerk seasoning evenly over roast. Place meat in a 3½-or 4-quart slow cooker, sprinkle with thyme, and pour water over roast.

2. Cover; cook on low-heat setting for 8 to 10 hours or on high-heat setting for 4 to 5 hours. Remove meat from cooker, reserving juices. Shred meat, discarding any fat. Skim fat from juices. Add enough of the juices to moisten meat (about ½ cup). Stir lime juice into meat.

3. To serve, use a slotted spoon to place pork mixture onto roll bottoms. If desired, layer with lettuce leaves, sweet pepper rings, and mango slices. Spoon Lime Mayo onto each sandwich; cover with roll tops.

Lime Mayo: In a bowl stir together ½ cup light mayonnaise dressing or regular mayonnaise, ¼ cup finely chopped red onion, ¼ teaspoon finely shredded lime peel, 1 tablespoon lime juice, and 1 clove garlic, minced. Cover; chill until ready to serve.

Nutrition Facts per serving: **430 calories, 21 g total fat, 74 mg cholesterol, 609 mg sodium, 34 g carbohydrate, 26 g protein.**

1 1½-to 2-pound boneless pork shoulder roast
1 tablespoon Jamaican jerk seasoning
¼ teaspoon dried thyme, crushed
1 cup water
1 tablespoon lime juice
6 to 8 kaiser rolls, split and toasted
6 to 8 lettuce leaves (optional)
6 thinly sliced red or green sweet pepper rings (optional)
1 medium mango, peeled and thinly sliced (optional)
1 recipe Lime Mayo

Barbecue-Style Ribs

Love ribs but don't want to stand over a hot grill? Let meaty pork ribs "barbecue" on your countertop all day. Shred leftover meat for sandwiches.

Prep: 5 minutes **Cook:** 10 hours on low or 5 hours on high **Broil:** 10 minutes **Makes:** 4 servings

---

3 to 3½ pounds pork
    country-style ribs,
    cut crosswise in half
    and cut into 2-rib portions
1 cup catsup
½ cup finely chopped onion
¼ cup packed brown sugar
1 tablespoon Worcestershire
    sauce
½ teaspoon chili powder
½ teaspoon liquid smoke
¼ teaspoon garlic powder
¼ teaspoon bottled hot
    pepper sauce

1. Preheat broiler. Place ribs on the unheated rack of a broiler pan. Broil 6 inches from the heat until brown, about 10 minutes, turning once. Transfer ribs to a 3½- or 4-quart slow cooker.

2. In a small bowl combine catsup, onion, brown sugar, Worcestershire sauce, chili powder, liquid smoke, garlic powder, and bottled hot pepper sauce. Pour sauce over ribs, turning to coat.

3. Cover; cook on low-heat setting for 10 to 12 hours or on high-heat setting for 5 to 6 hours.

4. Transfer ribs to a platter. If desired, skim fat from surface of sauce; pour sauce into a medium saucepan. Simmer sauce until reduced and thickened. Pass sauce with ribs.

Nutrition Facts per serving: **940 calories, 51 g total fat, 316 mg cholesterol, 1,115 mg sodium, 33 g carbohydrate, 86 g protein.**

Asian-Style Ribs

Three kinds of pepper—black, red, and hot pepper sauce—give these Chinese-style ribs their kick.

Prep: 15 minutes   **Cook:** 8 hours on low or 4 hours on high   **Makes:** 6 servings

1. Place ribs in a 3½- or 4-quart slow cooker, cutting as necessary to fit.

2. For sauce, in a small bowl combine green onions, soy sauce, molasses, hoisin sauce, brown sugar, vinegar, toasted sesame oil, lemon juice, hot pepper sauce, ginger, garlic powder, chili powder, ground red pepper, and ground black pepper. Pour the sauce over the ribs in cooker, turning to coat.

3. Cover and cook on low-heat setting for 8 to 10 hours or on high-heat setting for 4 to 5 hours. Transfer ribs to serving platter. Strain sauce; skim off fat. Serve sauce over ribs and rice.

Nutrition Facts per serving: 532 calories, 31 g total fat, 69 mg cholesterol, 511 mg sodium, 32 g carbohydrate, 30 g protein.

Sweet 'n' Peppery Country-Style Rib Sandwiches: Prepare the ribs as directed above, except omit the hot cooked rice. Remove the cooked meat from the bones. Using 2 forks, pull meat apart into shreds. To serve, add meat to split and toasted, large sesame buns or kaiser rolls. Serve the strained sauce on the side. Makes 8 to 10 sandwiches.

3½ pounds pork
    country-style ribs
6 green onions, chopped
¼ cup reduced-sodium
    soy sauce
¼ cup molasses
2 tablespoons hoisin sauce
2 tablespoons packed
    brown sugar
2 tablespoons white
    wine vinegar
2 teaspoons toasted
    sesame oil
2 teaspoons lemon juice
½ teaspoon bottled
    hot pepper sauce
½ teaspoon ground ginger
½ teaspoon garlic powder
½ teaspoon chili powder
¼ teaspoon ground red pepper
¼ teaspoon ground
    black pepper
2 cups hot cooked rice

Country Ribs

Serve these meaty ribs with baked beans, coleslaw, and cherry-peach cobbler.

Prep: 10 minutes **Cook:** 10 hours on low or 5 hours on high **Makes:** 4 to 6 servings

1 large onion, sliced and
    separated into rings
2½ to 3 pounds pork
    country-style ribs
1½ cups vegetable
    juice cocktail
½ of a 6-ounce can tomato
    paste (⅓ cup)
¼ cup molasses
3 tablespoons vinegar
1 teaspoon dry mustard
¼ teaspoon salt
¼ teaspoon pepper
⅛ teaspoon dried thyme,
    crushed
⅛ teaspoon dried rosemary,
    crushed

1. In a 3½-, 4-, 5-, or 6-quart slow cooker place onion rings. Place ribs atop onion. Combine vegetable juice cocktail, tomato paste, molasses, vinegar, dry mustard, salt, pepper, thyme, and rosemary. Reserve 1 cup for sauce; cover and refrigerate. Pour remaining mixture over ribs. Cover; cook on low-heat setting for 10 to 12 hours or on high-heat setting for 5 to 6 hours.

2. For sauce, in a small saucepan simmer reserved mixture, uncovered, for 10 minutes. Drain ribs; discard cooking liquid. Serve sauce with ribs.

Nutrition Facts per serving: **355 calories, 13 g total fat, 101 mg cholesterol, 519 mg sodium, 26 g carbohydrate, 33 g protein.**

Aloha Pork Steaks

These island-style steaks get their name from a sweet-and-sour pineapple sauce.

Prep: 15 minutes   **Cook:** 6 hours on low or 3 hours on high   **Makes:** 4 servings

1. In a large skillet brown pork steaks on both sides in hot oil. Drain off fat. Transfer steaks to a 3½- or 4-quart slow cooker.

2. In a bowl combine undrained pineapple, green sweet pepper, water, brown sugar, tapioca, catsup, soy sauce, and dry mustard; pour over steaks.

3. Cover; cook on low-heat setting for 6 to 8 hours or on high-heat setting for 3 to 4 hours. Skim fat from sauce. Serve over hot cooked rice.

Nutrition Facts per serving: **482 calories, 16 g total fat, 93 mg cholesterol, 356 mg sodium, 57 g carbohydrate, 27 g protein.**

4 pork shoulder steaks, cut ½-inch thick
2 teaspoons cooking oil
1 8-ounce can crushed pineapple
½ cup chopped green sweet pepper
½ cup water
⅓ cup packed brown sugar
2 tablespoons quick-cooking tapioca
2 tablespoons catsup
2 teaspoons soy sauce
½ teaspoon dry mustard
2 cups hot cooked rice

Pork Chops with Apples and Sauerkraut

If you like sauerkraut a little less lip-puckering, rinse and drain it in a colander before placing it in the slow cooker.

Prep: 20 minutes **Cook:** 6 hours on low or 3 hours on high **Makes:** 4 servings

---

4 pork sirloin chops,
  cut ¾ inch thick
  (about 1½ pounds)
1 tablespoon cooking oil
2 medium potatoes,
  cut into ¼-inch slices
2 medium carrots,
  cut into ½-inch pieces
1 medium onion, thinly sliced
1 16-ounce can sauerkraut,
  drained
2 small cooking apples,
  cut into ¼-inch slices
½ cup apple cider
  or apple juice
¼ cup catsup
½ teaspoon caraway seeds
  Snipped fresh parsley
  (optional)

1. In a large skillet brown pork chops on both sides in hot oil.

2. In a 3½- or 4-quart slow cooker place potatoes, carrots, onion, browned pork chops, sauerkraut, and apples. In a bowl combine apple cider or apple juice, catsup, and caraway seeds; pour over apples.

3. Cover; cook on low-heat setting for 6 to 8 hours or on high-heat setting for 3 to 4 hours. Garnish with snipped fresh parsley, if desired.

Nutrition Facts per serving: 413 calories, 15 g total fat, 77 mg cholesterol, 934 mg sodium, 43 g carbohydrate, 28 g protein.

Pork Chops and Mustard-Sauced Potatoes

If you can't find ¾-inch-thick chops in the self-serve meat case, ask a butcher to carve a bone-in top loin roast into ¾-inch slices.

Prep: 20 minutes   **Cook:** 7 hours on low or 3½ hours on high   **Makes:** 6 servings

1. In a large skillet brown pork chops on both sides, half at a time, in hot oil. Drain off fat.

2. In a large mixing bowl combine soup, wine or chicken broth, mustard, thyme, garlic, and pepper. Add potatoes and onion, stirring to coat. Transfer to a 3½- or 4-quart slow cooker. Place browned chops atop potatoes.

3. Cover; cook on low-heat setting for 7 to 8 hours or on high-heat setting for 3½ hours.

Nutrition Facts per serving: **335 calories, 11 g total fat, 39 mg cholesterol, 705 mg sodium, 39 g carbohydrate, 17 g protein.**

6 pork loin chops,
   cut ¾ inch thick
1 tablespoon cooking oil
1 10¾-ounce can condensed
   cream of mushroom soup
¼ cup dry white wine
   or chicken broth
¼ cup Dijon-style mustard
1 teaspoon dried thyme,
   crushed
1 clove garlic, minced
¼ teaspoon pepper
6 medium potatoes,
   cut into ¼-inch slices
1 medium onion, sliced

Pork Chops with Mushroom Sauce

Serve these mushroom-sauced chops with hot cooked rice, buttered egg noodles, or spaetzle, which can be found in the pasta aisle.

Prep: 20 minutes **Cook:** 10 hours on low or 4½ hours on high **Makes:** 4 servings

4 **pork loin chops,**
   cut ¾ inch thick

1 **tablespoon cooking oil**

1 **small onion, thinly sliced**

1 **10¾-ounce can condensed**
   cream of mushroom soup

¾ **cup dry white wine**

1 **4-ounce can sliced**
   mushrooms, drained

2 **tablespoons quick-cooking**
   tapioca

2 **teaspoons Worcestershire**
   sauce

1 **teaspoon instant beef**
   bouillon granules

¾ **teaspoon dried thyme,**
   crushed

¼ **teaspoon garlic powder**
   Hot cooked rice

1. In a skillet brown chops on both sides in hot oil. In a 3½- or 4-quart slow cooker place onion; add chops. In a bowl combine soup, wine, mushrooms, tapioca, Worcestershire sauce, bouillon granules, thyme, and garlic powder; pour over chops.

2. Cover; cook on low-heat setting for 10 to 12 hours or on high-heat setting for 4½ to 5 hours. Serve over rice.

For 5- or 6-quart slow cooker: Use 6 pork chops, cut in ¾ inch slices. Leave remaining ingredient amounts the same. Prepare as above. Makes 6 servings.

Nutrition Facts per serving: **539 calories, 19 g total fat, 103 mg cholesterol, 979 mg sodium, 37 g carbohydrate, 45 g protein.**

Southwest Pork Chops

In the mood for chili, but only have pork chops in the freezer? Thaw them out, toss them in the slow cooker with a few other ingredients, and warm up with this spicy one-dish meal.

Prep: 15 minutes **Cook:** 5 hours on low plus 30 minutes on high or 3 hours on high **Makes:** 6 servings

---

1. Trim excess fat from chops. Place chops in the bottom of a 3½- or 4-quart slow cooker. Add chili beans and salsa. Cover; cook on high-heat setting for 2 ½ hours or low-heat setting for 5 hours. If using low-heat setting, turn to high-heat setting. Stir in corn. Cover and cook 30 minutes longer. Serve over rice. Sprinkle with cilantro, if desired.

2. For all-day cooking: Substitute 8 boneless pork chops for the 6 rib chops. (When cooked this long, chops with bone may leave bony fragments in the cooked mixture.) Cover and cook on low-heat setting for 9½ hours. Turn to high-heat setting. Stir in corn. Cover and cook 30 minutes longer. Serve as above.

Note: 2 medium ears of fresh corn equal about 1 cup of whole kernel corn.

Nutrition Facts per serving: **334 calories, 7 g total fat, 77 mg cholesterol, 716 mg sodium, 34 g carbohydrate, 33 g protein.**

6 pork rib chops, cut ¾-inch thick (about 2 ½ lb.)
1 15-oz. can Mexican-style or Tex-Mex-style chili beans
1¼ cups bottled salsa
1 cup fresh* or frozen whole kernel corn
2 cups hot cooked rice
  Snipped fresh cilantro (optional)

Spicy Peanut Pork Chops

Creamy peanut sauce spiked with crushed red pepper cloaks these Thai-style chops. Be sure to use unsweetened coconut milk. Look for it in the Asian foods section of your supermarket.

Prep: 20 minutes **Cook:** 6 hours on low or 3 hours on high **Makes:** 8 servings

8 boneless pork chops,
    cut ¾ inch thick
    (about 2 pounds)
1 tablespoon cooking oil
2 cups purchased shredded
    carrots
2 medium onions,
    chopped (1 cup)
1 14-ounce can light
    coconut milk
½ cup chicken broth
½ cup creamy peanut butter
½ teaspoon crushed
    red pepper
6 cups hot cooked basmati
    rice or shredded Chinese
    cabbage (Napa)

1. In a large skillet brown pork chops, half at a time, on both sides in hot oil.

2. In a 3½- or 4-quart slow cooker place carrots and onions. In a bowl combine coconut milk, chicken broth, peanut butter, and red pepper; pour over vegetables. Place browned chops on top of vegetables.

3. Cover and cook on low-heat setting for 6 to 8 hours or on high-heat setting for 3 to 4 hours. Serve with rice or cabbage.

Nutrition Facts per serving: **500 calories, 18 g total fat, 62 mg cholesterol, 212 mg sodium, 47 g carbohydrate, 32 g protein.**

Cranberry-Raspberry-Sauced Pork Chops

Slices of fresh apricots or plums are stirred in right before serving so they stay juicy and sweet rather than fall apart from overcooking.

Prep: 10 minutes **Cook:** 7 hours on low or 3½ hours on high **Stand:** 5 minutes **Makes:** 6 servings

1. In a 3½- or 4-quart slow cooker place pork chops.

2. For sauce, in a small bowl combine cranberry-orange sauce, raspberry preserves, tapioca, lemon peel, and cardamom. Pour over chops.

3. Cover; cook on low-heat setting for 7 to 8 hours or on high-heat setting for 3½ to 4 hours. Stir in sliced fruit. Cover; let stand 5 minutes. Serve with hot couscous.

Nutrition Facts per serving: 340 calories, 5 g total fat, 27 mg cholesterol, 1,040 mg sodium, 50 g carbohydrate, 23 g protein.

6 boneless smoked pork chops

1 cup cranberry-orange sauce

½ cup seedless red raspberry preserves

1 teaspoon quick-cooking tapioca

1 teaspoon finely shredded lemon peel

¼ teaspoon ground cardamom

3 fresh apricots or plums, pitted and sliced

3 cups hot cooked couscous

Fruit-Stuffed Ham Loaf

A quick-read thermometer is the best way to make sure meat is thoroughly cooked and safe to eat. For this ham loaf, it should register 170 °F.

Prep: 25 minutes **Cook:** 6½ hours on low or 3½ hours on high **Makes:** 6 servings

¾ cup mixed dried fruit bits

2 tablespoons apple butter

1 beaten egg

¼ cup milk

½ cup graham cracker crumbs

¼ teaspoon pepper

1 pound ground fully
  cooked ham

½ pound ground pork

½ cup packed brown sugar

2 tablespoons apple juice

½ teaspoon dry mustard

1. In a small bowl combine fruit bits and apple butter. In a medium bowl combine egg, milk, graham cracker crumbs, and pepper. Add ground ham and pork to egg mixture; mix well.

2. Crisscross three 18x2-inch foil strips (layered on a sheet of waxed paper to keep counter clean). In center of the foil strips pat half of the meat mixture into a 6-inch circle. Spread fruit mixture on meat circle to within ½ inch of edges. On another sheet of waxed paper pat remaining meat mixture into a 6½-inch circle. Invert atop the first circle. Remove paper. Press edges of meat to seal well. Bringing up foil strips, lift and transfer meat and foil to a 3½-, 4-, or 5-quart slow cooker. Press meat away from sides of the cooker to avoid burning.

3. Cover; cook on low-heat setting for 6 to 7 hours or on high-heat setting for 3 to 3½ hours.

4. In a small bowl combine brown sugar, apple juice, and dry mustard. Spread over meat. Cover; cook on low-heat or high-heat setting for 30 minutes more.

5. Using foil strips, carefully lift meat loaf and transfer to a serving plate; discard the foil strips. Serve ham loaf with glaze.

Nutrition Facts per serving: **336 calories, 10 g total fat, 91 mg cholesterol, 1,049 mg sodium, 40 g carbohydrate, 22 g protein.**

Choucroute Garni

This melange (pronounced "shoo-kroot gar-nee") of sauerkraut and meats seasoned with white wine and juniper berries hails from the Alsatian region of France.

Prep: 15 minutes **Cook:** 10 hours on low or 4½ hours on high **Makes:** 4 servings

1. Core apples and cut into quarters. Score knackwurst diagonally. In a 3½- or 4-quart slow cooker place potatoes; carrots; onion; juniper berries, if desired; bay leaf; pork chops or ham; sauerkraut; apples; and knackwurst. Combine water, wine, bouillon granules, cloves, and pepper; add to cooker.

2. Cover; cook on low-heat setting for 10 to 12 hours or on high heat setting for 4½ to 5 hours. Discard bay leaf.

For 5- or 6-quart slow cooker: Use 3 cooking apples; 3 fully cooked knackwurst; 3 potatoes, quartered; 3 carrots, cut into ½-inch pieces; ¾ cup chopped onion; 5 juniper berries, crushed (optional); 2 bay leaves; 3 medium smoked pork loin chops, cut ¾ inch thick, or ¾ pound fully cooked ham slice, cut into pieces; one 27-ounce can sauerkraut, drained; ¾ cup water; ¾ cup dry white wine; 1½ teaspoons instant chicken bouillon granules; ⅛ teaspoon ground cloves; and ¼ teaspoon pepper. Prepare as above. Makes 6 servings.

Nutrition Facts per serving: 361 calories, 17 g total fat, 46 mg cholesterol, 1,745 mg sodium, 34 g carbohydrate, 16 g protein.

- 2 small cooking apples
- 2 fully cooked knackwurst
- 2 medium potatoes, quartered
- 2 medium carrots, cut into ½-inch pieces (1 cup)
- ½ cup chopped onion
- 3 juniper berries, crushed (optional)
- 1 bay leaf
- 2 medium smoked pork loin chops, cut ¾ inch thick, or ½ pound fully cooked ham slice, cut into pieces
- 1 16-ounce can sauerkraut, drained
- ½ cup water
- ½ cup dry white wine
- 1 teaspoon instant chicken bouillon granules
- ⅛ teaspoon ground cloves
- ⅛ teaspoon pepper

Smoked Sausage and Beans

Top each serving of this four-bean and sausage dish with sour cream or plain yogurt.

Prep: 10 minutes **Cook:** 8 hours on low or 4 hours on high **Makes:** 8 servings

1 15½-ounce can
    red kidney beans

1 15-ounce can black beans,
    rinsed and drained

1 15-ounce can Great
    Northern beans, drained

1 15-ounce can butter beans,
    drained

1 pound fully cooked smoked
    turkey sausage, halved
    lengthwise and cut into
    ½-inch slices

1½ cups catsup

1 medium green sweet pepper,
    chopped

½ cup chopped onion

¼ cup packed brown sugar

2 cloves garlic, minced

1 teaspoon Worcestershire
    sauce

½ teaspoon dry mustard

½ teaspoon bottled hot
    pepper sauce

1. In a 3½-, 4-, or 5-quart slow cooker combine undrained kidney beans, drained black beans, drained Great Northern beans, butter beans, sausage, catsup, green sweet pepper, onion, brown sugar, garlic, Worcestershire sauce, dry mustard, and hot pepper sauce. Stir all ingredients together.

2. Cover; cook on low-heat setting for 8 to 10 hours or on high-heat setting for 4 to 5 hours.

Nutrition Facts per serving: **372 calories, 8 g total fat, 30 mg cholesterol, 1,499 mg sodium, 58 g carbohydrate, 24 g protein.**

Italian-Sausage Heros

These state-fair favorites can easily be made at home. Enjoy them with cold lemonade.

Prep: 20 minutes **Cook:** 10 hours on low **Makes:** 8 servings

1. In a large skillet cook sausage, ground beef, and onion until meat is brown and onion is tender. Drain off fat.

2. Meanwhile, in a 3½- or 4-quart slow cooker combine tomato sauce, undrained tomatoes, mushrooms, olives, tapioca, sugar, oregano, pepper, and garlic powder. Stir in meat mixture. Cover; cook on low-heat setting for 10 to 12 hours.

3. Using a fork, hollow out bottom halves of rolls, leaving ¼-inch-thick shells. (Reserve bread pieces for another use.) Place cheese in bottom halves, trimming as necessary to fit. Spoon meat mixture into rolls. Cut remaining cheese into strips and place atop meat mixture. Cover with bun tops.

For 5- or 6-quart slow cooker: Double all ingredients; prepare as above. Makes 16 servings.

Nutrition Facts per serving: 425 calories, 22 g total fat, 68 mg cholesterol, 1,073 mg sodium, 29 g carbohydrate, 23 g protein.

1 pound bulk Italian sausage
½ pound ground beef
1 cup chopped onion
1 15-ounce can tomato sauce
1 7½-ounce can tomatoes, cut up
1 4-ounce can mushroom stems and pieces, drained
½ cup sliced pitted ripe olives
4 teaspoons quick-cooking tapioca
1 teaspoon sugar
1 teaspoon dried oregano, crushed
⅛ teaspoon pepper
   Dash garlic powder
8 French-style rolls, split lengthwise
6 ounces sliced mozzarella cheese

Chorizo Sausage Sandwiches

Chorizo is a spicy Mexican sausage seasoned with lots of garlic and chili powder. If you can't find it at your local supermarket, you'll no doubt find it an Hispanic food market.

Prep: 25 minutes   **Cook:** 8 hours on low or 4 hours on high   **Makes:** 16 servings

 1 pound chorizo sausage
   or bulk Italian sausage
 2 pounds ground raw turkey
   or lean ground beef
 2 cups chopped onion
 1 15-ounce can tomato sauce
 1 14½-ounce can
   diced tomatoes
 2 tablespoons quick-cooking
   tapioca
 2 tablespoons finely chopped,
   seeded jalapeño peppers
 2 teaspoons sugar
 2 teaspoons dried oregano,
   crushed
16 French-style rolls, split
   lengthwise
   Sliced pitted ripe olives
   (optional)
   Shredded Monterey jack
   cheese (optional)
   Mild sliced cherry peppers
   (optional)

1. Remove casing from chorizo (if using). In a large skillet cook sausage and ground turkey or beef, half at a time, until meat is cooked through. Drain off fat. In a 5- or 6-quart slow cooker combine onion, tomato sauce, undrained tomatoes, tapioca, jalapeño peppers, sugar, and oregano. Stir in the meat.

2. Cover; cook on low-heat setting for 8 to 10 hours or on high-heat setting for 4 to 5 hours. Using a fork, hollow out bottom halves of rolls, leaving a ¼-inch-thick shell. Spoon meat mixture into roll bottoms. Add roll tops. If desired, serve with sliced olives, shredded cheese, and/or cherry peppers.

Nutrition Facts per serving: 253 calories, 8 g total fat, 21 mg cholesterol, 593 mg sodium, 35 g carbohydrate, 14 g protein.

Fettuccine with Sausage and Mushrooms

Earthy cremini mushrooms are immature portobello mushrooms. They impart a woodsy flavor to this pasta sauce. Button mushrooms would be a fine substitute.

Prep: 15 minutes   **Cook:** 6 hours on low or 3 hours on high   **Makes:** 6 to 8 servings

1. In a large skillet brown sausage. Drain off fat. In a 3½- or 4-quart slow cooker combine mushrooms, tomatoes, tomato sauce, tomato paste, water, onion, sugar, rosemary, pepper, and garlic. Stir in sausage.

2. Cover; cook on low-heat setting for 6 to 8 hours or on high-heat setting for 3 to 4 hours.

3. Just before serving, cook pasta according to package directions; drain. Serve sausage mixture over pasta. If desired, sprinkle with Parmesan cheese.

Nutrition Facts per serving: 358 calories, 10 g total fat, 22 mg cholesterol, 938 mg sodium, 54 g carbohydrate, 14 g protein.

- 12 ounces bulk sweet Italian sausage
- 2 cups sliced fresh cremini and/or button mushrooms
- 1 28-ounce can crushed tomatoes
- 1 8-ounce can tomato sauce
- 1 6-ounce can tomato paste
- ⅔ cup water
- 1 medium onion, chopped
- 1 tablespoon sugar
- 1 teaspoon dried rosemary, crushed, or 1 tablespoon snipped fresh rosemary
- ¼ teaspoon pepper
- 2 cloves garlic, minced
- 9 to 12 ounces dried fettuccine, spaghetti, or mafalda
- Freshly shredded or grated Parmesan cheese (optional)

Curried Lamb and Rice

Serve this classic curried lamb with a salad of fresh spinach, cucumber, and tomato.

Prep: 20 minutes **Cook:** 7 hours on low or 3½ hours on high **Stand:** 5 minutes **Makes:** 6 servings

1 2- to 2½-pound boneless
   lamb shoulder roast
1 tablespoon cooking oil
2½ cups hot-style
   vegetable juice
1 cup regular brown rice
1 teaspoon curry powder
¼ teaspoon salt
2 medium carrots,
   cut into ½-inch pieces
1 medium green sweet pepper,
   cut into ½-inch strips

1. Trim fat from lamb roast. In a large skillet brown roast on all sides in hot oil.

2. Meanwhile, in a 3½- or 4-quart slow cooker combine vegetable juice, uncooked rice, curry powder, and salt. Add carrots. Place meat on carrots.

3. Cover; cook on low-heat setting for 7 to 8 hours or on high-heat setting for 3½ to 4 hours.

4. Add the green sweet pepper to the slow cooker. Cover and let stand 5 to 10 minutes.

Nutrition Facts per serving: **367 calories, 13 g total fat, 89 mg cholesterol, 544 mg sodium, 32 g carbohydrate, 29 g protein.**

Greek Lamb with Spinach and Orzo

Mediterranean flavorings—oregano, lemon, garlic, and feta cheese—enliven tender chunks of lamb in this robust dish.

Prep: 20 minutes   **Cook:** 8 hours on low or 4 hours on high   **Makes:** 8 servings

1. Trim fat from roast. If necessary, cut roast to fit into a 3½-, 4-, 5-, or 6-quart slow cooker. In a small bowl combine oregano, lemon peel, garlic, and salt. Sprinkle evenly over sides of lamb roast; rub lightly with fingers. Place lamb in cooker. Sprinkle lamb with lemon juice.

2. Cover and cook on low-heat setting for 8 to 10 hours or on high-heat setting for 4 to 5 hours.

3. Remove lamb from cooker. Remove meat from bones; discard bones and fat. Chop meat; set aside. Add spinach to cooking juices in cooker, stirring until spinach is wilted. Add cooked orzo, feta, and lamb; stir to mix.

Nutrition Facts per serving: **409 calories, 16 g total fat, 120 mg cholesterol, 338 mg sodium, 25 g carbohydrate, 38 g protein.**

- 1 3- to 3½-pound lamb shoulder roast (bone-in)
- 1 tablespoon dried oregano, crushed
- 1 tablespoon finely shredded lemon peel
- 4 cloves garlic, minced
- ¼ teaspoon salt
- ¼ cup lemon juice
- 1 10-ounce bag pre-washed fresh spinach, chopped
- 5 cups cooked orzo
- 4 ounces crumbled feta cheese

Honey-Spiced Lamb and Vegetables

An unusual combination of spices—ginger, anise, cinnamon, and red pepper—gives this lamb roast an exotic richness. Serve it with hot cooked couscous and tender sweet beans (cooked green soybeans).

Prep: 25 minutes **Cook:** 10 hours on low or 5 hours on high **Makes:** 6 to 8 servings

1 2½- to 3-pound boneless lamb shoulder roast
1 tablespoon cooking oil
1½ pounds whole tiny new potatoes or 5 medium potatoes
2 cups whole tiny carrots
2 small onions, cut into wedges
1¼ cups beef broth
1 tablespoon honey
1 tablespoon grated gingerroot or ¾ teaspoon ground ginger
½ teaspoon salt
½ teaspoon anise seeds or ¼ teaspoon ground allspice
½ teaspoon ground cinnamon
⅛ to ¼ teaspoon ground red pepper
½ cup cold water
¼ cup all-purpose flour
1½ teaspoons finely shredded orange peel

1. Trim the fat from the lamb roast. If necessary, cut roast to fit into slow cooker. In a large skillet brown roast on all sides in hot oil.

2. Meanwhile, remove a narrow strip of peel from the center of each new potato, or peel (if desired) and quarter each medium potato.

3. In a 3½-, 4-, or 5-quart slow cooker place potatoes, carrots, and onions. Place meat on vegetables. In a bowl combine beef broth, honey, gingerroot, salt, anise seeds or allspice, cinnamon, and red pepper. Pour over meat and vegetables.

4. Cover; cook on low-heat setting for 10 to 12 hours or on high-heat setting for 5 to 6 hours.

5. Remove meat and vegetables with slotted spoon; keep warm. For gravy, skim fat from juices; measure 1½ cups juices. In a saucepan, combine cold water, flour, and orange peel. Stir in the reserved 1½ cups of juices. Cook and stir until thickened and bubbly. Cook and stir 1 minute more. If desired, season to taste. Pass gravy with the meat and vegetables.

Nutrition Facts per serving: **462 calories, 17 g total fat, 111 mg cholesterol, 468 mg sodium, 41 g carbohydrate, 37 g protein.**

Mustard-Sauced Lamb and Artichokes

The best way to make finely shredded lemon peel is to use a small tool called a citrus zester to create long strips of peel, then use a pair of clean kitchen shears to snip the strips into small shreds.

Prep: 30 minutes   **Cook:** 10 hours on low plus 30 minutes on high or 4½ hours on high   **Makes:** 4 servings

1. Trim fat from lamb roast. If necessary, cut roast to fit into slow cooker. In a small bowl combine lemon-pepper seasoning and dry mustard. Sprinkle evenly over sides of lamb roast; rub lightly with fingers. In a large skillet brown the roast on all sides in hot oil.

2. Meanwhile, in a 3½- or 4-quart slow cooker place potatoes and carrots. Place meat atop vegetables. In a bowl combine broth, Dijon-style mustard, tapioca, lemon juice, rosemary, lemon peel, pepper, and garlic; pour over all in slow cooker.

3. Cover; cook on low-heat setting for 10 to 12 hours or on high-heat setting for 4 to 5 hours.

4. If using low-heat setting, turn to high-heat setting. Add thawed artichoke hearts. Cover and cook 30 minutes longer on high-heat setting. Skim fat from gravy and serve with roast.

Nutrition Facts per serving: **590 calories, 21 g total fat, 133 mg cholesterol, 824 mg sodium, 52 g carbohydrate, 47 g protein.**

1 2- to 2½-pound boneless lamb shoulder roast
½ teaspoon lemon-pepper seasoning
½ teaspoon dry mustard
1 tablespoon cooking oil
4 medium potatoes, quartered
1½ cups whole tiny carrots
1 cup chicken broth
3 tablespoons Dijon-style mustard
2 tablespoons quick-cooking tapioca
1 tablespoon lemon juice
½ teaspoon dried rosemary, crushed
¼ teaspoon finely shredded lemon peel
¼ teaspoon pepper
2 cloves garlic, minced
1 9-ounce package frozen artichoke hearts, thawed

Moroccan-Style Lamb

Fill your kitchen with the exotic aromas of a North African spice market. Substitute raisins or golden raisins for the currants, if you like.

Prep: 15 minutes **Cook:** 9 hours on low or 4½ hours on high **Makes:** 8 servings

2 pounds lean boneless, cut-up lamb, fat removed

2 large carrots, peeled and cut into 1-inch pieces

2 large onions, peeled and quartered

2 cups chicken broth

3 medium tomatoes, chopped

1½ teaspoons ground cumin

¼ teaspoon crushed red pepper (optional)

1 teaspoon ground turmeric

1 10-ounce package quick-cooking couscous (1½ cups)

¼ cup currants

1. In a 3½- or 4-quart slow cooker combine lamb, carrots, onions, broth, chopped tomatoes, cumin, pepper, and half of the turmeric.

2. Cover; cook on low-heat setting for 9 to 10 hours or on high-heat setting for 4½ to 5½ hours.

3. Transfer lamb mixture to a serving bowl using a slotted spoon, leaving juices in cooker. If using low-heat setting, turn to high-heat setting. Stir in remaining turmeric, couscous, and currants. Cover and cook for 5 to 7 minutes. Fluff couscous with a fork. Divide couscous among eight pasta dishes. Spoon lamb mixture over couscous.

Nutrition Facts per serving: 330 calories, 5 g total fat, 73 mg cholesterol, 339 mg sodium, 39 g carbohydrate, 30 g protein.

Winter Night Osso Buco

The squash and Brussels sprouts are poetic license—additions to this traditional Italian dish. Serve it as the Italians do—with saffron risotto—and a garnish of minced parsley, lemon peel, and garlic.

Prep: 25 minutes **Cook:** 8 hours on low plus 45 minutes on high or 4 hours 45 minutes on high **Makes:** 4 servings

1. In a 10-inch skillet heat oil over medium-high heat. Brown veal shanks or beef ribs, half at a time, in hot oil. Transfer the meat to a 3½- to 4-quart slow cooker, reserving drippings in skillet. Sprinkle the meat with pepper.

2. Add onion and garlic to skillet. Add more oil if necessary. Reduce heat to medium; cook until onion is tender, stirring occasionally. Add chicken broth, scraping bottom of the pan to loosen any browned bits.

3. Transfer the onion mixture with juices to the slow cooker. Add potatoes. Cover and cook on the low-heat setting for 8 to 9 hours or on high-heat setting for 4 to 4½ hours or until meat is nearly tender.

4. Add squash, Brussels sprouts, and horseradish to cooker, rearranging so vegetables are in cooking liquid. Stir together cornstarch and water; stir into mixture in cooker. Increase heat to high. Cook, covered, for 45 to 60 minutes or until vegetables are just tender. Transfer meat and vegetables to a serving platter. Sprinkle with parsley, if desired.

Nutrition Facts per serving: **474 calories, 14 g total fat, 139 mg cholesterol, 626 mg sodium, 42 g carbohydrate, 46 g protein.**

2 tablespoons olive oil
4 veal shank cross cuts
  (2 pounds) or 1½ pounds
  boneless beef short ribs
¼ teaspoon pepper
1 large onion, chopped
3 cloves garlic, minced
1 10½-ounce can condensed
  chicken broth
8 new potatoes, halved
1½ cups cubed, peeled butternut
  squash (1- to 1½-inch
  cubes) (about 1 pound
  unpeeled)
1 10-ounce package frozen
  brussels sprouts
1 tablespoon prepared
  horseradish
2 tablespoons cornstarch
2 tablespoons cold water
  Snipped parsley (optional)

poultry

A chicken in every pot is an attractive proposition, especially when it happens to be a slow cooker that can turn any bird (turkey too!) into succulent eating.

Chicken with Creamy Chive Sauce, page 204

Barbecue-Style Chicken

Too cold to fire up the grill and you have a craving for some all-American barbecued chicken? Fire up the slow cooker instead.

Prep: 25 minutes **Cook:** 10 hours on low or 5 hours on high **Makes:** 4 to 5 servings

2 medium unpeeled potatoes, cut into ½-inch pieces

1 large green sweet pepper, cut into strips

1 medium onion, sliced

1 tablespoon quick-cooking tapioca

2 pounds chicken thighs or drumsticks, skin and fat removed

1 8-ounce can tomato sauce

2 tablespoons packed brown sugar

1 tablespoon Worcestershire sauce

1 tablespoon yellow mustard

1 clove garlic, minced

¼ teaspoon salt

1. In a 3½- to 4-quart slow cooker place potatoes, sweet pepper, and onion. Sprinkle tapioca over vegetables. Place chicken pieces on top.

2. In a small mixing bowl stir together tomato sauce, brown sugar, Worcestershire sauce, mustard, garlic, and salt. Pour mixture over chicken in slow cooker. Cover and cook on low-heat setting for 10 to 12 hours or on high-heat setting for 5 to 6 hours. To serve, transfer the chicken and vegetables to a serving bowl. Skim fat from the sauce, then pour sauce over chicken and vegetables.

Nutrition Facts per serving: **282 calories, 5 g total fat, 107 mg cholesterol, 670 mg sodium, 30 g carbohydrate, 29 g protein.**

Cashew-Ginger Chicken

Serve this Chinese-style dish with oolong tea and fortune cookies or almond cookies for dessert.

Prep: 15 minutes **Cook:** 6 hours on low or 3 hours on high **Makes:** 6 servings

1. In a 3½- or 4-quart slow cooker stir together the soup, soy sauce, and ginger until well combined. Stir in the chicken tenders, celery, carrot, water chestnuts, and mushrooms.

2. Cover; cook on low-heat setting for 6 to 8 hours or on high-heat setting for 3 to 4 hours. Stir cashews into chicken mixture. Serve over hot cooked rice.

Nutrition Facts per serving: 368 calories, 9 g total fat, 68 mg cholesterol, 789 mg sodium, 38 g carbohydrate, 33 g protein.

1 10¾-ounce can condensed golden mushroom soup
2 tablespoons soy sauce
½ teaspoon ground ginger
1½ pounds chicken tenders
1 cup sliced celery
1 cup purchased shredded carrot
1 8-ounce can sliced water chestnuts, drained
1 cup sliced fresh mushrooms or one 4-ounce can sliced mushrooms, drained
½ cup cashews
3 cups hot cooked rice

Chicken a la Roma

Artichokes and olives give tender chicken pieces an Italian accent. Serve them with hot cooked linguine and sprinkle a little fresh-grated Romano cheese on top, if you like.

Prep: 15 minutes **Cook:** 7 hours on low or 3½ hours on high **Makes:** 4 to 6 servings

2 cups sliced fresh
  mushrooms
1 14½-ounce can tomato
  wedges, drained
1 9-ounce package frozen
  artichoke hearts
½ cup sliced, pitted ripe olives
3 tablespoons quick-cooking
  tapioca
2 to 2½ pounds chicken
  breasts, thighs,
  and/or legs, skinned
¾ cup chicken broth
¼ cup dry white wine
  or chicken broth
1 tablespoon dried Italian
  seasoning, crushed
4 ounces linguine, cooked
  and drained

1. In a 3½- or 4-quart slow cooker combine the mushrooms, tomato wedges, frozen artichoke hearts, and olives. Sprinkle with tapioca. Place the chicken pieces atop the vegetables.

2. In a bowl combine the chicken broth, white wine, and Italian seasoning. Pour over the chicken.

3. Cover; cook on low-heat setting for 7 to 8 hours or on high-heat setting for 3½ to 4 hours. Serve with hot cooked linguine.

Nutrition Facts per serving: 397 calories, 10 g total fat, 81 mg cholesterol, 538 mg sodium, 42 g carbohydrate, 35 g protein.

Chicken and Dumplings

Sometimes nothing but comfort food will do. Old-fashioned stewed chicken topped with fluffy cheddar-cheese dumplings is a sure cure for anything that ails you.

Prep: 25 minutes **Cook:** 8 hours on low plus 25 minutes on high or 4 hours and 25 minutes on high **Makes:** 8 servings

1. In a 4- or 5-quart slow cooker place carrots, potatoes, parsnips, garlic, bay leaves, sage, ½ teaspoon salt, and pepper. Top with chicken pieces. In a medium bowl gradually whisk broth into soup. Pour broth mixture over chicken and vegetables.

2. Cover; cook on low-heat setting for 8 to 10 hours or on high-heat setting for 4 to 5 hours.

3. If using low-heat setting, turn to high heat setting. In a medium mixing bowl combine flour, cheddar cheese, cornmeal, baking powder, and ¼ teaspoon salt. Combine egg, milk, and melted butter and stir into flour mixture until just combined. Stir stew and remove bay leaves from stew. Combine water and cornstarch; stir into stew. Drop dumplings by tablespoons on top of stew.

4. Cover; cook for 25 to 30 minutes more or until toothpick inserted into dumplings comes out clean.

Nutrition Facts per serving: 361 calories, 14 g total fat, 140 mg cholesterol, 948 mg sodium, 29 g carbohydrate, 29 g protein.

2 cups chopped carrots
2 cups chopped potatoes, peeled if desired
1½ cups chopped parsnips
1 clove garlic, minced
2 bay leaves
1 teaspoon dried sage, crushed
½ teaspoon salt
¼ teaspoon pepper
2 pounds boneless, skinless chicken thighs, cut in 1-inch pieces
1 14-ounce can chicken broth
1 10¾-ounce can condensed cream of chicken soup
½ cup all-purpose flour
½ cup shredded cheddar cheese
⅓ cup yellow cornmeal
1 teaspoon baking powder
¼ teaspoon salt
1 beaten egg
2 tablespoons milk
2 tablespoons butter, melted
2 tablespoons water
1 tablespoon cornstarch

Chicken and Mushrooms

You can certainly use just one kind of mushroom for this earthy chicken dish, but a variety will give it more interesting texture and flavor.

Prep: 25 minutes **Cook:** 7 hours on low or 3½ hours on high **Makes:** 6 servings

---

5 cups sliced, assorted fresh
   mushrooms, such as
   shiitake, button, crimini,
   and oyster
1 medium onion, chopped
½ cup chopped carrot
¼ cup dried tomato pieces
   (not oil-packed)
¾ cup chicken broth
¼ cup dry white wine
   or chicken broth
3 tablespoons quick-cooking
   tapioca
1 teaspoon dried thyme,
   crushed
½ teaspoon dried basil,
   crushed
½ teaspoon garlic salt
¼ to ½ teaspoon pepper
3 pounds chicken thighs
   or drumsticks (with bone),
   skinned
4½ cups hot cooked plain
   and/or spinach linguine
   or fettuccine,
   or hot cooked rice

1. In a 4- or 5-quart slow cooker combine mushrooms, onion, carrot, and dried tomato pieces. Pour chicken broth and wine over all. Sprinkle with tapioca, thyme, basil, garlic salt, and pepper. Place chicken pieces on top of vegetables.

2. Cover and cook on low-heat setting for 7 to 8 hours or on high-heat setting for 3½ to 4 hours. To serve, arrange chicken and vegetables over pasta or rice; spoon juices on top.

Nutrition Facts per serving: 360 calories, 7 g total fat, 107 mg cholesterol, 350 mg sodium, 39 g carbohydrate, 34 g protein.

Chicken and Rice Burritos

You're no longer limited to plain flour or corn tortillas. Exercise your flatbread options and wrap this zippy chicken and rice filling in green spinach or orange chile flour tortillas.

Prep: 25 minutes **Cook:** 6 hours on low or 3 hours on high **Stand:** 5 minutes **Makes:** 6 to 8 servings

1. Cut zucchini in half lengthwise and then into ¾-inch slices. In a 3½- or 4-quart slow cooker combine zucchini, sweet pepper, onion, and celery. Top with chicken strips. In a small bowl combine taco sauce, bouillon granules, and cumin. Pour over chicken.

2. Cover and cook on low-heat setting for 6 to 7 hours or on high-heat setting for 3 to 3½ hours. Stir in rice. Cover and let stand for 5 minutes.

3. Warm tortillas according to package directions. Divide chicken mixture evenly among warmed tortillas. Top with shredded cheese, tomato, and green onion. Fold bottom edge of each tortilla up and over filling. Fold opposite sides in, just until they meet. Roll up from bottom. Secure with wooden toothpicks, if necessary.

Nutrition Facts per serving: 408 calories, 10 g total fat, 81 mg cholesterol, 735 mg sodium, 43 g carbohydrate, 35 g protein.

1 medium zucchini
1 large green sweet pepper, cubed
1 medium onion, coarsely chopped
½ cup coarsely chopped celery
1½ pounds skinless, boneless chicken breast halves, cut into ½-inch strips
1 8-ounce bottle green taco sauce
1 teaspoon instant chicken bouillon granules
½ teaspoon ground cumin
1 cup instant rice
6 to 8 nine- to ten-inch spinach, chile, or plain flour tortillas
¾ cup shredded Monterey Jack cheese with jalapeño peppers (3 ounces)
2 small tomatoes, chopped
2 green onions, sliced

Chicken and Sausage Cassoulet

Traditionally, this slow-cooked French dish is made with white beans and a variety of meats that vary by region. Serve this easy version with crusty bread and a salad dressed with Dijon vinaigrette.

Prep: 15 minutes **Cook:** 5 hours on low or 2½ hours on high **Makes:** 4 servings

3 medium carrots, cut into
   ½-inch pieces (1 cup)
1 medium onion, chopped
   (½ cup)
⅓ cup water
1 6-ounce can tomato paste
½ cup dry red wine or water
1 teaspoon garlic powder
½ teaspoon dried thyme,
   crushed
⅛ teaspoon ground cloves
2 bay leaves
2 15-ounce cans navy beans,
   drained
4 skinless, boneless chicken
   breast halves
8 ounces fully cooked
   Polish sausage, cut into
   ¼-inch slices

1. In a small saucepan combine the carrots, onion, and ⅓ cup water. Bring to boiling; reduce heat. Simmer, covered, for 8 minutes. Transfer the mixture to a 3½- or 4-quart slow cooker.

2. Stir in tomato paste, wine or water, garlic powder, thyme, cloves, and bay leaves; add beans. Place chicken atop bean mixture. Place sausage atop chicken.

3. Cover; cook on low-heat setting for 5 to 7 hours or on high-heat setting for 2½ to 3½ hours. Before serving, discard bay leaves and skim off fat.

Nutrition Facts per serving: 657 calories, 21 g total fat, 99 mg cholesterol, 1,659 mg sodium, 64 g carbohydrate, 49 g protein.

Chicken and Shrimp Jambalaya

If you like your Cajun food spicy, use the Homemade Cajun Seasoning blend. Our three-pepper combo packs more wallop than the supermarket variety.

Prep: 20 minutes **Cook:** 5 hours on low or 2½ hours on high **Stand:** 10 minutes **Makes:** 6 servings

1. In a 3½- or 4-quart slow cooker combine celery, onion, undrained tomatoes, broth, tomato paste, Worcestershire sauce, and Cajun seasoning. Stir in chicken.

2. Cover and cook on low-heat setting for 5 to 6 hours or on high-heat setting for 2½ to 3 hours. Stir in rice, shrimp, and sweet pepper. Cover and let stand 10 to 15 minutes or until most of the liquid is absorbed and rice is tender.

Homemade Cajun Seasoning: In a small bowl combine ¼ teaspoon white pepper, ¼ teaspoon garlic powder, ¼ teaspoon onion powder, ⅛ to ¼ teaspoon ground red pepper, ¼ teaspoon paprika, and ¼ teaspoon black pepper.

Nutrition Facts per serving: **261 calories, 2 g total fat, 118 mg cholesterol, 391 mg sodium, 30 g carbohydrate, 30 g protein.**

- 1 cup sliced celery
- 1 large onion, chopped
- 1 14½-ounce can reduced-sodium tomatoes, cut-up
- 1 14½-ounce can reduced-sodium chicken broth
- ½ of a 6-ounce can tomato paste (⅓ cup)
- 1 tablespoon Worcestershire sauce
- 1½ teaspoons Cajun seasoning or 1 recipe Homemade Cajun Seasoning
- 1 pound skinless, boneless chicken breast halves or thighs, cut into ¾-inch pieces
- 1½ cups instant rice
- 8 ounces cooked peeled, deveined shrimp
- ¾ cup chopped green sweet pepper

Chicken Cacciatore

"Cacciatora" is Italian for hunter. The Italian-American phrase "cacciatore" refers to anything served "hunter-style"—with onions, mushrooms, tomatoes, and herbs.

Prep: 25 minutes **Cook:** 6 hours on low plus 15 minutes on high or 3¼ hours on high **Makes:** 6 servings

2 cups sliced fresh
   mushrooms
1 cup sliced celery
1 cup chopped carrot
2 medium onions, cut into
   wedges
1 green, yellow, or red sweet
   pepper, cut into strips
4 cloves garlic, minced
12 chicken drumsticks, skinned
   (about 3½ pounds)
½ cup chicken broth
¼ cup dry white wine
2 tablespoons quick-cooking
   tapioca
2 bay leaves
1 teaspoon dried oregano,
   crushed
1 teaspoon sugar
½ teaspoon salt
¼ teaspoon pepper
1 14½-ounce can diced
   tomatoes
⅓ cup tomato paste
   Hot cooked pasta or rice

1. In a 5- or 6-quart slow cooker combine mushrooms, celery, carrot, onions, sweet pepper, and garlic. Place chicken on top of vegetables. Combine broth, wine, tapioca, bay leaves, oregano, sugar, salt, and pepper; pour over chicken.

2. Cover and cook on low-heat setting for 6 to 7 hours or on high-heat setting for 3 to 3½ hours.

3. Remove chicken and keep warm. Remove bay leaves and discard. If using low-heat setting, turn to high-heat setting. Stir in undrained tomatoes and tomato paste. Cover and cook 15 minutes longer on high-heat setting. Spoon vegetable mixture over chicken and pasta to serve.

Nutrition Facts per serving: 365 calories, 6 g total fat, 114 mg cholesterol, 507 mg sodium, 37 g carbohydrate, 38 g protein.

Chicken and Shrimp with Orzo

This elegant dish is ideal for entertaining, served with a salad of baby greens and a light white wine, such as a Sauvignon Blanc. Finish the meal sweetly with a fresh fruit tart and coffee.

Prep: 15 minutes   **Cook:** 6 hours on low plus 5 minutes on high or 3 hours on high   **Makes:** 4 to 5 servings

---

1. Cut chicken thighs into quarters. In a 3½-, 4-, or 5-quart slow cooker place the onion and garlic. Top with the chicken pieces. In a bowl combine the undrained tomatoes, tomato paste, wine or broth, lemon juice, bay leaves, salt, and crushed red pepper. Pour over all.

2. Cover; cook on low-heat setting for 6 to 7 hours or on high-heat setting for 3 to 3½ hours.

3. If using low-heat setting, turn to high-heat setting. Remove bay leaves. Stir in shrimp and artichoke hearts. Cover; cook for 5 minutes more. Serve chicken and shrimp mixture over hot cooked orzo. Sprinkle with feta cheese.

Nutrition Facts per serving: **615 calories, 21 g total fat, 187 mg cholesterol, 1,203 mg sodium, 56 g carbohydrate, 46 g protein.**

12 ounces skinless, boneless
  chicken thighs
1 large onion, chopped
3 cloves garlic, minced
1 14½-ounce can diced
  tomatoes with basil, garlic,
  and oregano, or diced
  tomatoes with onion
  and garlic
2 tablespoons tomato paste
½ cup port wine
  or chicken broth
2 tablespoons lemon juice
2 bay leaves
½ teaspoon salt
¼ teaspoon crushed red pepper
1 8-ounce package frozen
  peeled, cooked shrimp,
  thawed and drained
1 9-ounce package frozen
  artichoke hearts, thawed
  and coarsely chopped
2 cups hot cooked orzo
  (rosamarina)
½ cup crumbled feta cheese
  (2 ounces)

Chicken Curry

If you're just getting acquainted with Indian-style cooking, this classic dish is a terrific place to start. Curry powder ranges from mild to hot; read the label to discern the heat level of the bottle you buy.

Prep: 30 minutes   **Cook:** 6 hours on low plus 30 minutes on high or 3½ hours on high   **Makes:** 8 servings

3 tablespoons all-purpose flour
3 tablespoons curry powder
1½ teaspoons ground cumin
1 teaspoon salt
1½ pounds boneless, skinless
   chicken breasts or thighs,
   cut in 1-inch pieces
2 cups peeled and
   chopped potatoes
1½ cups bias-sliced carrots
1 cup coarsely chopped
   cooking apple
¾ cup chopped onion
2 cloves garlic, minced
1 jalapeño pepper, seeded
   and finely chopped
1 teaspoon instant chicken
   bouillon granules
½ cup water
1 13½-ounce can
   unsweetened coconut milk
   Hot cooked rice
   Raisins
   Chopped peanuts

1. In a large resealable plastic bag place flour, curry powder, cumin, and salt. Add chicken pieces; seal and shake to coat.

2. In a 3½- or 4-quart slow cooker place potatoes, carrots, apple, onion, garlic, jalapeño, and chicken bouillon. Top with chicken pieces. Pour water over chicken.

3. Cover; cook on low-heat setting for 6 to 8 hours or on high-heat setting for 3 to 4 hours.

4. If using low-heat setting, turn to high-heat setting. Stir in coconut milk; cover and cook on high-heat 30 minutes more. Serve over cooked rice and top with raisins and chopped peanuts.

Nutrition Facts per serving: 409 calories, 14 g total fat, 49 mg cholesterol, 513 mg sodium, 45 g carbohydrate, 26 g protein.

Chicken Mole

Mexican cooking encompasses far more than burritos and tacos. The complex flavors of this mole (pronounced MO-lay) made with chiles and chocolate pair beautifully with the mild taste of chicken.

Prep: 15 minutes **Cook:** 9 hours on low or 4½ hours on high **Makes:** 6 servings

---

1. For mole sauce, in a blender container or food processor bowl combine undrained tomatoes, chicken broth, onion, ¼ cup almonds, jalapeño peppers, cocoa powder, raisins, sesame seeds, garlic, sugar, cinnamon, nutmeg, and coriander. Cover and blend or process to a coarse puree.

2. In a 3½-, 4-, 5-, or 6-quart slow cooker place tapioca. Add chicken; then sauce. Cover; cook on low-heat setting for 9 to 11 hours or on high-heat setting for 4½ to 5½ hours.

3. Arrange chicken over rice on a platter. Skim fat from sauce; pour sauce over chicken. Sprinkle with almonds.

Nutrition Facts per serving: **448 calories, 23 g total fat, 99 mg cholesterol, 586 mg sodium, 24 g carbohydrate, 36 g protein.**

1 7½-ounce can tomatoes
¾ cup chicken broth
½ cup chopped onion
¼ cup slivered almonds
1 to 2 canned jalapeño peppers, drained
3 tablespoons unsweetened cocoa powder
3 tablespoons raisins
1 tablespoon sesame seeds
3 cloves garlic
1 teaspoon sugar
¼ teaspoon ground cinnamon
⅛ teaspoon ground nutmeg
⅛ teaspoon ground coriander
2 tablespoons quick-cooking tapioca
1 2½- to 3-pound broiler-fryer chicken, cut up and skinned
Hot cooked rice
2 tablespoons slivered almonds, toasted

Chicken Merlot with Mushrooms

Although it's called Chicken Merlot, you can use any dry red wine—such as a Cabernet Sauvignon, Syrah, or Burgundy—to make this wine-and-mushroom chicken dish.

Prep: 25 minutes **Cook:** 7 hours on low or 3½ hours on high **Makes:** 4 to 6 servings

3 cups sliced fresh
    mushrooms

1 large onion, chopped

2 cloves garlic, minced

2½ to 3 pounds meaty chicken
    pieces (breasts, thighs,
    and drumsticks), skinned

¾ cup chicken broth

1 6-ounce can tomato paste

¼ cup dry red wine (such as
    Merlot) or chicken broth

2 tablespoons quick-cooking
    tapioca

2 tablespoons snipped fresh
    basil or 1½ teaspoons
    dried basil, crushed

2 teaspoons sugar

¼ teaspoon salt

¼ teaspoon pepper

2 cups hot cooked noodles

2 tablespoons finely shredded
    Parmesan cheese

1. In a 3½-, 4-, or 5-quart slow cooker place mushrooms, onion, and garlic. Place chicken pieces on top of the vegetables. In a bowl combine broth, tomato paste, wine or chicken broth, tapioca, dried basil (if using), sugar, salt, and pepper. Pour over all.

2. Cover; cook on low-heat setting for 7 to 8 hours or on high-heat setting for 3½ to 4 hours. If using, stir in fresh basil. To serve, spoon chicken, mushroom mixture, and sauce over hot cooked noodles. Sprinkle with Parmesan cheese.

Nutrition Facts per serving: 469 calories, 12 g total fat, 144 mg cholesterol, 468 mg sodium, 41 g carbohydrate, 46 g protein.

Chicken Spaghetti Sauce

Everybody loves spaghetti with tomato sauce! Try this version made with ground turkey or chicken. To make it extra-lean, look for white-meat-only ground poultry that is ground without the skin.

Prep: 25 minutes **Cook:** 8 hours on low or 4 hours on high **Makes:** 8 to 10 servings

1. Brown meat with garlic in a large skillet until no longer pink. Drain fat.

2. In a 3½- or 4-quart slow cooker place meat mixture, undrained tomatoes, tomato paste, green pepper, Italian seasoning, salt, bay leaf, and hot pepper sauce, if desired.

3. Cover; cook on low-heat setting for 8 to 9 hours or on high-heat setting for 4 to 4½ hours. Remove bay leaf and discard. Serve sauce over pasta. Sprinkle with grated Parmesan cheese, if desired.

Nutrition Facts per serving: **379 calories, 6 g total fat, 45 mg cholesterol, 540 mg sodium, 60 g carbohydrate, 21 g protein.**

1 pound ground raw turkey
  or chicken
6 cloves garlic, minced
3 14½-ounce cans
  stewed tomatoes
2 6-ounce cans tomato paste
½ cup chopped green
  sweet pepper
1½ teaspoons dried Italian
  seasoning, crushed
½ teaspoon salt
1 bay leaf
⅛ teaspoon bottled
  hot pepper sauce (optional)
Hot cooked pasta
Grated Parmesan cheese
  (optional)

Chicken with Creamy Chive Sauce

Delicate strands of angel hair pasta cloaked in a creamy mushroom and onion sauce make this chicken dish just heavenly. It's also terrific served over hot cooked rice.

Prep: 15 minutes **Cook:** 4 hours on low **Makes:** 6 servings

6 skinless, boneless
   chicken breast halves
   (about 1½ pounds)
¼ cup butter
1 0.7-ounce package
   Italian salad dressing mix
1 10¾-ounce can condensed
   golden mushroom soup
½ cup dry white wine
½ of an 8-ounce tub cream
   cheese with chives
   and onion
   Hot cooked angel hair pasta
   Snipped fresh chives
   (optional)

1. Place chicken in a 3½- or 4-quart slow cooker. In a medium saucepan melt the butter. Stir in the dry Italian salad dressing mix. Stir in mushroom soup, white wine, and cream cheese until combined. Pour over the chicken. Cover and cook on low-heat setting for 4 to 5 hours.

2. Serve chicken and sauce over hot cooked pasta. Sprinkle with chives, if desired.

Nutrition Facts per serving: **405 calories, 17 g total fat, 110 mg cholesterol, 1,043 mg sodium, 26 g carbohydrate, 32 g protein.**

Chicken with Vegetables and Stuffing

Here's chicken and stuffing the easy way—and it's a great use for leftover chicken or turkey.

Prep: 25 minutes **Cook:** 5 hours on low or 2½ hours on high **Makes:** 6 servings

1. Prepare stuffing mix according to package instructions, except reduce water to ½ cup. (Stuffing will not be completely moistened.) Set aside.

2. In a large bowl combine chicken, zucchini, mushrooms, red or green sweet pepper, and onion. Stir in soup.

3. In a 3½-, 4-, or 5-quart slow cooker place half of the chicken-vegetable mixture; top with half of the stuffing. Repeat.

4. Cover; cook on low-heat setting for 5 to 6 hours or on high-heat setting for 2½ to 3 hours.

Nutrition Facts per serving: 315 calories, 11 g total fat, 52 mg cholesterol, 976 mg sodium, 29 g carbohydrate, 24 g protein.

1 6-ounce package chicken flavor stuffing mix
2½ cups chopped cooked chicken
2 cups zucchini, cut into ½-inch pieces
2 cups sliced fresh mushrooms
1 medium red or green sweet pepper, cut into ½-inch pieces
½ cup chopped onion
1 10¾-ounce can condensed cream of chicken soup or cream of mushroom soup

Cranberry Lemon Chicken

A kiss of honey gives this citrus and cranberry chicken just a touch of sweetness.

Prep: 15 minutes **Cook:** 6 hours on low or 3 hours on high **Makes:** 6 servings

1 medium onion, thinly sliced

2 medium apples, cored and
   cut into wedges

1 16-ounce can whole
   cranberry sauce

¼ cup frozen lemonade
   concentrate, thawed

2 tablespoons quick-cooking
   tapioca

2 tablespoons honey

¼ teaspoon salt

6 skinless, boneless
   chicken breast halves
   (about 2 pounds)

2 6-ounce packages long
   grain and wild rice mix

1. In a 3½- or 4-quart slow cooker layer onion and apples. In a medium bowl stir together cranberry sauce, lemonade concentrate, tapioca, honey, and salt. Add chicken breasts, one at a time, to cranberry mixture, turning to coat. Place chicken breasts atop apples. Pour cranberry mixture over chicken breasts.

2. Cover; cook on low-heat setting for 6 to 7 hours or on high-heat setting for 3 to 3½ hours.

3. Meanwhile, prepare long grain and wild rice according to package directions. Serve chicken and sauce over rice.

Nutrition Facts per serving: 565 calories, 2 g total fat, 88 mg cholesterol, 993 mg sodium, 96 g carbohydrate, 40 g protein.

Creamy Chicken and Noodles

Long-cooking chicken and noodles isn't just for Sunday dinner anymore. The slow cooker version of this family favorite can be enjoyed any day of the week.

Prep: 25 minutes **Cook:** 8 hours on low or 4 hours on high **Makes:** 6 servings

1. In a 3½- or 4-quart slow cooker place carrots, onion, celery, parsley, and bay leaf. Place chicken on top of vegetables. In a bowl stir together soup, water, thyme, and pepper. Pour over chicken and vegetables.

2. Cover and cook on low-heat setting for 8 to 9 hours or on high-heat setting for 4 to 4½ hours. Remove chicken from cooker; cool slightly. Remove and discard bay leaf.

3. Meanwhile, cook noodles according to package directions; drain. Stir peas into soup mixture in cooker. Remove chicken from bones; discard bones. Cut meat into bite-size pieces; stir into cooker. To serve, pour chicken mixture over noodles; toss gently to combine. Season to taste with salt and pepper, if desired.

Nutrition Facts per serving: 406 calories, 7 g total fat, 122 mg cholesterol, 532 mg sodium, 56 g carbohydrate, 28 g protein.

2 cups sliced carrots
1½ cups chopped onion
1 cup sliced celery
2 tablespoons snipped fresh parsley
1 bay leaf
3 medium chicken legs (drumstick-thigh portion), skinned (about 2 pounds)
2 10¾-ounce cans reduced-fat and reduced-sodium condensed cream of chicken soup
½ cup water
1 teaspoon dried thyme, crushed
¼ teaspoon pepper
10 ounces dried wide noodles (about 5 cups)
1 cup frozen peas
Salt (optional)
Pepper (optional)

Garlic Chicken with Artichokes

A dozen cloves of garlic may sound like overload, but the garlic mellows and sweetens as it cooks, enveloping the chicken in aroma and flavor.

Prep: 20 minutes **Cook:** 6 hours on low or 3 hours on high **Makes:** 6 servings

12 cloves garlic, minced

1 medium onion, chopped

1 tablespoon olive oil
    or cooking oil

1 8- or 9-ounce package
    frozen artichoke hearts

1 red sweet pepper,
    cut into strips

½ cup chicken broth

1 tablespoon quick-cooking
    tapioca

2 teaspoons dried rosemary,
    crushed

1 teaspoon finely shredded
    lemon peel

½ teaspoon ground
    black pepper

1½ pounds skinless, boneless
    chicken breast halves
    or thighs

4 cups hot cooked brown rice

1. In a small skillet cook garlic and onion in hot oil over medium heat, stirring occasionally, 5 minutes or until tender. In a 3½- or 4-quart slow cooker combine the frozen artichoke hearts, garlic mixture, sweet pepper, chicken broth, tapioca, rosemary, lemon peel, and black pepper. Add chicken; spoon some of the garlic mixture over chicken.

2. Cover and cook on low-heat setting for 6 to 7 hours or on high-heat setting for 3 to 3½ hours. Serve with rice.

Nutrition Facts per serving: 341 calories, 6 g total fat, 66 mg cholesterol, 159 mg sodium, 39 g carbohydrate, 32 g protein.

One-Pot Winter Dinner

You don't have to cook the onion in the bacon drippings, but the bacon does add a delicious smoky flavor to this homey dish. Even with the bacon, it still has only 4 grams of fat per serving.

Prep: 15 minutes **Cook:** 7 hours on low or 3½ hours on high **Makes:** 6 to 8 servings

1. In a skillet cook chicken, bacon or cooking oil, and onion until chicken is no longer pink. Drain off fat. Transfer mixture to a 3½- or 4-quart slow cooker. Gently stir in the remaining ingredients.

2. Cover and cook on low-heat setting for 7 to 8 hours or on high-heat setting for 3½ to 4 hours.

Nutrition Facts per serving: **395 calories, 4 g total fat, 28 mg cholesterol, 1,685 mg sodium, 76 g carbohydrate, 25 g protein.**

½ pound ground raw chicken
5 slices bacon, cut up,
   or 2 tablespoons cooking oil
1 cup chopped onion
2 31-ounce cans pork and
   beans in tomato sauce
1 15½-ounce can butter
   beans, drained
1 15-ounce can dark red kidney
   beans, drained
1 cup catsup
¼ cup packed brown sugar
3 tablespoons vinegar
1 teaspoon liquid smoke
   Dash salt
   Dash pepper

Greek Chicken and Orzo

For the most authentic Greek flavor, use kalamata olives, which have a rich, salty, fruity flavor and grow in abundance all over the Greek islands.

Prep: 25 minutes **Cook:** 5 hours on low or 2½ hours on high **Makes:** 4 servings

4 medium chicken
    breast halves (about
    1½ pounds total)

2 tablespoons cooking oil

1 medium fennel bulb, cut into
    ½-inch pieces (2 cups)

1 medium onion,
    cut into wedges

2 cloves garlic, minced

2 cups water

2 tablespoons white
    balsamic vinegar

2 teaspoons instant chicken
    bouillon granules

1 tablespoon snipped fresh
    oregano or 1 teaspoon
    dried oregano, crushed

¼ teaspoon crushed
    red pepper

1⅓ cups orzo pasta
    (rosamarina)

1 medium tomato, chopped

¼ cup crumbled feta cheese
    (1 ounce)

¼ cup chopped pitted
    ripe olives

1 tablespoon snipped
    fresh oregano

1. Skin chicken. In a large skillet brown chicken breasts in hot oil. In a 3½- or 4-quart slow cooker combine fennel, onion, and garlic. Add the chicken breasts. In a bowl stir together water, balsamic vinegar, bouillon granules, dried oregano (if using), and crushed red pepper. Pour over all.

2. Cover; cook on low-heat setting for 5 to 6 hours or on high-heat setting for 2½ to 3 hours. If using, stir in the 1 tablespoon fresh oregano.

3. Cook the orzo according to package directions; drain. Stir tomato, cheese, olives, and the 1 tablespoon fresh oregano into orzo. Using a slotted spoon, remove chicken and vegetables from cooker. Serve with orzo mixture.

Nutrition Facts per serving: 439 calories, 12 g total fat, 58 mg cholesterol, 626 mg sodium, 53 g carbohydrate, 28 g protein.

Italian Chicken and Green Beans

Italian-style green beans are broad and thick and make for toothsome eating. You can also use regular cut green beans with no change in the flavor of this Italian-style dish.

Prep: 15 minutes **Cook:** 5 hours on low or 2½ hours on high **Makes:** 4 servings

1. Cut chicken into 1-inch pieces.

2. In a 3½- or 4-quart slow cooker place green beans, mushrooms, and onion. Place chicken atop vegetables.

3. In a small bowl combine undrained tomatoes, tomato paste, Italian seasoning, and garlic. Pour over chicken.

4. Cover; cook on low-heat setting for 5 to 6 hours or on high-heat setting for 2½ to 3 hours. Serve over hot cooked fettuccine. If desired, pass grated Parmesan cheese.

Nutrition Facts per serving: 308 calories, 4 g total fat, 45 mg cholesterol, 799 mg sodium, 44 g carbohydrate, 24 g protein.

12 ounces skinless, boneless chicken breast halves

1 9-ounce package frozen Italian-style green beans

1 cup fresh mushrooms, quartered

1 small onion, sliced ¼ inch thick

1 14½-ounce can Italian-style stewed tomatoes

1 6-ounce can Italian-style tomato paste

1 teaspoon dried Italian seasoning, crushed

2 cloves garlic, minced

4 ounces fettuccine, cooked and drained
Grated Parmesan cheese (optional)

Herbed Chicken and Vegetables

Use a fairly dry white wine such as a Chardonnay or Sauvignon Blanc to make this light dish of tender, falling-off-the-bone chicken and vegetables in an aromatic herbed wine sauce.

Prep: 25 minutes **Cook:** 8 hours on low or 4 hours on high **Makes:** 6 servings

3 pounds chicken legs, thighs, or drumsticks, skinned

2 tablespoons cooking oil

1 cup chicken broth

½ cup dry white wine

1 tablespoon snipped fresh parsley

½ teaspoon salt

½ teaspoon dried rosemary, crushed

½ teaspoon dried thyme, crushed

¼ teaspoon pepper

1 clove garlic, minced

4 medium potatoes, quartered

4 medium carrots, cut into ½-inch pieces

2 stalks celery, cut into 1-inch pieces

1 small onion, sliced

2 tablespoons cornstarch

2 tablespoons cold water

1. In a skillet brown chicken pieces, half at a time, in hot oil.

2. In a bowl combine the chicken broth, wine, parsley, salt, rosemary, thyme, pepper, and garlic.

3. In a 3½-, 4-, or 5-quart slow cooker place potatoes, carrots, celery, and onion. Place chicken pieces atop vegetables. Pour broth mixture over chicken.

4. Cover; cook on low-heat setting for 8 to 9 hours or on high-heat setting for 4 to 4½ hours.

5. Using a slotted spoon, remove chicken and vegetables to a platter. Keep chicken and vegetables warm.

6. For gravy, skim fat from cooking juices. Strain juices into a saucepan. Combine cornstarch and cold water; stir into juices in saucepan. Cook and stir until thickened and bubbly. Cook and stir 2 minutes more. Pass the gravy with the chicken and vegetables.

Nutrition Facts per serving: 338 calories, 10 g total fat, 79 mg cholesterol, 416 mg sodium, 31 g carbohydrate, 27 g protein.

Orange Teriyaki Chicken

Garnish each serving of this sweet and fruity chicken with fresh orange slices and toasted almonds.

Prep: 15 minutes **Cook:** 4 hours on low or 2 hours on high **Makes:** 4 servings

1. Cut chicken into 1-inch pieces.

2. In a 3½-, 4-, or 5-quart slow cooker place frozen vegetables. Sprinkle tapioca over vegetables. Place chicken pieces atop vegetables.

3. For sauce, in a small bowl combine chicken broth, brown sugar, teriyaki sauce, mustard, orange peel, and ginger. Pour sauce over chicken pieces.

4. Cover; cook on low-heat setting for 4 to 6 hours or on high-heat setting for 2 to 3 hours. Serve with hot cooked rice.

Nutrition Facts per serving: **303 calories, 4 g total fat, 60 mg cholesterol, 543 mg sodium, 39 g carbohydrate, 27 g protein.**

1 pound skinless, boneless
  chicken breast halves
  or thighs
1 16-ounce package loose-pack
  frozen broccoli,
  baby carrots, and
  water chestnuts
2 tablespoons quick-cooking
  tapioca
½ cup chicken broth
2 tablespoons brown sugar
2 tablespoons teriyaki sauce
1 teaspoon dry mustard
1 teaspoon finely shredded
  orange peel
½ teaspoon ground ginger
2 cups hot cooked rice

Southwest Barbecue-Style Chicken

Sweet and hot jalapeño pepper jelly is the secret ingredient in this delicious barbecued chicken. Serve it with black beans, avocado slices, and warmed flour tortillas.

Prep: 10 minutes **Cook:** 6 hours on low or 3 hours on high **Makes:** 4 to 6 servings

½ cup tomato sauce
2 tablespoons jalapeño
    pepper jelly
2 tablespoons lime
    or lemon juice
2 tablespoons quick-cooking
    tapioca
1 teaspoon brown sugar
1 teaspoon ground cumin
¼ to ½ teaspoon crushed
    red pepper
2 to 2½ pounds chicken
    breasts, thighs,
    and/or legs, skinned

1. In a 3½- or 4-quart slow cooker combine tomato sauce, jelly, lime or lemon juice, tapioca, brown sugar, cumin, and red pepper. Place chicken atop sauce mixture, meaty side down.

2. Cover; cook on low-heat setting for 6 to 7 hours or on high-heat setting for 3 to 3½ hours.

Nutrition Facts per serving: **227 calories, 7 g total fat, 81 mg cholesterol, 264 mg sodium, 15 g carbohydrate, 26 g protein.**

Spicy Ginger and Tomato Chicken

Simple but sophisticated, this super-light dish gets its great flavor from a just-right balance of tomato, ginger, garlic, crushed red pepper—and a touch of brown sugar for sweetness.

Prep: 15 minutes **Cook:** 6 hours on low or 3 hours on high **Makes:** 6 servings

1. Place chicken pieces in a 3½- or 4-quart slow cooker.

2. Drain 1 can of tomatoes; chop tomatoes from both cans. For sauce, in a medium bowl combine both cans of tomatoes, tapioca, ginger, cilantro or parsley, garlic, brown sugar, crushed red pepper, and salt. Pour sauce over chicken.

3. Cover; cook on low-heat setting for 6 to 7 hours or on high-heat setting for 3 to 3½ hours. Skim fat from sauce. Serve sauce with chicken and couscous or rice.

Nutrition Facts per serving: 332 calories, 11 g total fat, 66 mg cholesterol, 507 mg sodium, 33 g carbohydrate, 25 g protein.

1 2½- to 3-pound cut up boiler-fryer chicken, skinned

2 16-ounce cans tomatoes

2 tablespoons quick-cooking tapioca

1 tablespoon grated ginger

1 tablespoon snipped fresh cilantro or parsley

4 cloves garlic, minced

2 teaspoons brown sugar

½ to 1 teaspoon crushed red pepper

½ teaspoon salt

3 cups hot cooked couscous or rice

Sweet and Tangy Spiced Chicken

A homemade citrus barbecue sauce made with the juices of lemon, pineapple, and orange—and spiced with cinnamon, allspice, and cloves—gives this easy chicken dish a pleasant tang.

Prep: 20 minutes **Cook:** 8 hours on low or 4 hours on high **Makes:** 6 servings

1 6-ounce can frozen
    pineapple-orange juice
    concentrate, thawed
½ cup catsup
2 tablespoons lemon juice
2 tablespoons quick-cooking
    tapioca
2 inches stick cinnamon,
    broken
8 whole allspice
4 whole cloves
2½ to 3 pounds meaty
    chicken pieces
    (breast halves, thighs,
    and drumsticks) skinned
Hot cooked couscous

1. For sauce, in a small bowl combine juice concentrate, catsup, and lemon juice. Pour about half of the sauce into a 3½- or 4-quart slow cooker. Add tapioca to the cooker; stir. For spice bag, place cinnamon, allspice, and cloves in cheesecloth and tie. Add bag to cooker. Place chicken pieces in slow cooker. Pour remaining sauce over chicken.

2. Cover; cook on low-heat setting for 8 hours or on high-heat setting for 4 hours. Discard spice bag. Transfer chicken to a serving platter. Skim fat from sauce. Serve sauce and hot couscous with chicken.

For 5- or 6-quart slow cooker: Double all ingredients. Prepare as above. Makes 12 servings.

Nutrition Facts per serving: 471 calories, 9 g total fat, 115 mg cholesterol, 479 mg sodium, 54 g carbohydrate, 41 g protein.

Thyme and Garlic Chicken Breasts

A few simple ingredients—garlic, thyme, orange juice, and a splash of balsamic vinegar—result in a big flavor payoff for these chicken breasts. Serve them with a package of saffron rice and steamed peas.

Prep: 15 minutes **Cook:** 5 hours on low or 2½ hours on high **Boil:** 10 minutes **Makes:** 6 to 8 servings

1. Sprinkle garlic and thyme over chicken. Place chicken pieces in a 3½- or 4-quart slow cooker. Pour orange juice and vinegar over chicken.

2. Cover and cook on low-heat setting for 5 to 6 hours or on high-heat setting for 2½ to 3 hours.

3. Remove chicken from cooker; cover and keep warm. Skim off fat from cooking juices. Strain juices into a saucepan. Bring to boiling; reduce heat. Boil gently, uncovered, for 10 minutes or until reduced to 1 cup. Pass juices to spoon over chicken.

Nutrition Facts per serving: **178 calories, 2 g total fat, 85 mg cholesterol, 78 mg sodium, 3 g carbohydrate, 34 g protein.**

- **6 cloves garlic, minced**
- **1½ teaspoons dried thyme, crushed**
- **3 to 4 pounds whole chicken breasts (with bone), halved and skinned**
- **¼ cup orange juice**
- **1 tablespoon balsamic vinegar**

Rosemary Chicken with Pasta

As this aromatic meal finishes cooking, make a spinach salad with baby spinach, blue cheese crumbles, croutons, Italian dressing—and lots of coarsely ground black pepper.

Prep: 10 minutes **Cook:** 7 hours on low or 3½ hours on high **Makes:** 4 servings

2 medium onions, sliced or chopped

2 teaspoons bottled minced garlic or 4 cloves garlic, minced

¾ pound skinless, boneless chicken breasts or thighs

1 14½-ounce can diced tomatoes

1 6-ounce can tomato paste

2 tablespoons wine vinegar

2 bay leaves

1 teaspoon sugar

½ teaspoon dried rosemary, crushed

¼ teaspoon salt

¼ teaspoon pepper

1 4-ounce can sliced mushrooms, drained

8 ounces dried pasta (such as penne, mostaccioli, or elbow macaroni)

Grated Parmesan cheese

1. In a 3½-, 4-, or 4½-quart slow cooker place the onions and garlic. Add chicken to cooker.

2. In a mixing bowl combine undrained tomatoes, tomato paste, vinegar, bay leaves, sugar, rosemary, salt, and pepper; mix well. Pour over chicken.

3. Cover and cook on low-heat setting for 7 hours or on high-heat setting for 3½ hours.

4. When ready to serve, remove bay leaves. Stir mushrooms into chicken mixture; cook for 5 to 10 minutes more to heat through. Meanwhile, cook pasta according to package directions. Serve the chicken and sauce over the hot cooked pasta; sprinkle with Parmesan cheese.

Nutrition Facts per serving: 415 calories, 5 g total fat, 47 mg cholesterol, 568 mg sodium, 65 g carbohydrate, 29 g protein.

Sweet-and-Sour Chicken with Almonds

Five ingredients add up to a terrific Chinese-style dinner.

Prep: 10 minutes **Cook:** 5 hours on low or 2½ hours on high **Makes:** 4 servings

---

1. Cut chicken into 1-inch pieces.

2. In a 3½- or 4-quart slow cooker combine chicken, sweet-and-sour cooking sauce, and frozen vegetables.

3. Cover; cook on low-heat setting for 5 to 6 hours or on high-heat setting for 2½ to 3 hours. Serve with hot cooked rice. Sprinkle with almonds.

Nutrition Facts per serving: **415 calories, 7 g total fat, 59 mg cholesterol, 526 mg sodium, 62 g carbohydrate, 27 g protein.**

1 pound skinless, boneless chicken breast halves
1 24½-ounce jar sweet-and-sour cooking sauce for chicken
1 16-ounce package loose-pack frozen broccoli, carrots, water chestnuts, and red sweet peppers
2 cup hot cooked rice
¼ cup toasted, chopped almonds

Weeknight Chicken and Rice

After a long day at work, school, or errand-running, having this satisfying chicken and rice dish ready and waiting is a simple pleasure.

Prep: 15 minutes **Cook:** 5 hours on low plus 10 minutes on high or 2½ hours on high **Makes:** 4 servings

---

2 cups sliced fresh
   mushrooms
1 cup sliced celery
½ cup chopped onion
1½ teaspoons dried dillweed
¼ teaspoon pepper
2 pounds chicken thighs,
   skinned
1 10¾-ounce can condensed
   cream of mushroom
   or cream of chicken soup
¾ cup chicken broth
1½ cups instant rice

1. In a 3½- or 4-quart slow cooker combine mushrooms, celery, onion, dillweed, and pepper. Place chicken on top of vegetables. Combine soup and broth and pour over chicken mixture.

2. Cover; cook on low-heat setting for 5 to 6 hours or on high-heat setting for 2½ to 3 hours. Stir in rice. If using low heat setting, turn to high; cover and cook for 10 more minutes.

Nutrition Facts per serving: 516 calories, 12 g total fat, 108 mg cholesterol, 840 mg sodium, 66 g carbohydrate, 34 g protein.

Barbecue-Style Turkey Thighs

Add an extra pinch of crushed red pepper if you like your barbecue on the spicy side.

Prep: 10 minutes **Cook:** 10 hours on low or 5 hours on high **Makes:** 4 to 6 servings

1. In a 3½ or 4-quart slow cooker combine catsup, brown sugar, tapioca, vinegar, Worcestershire sauce, cinnamon, and red pepper. Place turkey thighs or chicken pieces atop catsup mixture, meaty side down and flat in the cooker.

2. Cover; cook on low-heat setting for 10 to 12 hours or high-heat setting for 5 to 6 hours. Serve turkey or chicken and sauce over rice or noodles, if desired.

For 5- or 6-quart slow cooker: Use ¾ cup catsup, 3 tablespoons brown sugar, 4 teaspoons quick-cooking tapioca, 4 teaspoons vinegar, 2 teaspoons Worcestershire sauce, ¼ teaspoon ground cinnamon, ¼ teaspoon crushed red pepper, and 3 to 3½ pounds turkey thighs or meaty chicken pieces, skinned and frozen. Prepare as above. Makes 6 to 8 servings.

Nutrition Facts per serving: **239 calories, 6 g total fat, 100 mg cholesterol, 449 mg sodium, 16 g carbohydrate, 30 g protein.**

½ cup catsup

2 tablespoons brown sugar

1 tablespoon quick-cooking tapioca

1 tablespoon vinegar

1 teaspoon Worcestershire sauce

¼ teaspoon ground cinnamon

¼ teaspoon crushed red pepper

2 to 2½ pounds turkey thighs (about 2 thighs) or meaty chicken pieces (breasts, thighs, and drumsticks), skinned

Hot cooked rice or noodles (optional)

Fruited Turkey in Red Wine Sauce

Turkey thighs get dressed up with a savory compote of dried apricots, prunes, red wine, garlic, thyme, and honey. Serve it with hot cooked rice or couscous.

Prep: 30 minutes   **Cook:** 6 hours on low or 3 hours on high   **Makes:** 4 or 5 servings

3 pounds turkey thighs
1 tablespoon cooking oil
½ cup pitted prunes
½ cup dried apricot halves
½ cup orange juice
¼ cup dry red wine
4 cloves garlic, minced
1 tablespoon honey
1 tablespoon finely shredded lemon peel
2 teaspoons dried thyme, crushed
½ teaspoon salt
1 tablespoon cornstarch
1 tablespoon cold water
Hot cooked rice

1. Remove skin from turkey thighs. In a large skillet brown turkey in hot oil. Transfer turkey to a 3½- or 4-quart slow cooker. Place prunes and apricots on top of turkey.

2. Stir together orange juice, wine, garlic, honey, lemon peel, thyme, and salt. Pour orange juice mixture over turkey.

3. Cover and cook on low-heat setting for 6 to 7 hours or on high-heat setting for 3 to 3½ hours.

4. Using a slotted spoon, transfer turkey and fruit to a serving platter; cover turkey and keep warm. Pour cooking juices into a glass measure; skim off fat. For sauce, measure 1¼ cups juices. Transfer to a saucepan. Combine the cornstarch and cold water; stir into juices in saucepan. Cook and stir over medium heat until thickened and bubbly. Cook and stir for 2 minutes more. Spoon sauce over turkey and hot cooked rice.

Nutrition Facts per serving: **531 calories, 14 g total fat, 156 mg cholesterol, 406 mg sodium, 49 g carbohydrate, 47 g protein.**

Maple-Mustard Turkey Thighs

Round out this yummy anytime meal with mashed potatoes (stir in some bottled minced and roasted garlic for flavor) and steamed green beans.

Prep: 10 minutes **Cook:** 6 hours on low or 2½ hours on high **Makes:** 6 servings

1. Place turkey thighs in the bottom of a 3½- or 4-quart slow cooker.

2. In a small bowl stir together syrup, mustard, and tapioca. Pour over turkey.

3. Cover; cook on low-heat setting for 6 to 7 hours or on high-heat setting for 2½ to 3 hours.

Nutrition Facts per serving: **263 calories, 8 g total fat, 81 mg cholesterol, 255 mg sodium, 19 g carbohydrate, 28 g protein.**

2 to 2½ pounds turkey thighs (about 2 thighs), skinned

½ cup maple syrup or maple-flavored syrup

⅓ cup coarse-grain brown mustard

1 tablespoon quick-cooking tapioca

Mexican-Style Turkey Sausage and Beans

Pick your salsa—mild, medium, or hot—to make this bean and sausage mélange mild or tongue-tingling. Serve it with warm corn bread or muffins.

Prep: 15 minutes   **Cook:** 6 hours on low or 3 hours on high   **Makes:** 6 servings

1 cup chopped green
   sweet pepper
1 large onion, chopped
3 cloves garlic, minced
1 15-ounce can white kidney
   beans (cannellini),
   rinsed and drained
1 15-ounce can black beans,
   rinsed and drained
1 15-ounce can red kidney
   beans, rinsed and drained
1½ cups frozen whole
   kernel corn
1½ cups bottled salsa
1 teaspoon ground cumin
1 pound smoked turkey
   sausage, sliced

1. In a 3½- or 4-quart slow cooker combine sweet pepper, onion, garlic, beans, corn, salsa, cumin, and sausage.

2. Cover and cook on low-heat setting for 6 to 7 hours or on high-heat setting for 3 to 3½ hours.

Nutrition Facts per serving: **307 calories, 8 g total fat, 47 mg cholesterol, 1,213 mg sodium, 47 g carbohydrate, 28 g protein.**

Turkey Roast Chablis

Here's the perfect dish for a small holiday gathering when a whole bird is just too much.

Serve it with a crisp green salad topped with toasted pecans and dried cranberries.

Prep: 20 minutes   **Cook:** 10 hours on low or 4½ hours on high   **Makes:** 6 to 8 servings

---

1. In a 3½, 4-, 5-, or 6-quart slow cooker combine white wine, onion, garlic, and bay leaf. If turkey roast is wrapped in netting, remove and discard. If gravy packet is included, remove packet from roast; refrigerate packet for another use. Combine rosemary and pepper. Rub roast with rosemary mixture. Place turkey roast in cooker.

2. Cover; cook on low-heat setting for 10 to 12 hours or on high-heat setting for 4½ to 5½ hours. Remove roast and keep warm. For gravy, strain cooking juices; discard solids. Skim fat from juices. Measure 1⅓ cups juices into a small saucepan. Combine cream or milk, cornstarch, and salt; stir into juices. Cook and stir until thickened and bubbly. Cook and stir 2 minutes more.

3. Slice turkey roast. Spoon some gravy over roast. Pass remaining gravy with roast.

Nutrition Facts per serving: **324 calories, 6 g total fat, 125 mg cholesterol, 1,594 mg sodium, 19 g carbohydrate, 41 g protein.**

¾ cup dry white wine

½ cup chopped onion

1 clove garlic, minced

1 bay leaf

1 3 to 3½-pound frozen boneless turkey roast, thawed

1 teaspoon dried rosemary, crushed

¼ teaspoon pepper

⅓ cup light cream or milk

2 tablespoons cornstarch

⅛ teaspoon salt

Turkey Meatballs and Gravy

Using a package of gravy mix as a starter for a savory herbed gravy makes this family-pleasing dinner doable any day of the week.

Prep: 30 minutes **Cook:** 6 hours on low or 3 hours on high **Makes:** 8 servings

2 beaten eggs

¾ cup fine dry seasoned bread crumbs

½ cup finely chopped onion

½ cup finely chopped celery

2 tablespoons snipped fresh parsley

¼ teaspoon pepper

⅛ teaspoon garlic powder

2 pounds ground raw turkey

1½ teaspoons cooking oil

1 10¾-ounce can reduced-sodium condensed cream of mushroom soup

1 cup water

1 ¹⁵⁄₁₆-ounce envelope turkey gravy mix

½ teaspoon finely shredded lemon peel

½ teaspoon dried thyme, crushed

1 bay leaf

Hot cooked mashed potatoes or buttered noodles

Snipped fresh parsley (optional)

1. In a large bowl combine eggs, bread crumbs, onion, celery, 2 tablespoons parsley, pepper, and garlic powder. Add ground turkey and mix well. Shape into 1½-inch balls.

2. In a large skillet brown meatballs, half at a time, in hot oil. If necessary add additional oil. Drain meatballs. Transfer to a 3½- or 4-quart slow cooker.

3. In a bowl combine soup, water, gravy mix, lemon peel, thyme, and bay leaf. Pour over meatballs.

4. Cover; cook on low-heat setting for 6 to 8 hours or on high-heat setting for 3 to 4 hours. Discard bay leaf. Serve with mashed potatoes or noodles. Sprinkle with additional snipped fresh parsley.

Nutrition Facts per serving: **314 calories, 14 g total fat, 98 mg cholesterol, 916 mg sodium, 25 g carbohydrate, 21 g protein.**

Turkey Sausage and Sweet Pepper Sauce

To easily peel fresh tomatoes, plunge them in boiling water for 10 seconds, then quickly remove with a slotted spoon and run under cold water. The skins will slip right off.

Prep: 15 minutes **Cook:** 8 hours on low or 4 hours on high **Makes:** 6 to 8 servings

1. Remove casings from sausage, if present. In a large skillet cook turkey sausage until brown. Drain off fat Transfer cooked sausage to a 3½-, 4, or 5-quart slow cooker. Stir in fresh or undrained canned tomatoes, sweet peppers, mushrooms, onion, tomato paste, garlic, sugar, pepper, and bay leaf.

2. Cover and cook on low-heat setting for 8 to 10 hours or on high-heat setting for 4 to 5 hours.

3. Cook pasta on range top according to package directions; drain. Remove and discard bay leaf from sauce. Serve sauce over pasta. Sprinkle with Parmesan cheese, if desired.

Nutrition Facts per serving: **517 calories, 14 g total fat, 60 mg cholesterol, 1,394 mg sodium, 69 g carbohydrate, 30 g protein.**

1½ pounds uncooked turkey
  Italian sausage
4 cups chopped, peeled
  tomatoes (6 large)
  or two 14½-ounce cans
  tomatoes, cut up
2 medium green
  and/or yellow sweet
  peppers, cut into strips
2 cups sliced fresh mushrooms
1 large onion, chopped
2 6-ounce cans Italian-style
  tomato paste
2 cloves garlic, minced
1 teaspoon sugar
½ teaspoon pepper
1 bay leaf
12 to 16 ounces dried penne,
  rigatoni, or other pasta
  Finely shredded Parmesan
  cheese (optional)

vegetables and sides

Think outside the box: Slow cookers aren't just for pot roast and stew anymore. The delicious evidence? This collection of meatless main dishes and vegetable and grain go-alongs.

Vegetable-Barley Medley, page 235

Bean and Rice Stuffed Peppers

Five easy ingredients make a delicious, healthy meatless meal. Just add some corn bread or whole wheat rolls and dinner is done!

Prep: 15 minutes **Cook:** 6 hours on low or 3 hours on high **Makes:** 4 main-dish servings

- 4 medium green, red, or yellow sweet peppers
- 1 cup cooked converted rice
- 1 15-ounce can chili beans with chili gravy
- 4 ounces Monterey Jack cheese, shredded (1 cup)
- 1 15-ounce can chunky tomato sauce with onion, celery, and green pepper

1. Remove tops, membranes, and seeds from sweet peppers. Stir together rice, beans, and ½ cup of the cheese; spoon into peppers. Pour tomato sauce into the bottom of a 5- or 6-quart slow cooker. Place peppers, filled side up, in cooker.

2. Cover and cook on low-heat setting for 6 to 6½ hours or on high heat setting for 3 to 3½ hours. Transfer peppers to serving plate. Spoon tomato sauce over peppers and sprinkle with remaining cheese.

Nutrition Facts per serving: 323 calories, 11 g total fat, 25 mg cholesterol, 918 mg sodium, 41 g carbohydrate, 16 g protein.

Curried Vegetable Rice

When you're shopping for coconut milk, be sure to buy the unsweetened variety to make this vegetable-rich main dish.

Prep: 25 minutes **Cook:** 7 hours on low or 3½ hours on high **Makes:** 6 main-dish servings

1. In a 3½- or 4-quart slow cooker place potatoes, sweet potato, carrot, onion, garlic, ginger, salt, curry powder, and cumin. Pour coconut milk and vegetable broth into cooker.

2. Cover; cook on low-heat setting for 7 to 8 hours or on high-heat setting for 3½ to 4 hours. Stir in rice and peas. Cover and cook for 5 minutes more. Garnish each serving with cashews.

Nutrition Facts per serving: 443 calories, 21 g total fat, 0 mg cholesterol, 804 mg sodium, 58 g carbohydrate, 10 g protein.

3 cups coarsely chopped red-skinned potatoes (1 pound)
2 cups peeled and coarsely chopped sweet potato (12 ounces)
1 cup coarsely chopped carrot
½ cup chopped onion
2 cloves garlic, minced
2 teaspoons grated fresh ginger
1 teaspoon salt
1 teaspoon curry powder
½ teaspoon ground cumin
1 13½-ounce can coconut milk
1 14-ounce can vegetable broth
1½ cups quick-cooking rice
1 cup frozen peas
½ cup roasted cashews

Ravioli with Mushroom-Wine Sauce

The sauce for these cheese-stuffed ravioli simmers for hours so it's rich and flavorful. The pasta is stirred into the slow cooker just 20 minutes before serving so it's cooked to a perfect al dente.

Prep: 20 minutes   **Cook:** 4 hours on low plus 20 minutes on high or 2 hours 20 minutes on high   **Makes:** 4 main-dish servings

4 cups sliced button
    mushrooms
4 cups sliced assorted exotic
    mushrooms (portobello,
    shiitake and/or crimini)
2 14½-ounce cans diced
    tomatoes
½ cup water
⅓ cup dry red wine
4 cloves garlic, minced
½ teaspoon salt
¼ teaspoon dried rosemary,
    crushed
¼ teaspoon crushed
    red pepper flakes
1 9-ounce package
    refrigerated cheese-filled
    ravioli
    Finely shredded Parmesan
    cheese

1. In a 4- or 5-quart slow cooker place mushrooms, tomatoes, water, red wine, garlic, salt, rosemary, and crushed red pepper.

2. Cover; cook on low-heat setting for 4 to 6 hours or on high-heat setting for 2 to 3 hours. If using low-heat setting, turn to high-heat setting. Stir in ravioli. Cover and cook 20 minutes more. Serve with Parmesan cheese.

Nutrition Facts per serving: **361 calories, 7 g total fat, 32 mg cholesterol, 1,068 mg sodium, 62 g carbohydrate, 18 g protein.**

Savory Beans and Rice

Brown rice is simply regular rice that is less processed. Layers of bran are left on the kernels which give the rice a nutty flavor and chewy texture—not to mention more nutritional value.

Prep: 20 minutes **Cook:** 9½ hours on low or 4½ hours on high **Stand:** 1 hour **Makes:** 5 main-dish servings

1. Rinse beans; place in a large saucepan. Add enough water to cover beans by 2 inches. Bring to boiling; reduce heat. Simmer for 10 minutes. Remove from heat. Cover and let stand for 1 hour. (Or place beans in water in a large saucepan. Cover; let soak in a cool place overnight.) Drain and rinse beans.

2. In a 3½- or 4-quart slow cooker combine beans, onion, celery, garlic, bouillon, basil, and bay leaf. Pour the 1¼ cups water over all.

3. Cover and cook on low-heat setting for 9 to 10 hours or on high heat setting for 4 to 5 hours.

4. Cook brown rice according to package directions; keep warm. Remove bay leaf from bean mixture; discard. Stir undrained stewed tomatoes, chile peppers, and hot pepper sauce into cooked beans. Cook 30 minutes more. Serve bean mixture over hot cooked rice.

Nutrition Facts per serving: **383 calories, 3 g total fat, 0 mg cholesterol, 406 mg sodium, 74 g carbohydrate, 16 g protein.**

1¼ cups dry red beans
   or dry red kidney beans
1 large onion, chopped (1 cup)
¾ cup sliced celery
2 cloves garlic, minced
½ of a vegetable bouillon cube
1 teaspoon dried basil, crushed
1 bay leaf
1¼ cups water
1¼ cups brown rice
1 14½-ounce can stewed
   tomatoes
1 4-ounce can diced green
   chile peppers, drained
Few dashes bottled
   hot pepper sauce

Spicy Black Beans and Rice

If you like your food spicy, leave the seeds in the jalapeño peppers. If you prefer just a little heat, scrape them out of the peppers before you begin chopping.

Prep: 20 minutes   **Cook:** 8 hours on low or 4 hours on high   **Stand:** 1 hour   **Makes:** 8 main-dish servings

2 cups dry black beans
1 cup chopped onion
1 cup chopped celery
1 cup chopped carrot
1 medium yellow or green
 sweet pepper, chopped
2 jalapeño peppers, chopped
4 cloves garlic, minced
1 tablespoon ground cumin
1 teaspoon ground coriander
1 teaspoon dried thyme,
 crushed
½ teaspoon salt
¼ teaspoon pepper
2 bay leaves
5 cups chicken broth
4 cups hot cooked rice

1. Rinse beans; place in a large saucepan. Add enough water to cover beans by 2 inches. Bring to boiling; reduce heat. Simmer for 2 minutes. Remove from heat and let stand, covered, for 1 hour. (Or omit simmering and soak beans in cold water overnight in a covered pan.) Drain beans.

2. In a 3½-, 4-, or 5-quart slow cooker combine onion, celery, carrot, yellow or green sweet pepper, jalapeño peppers, garlic, cumin, coriander, thyme, salt, pepper, and bay leaves. Stir in drained beans and chicken broth.

3. Cover; cook on low-heat setting for 8 to 10 hours or on high-heat setting for 4 to 5 hours. Discard bay leaves. If desired, mash beans slightly with a potato masher. Serve with hot rice.

Nutrition Facts per serving: **198 calories, 2 g total fat, 1 mg cholesterol, 789 mg sodium, 38 g carbohydrate, 10 g protein.**

Vegetable-Barley Medley

High in fiber and flavor, this meatless main dish is not only chock-full of good vegetables and grains but also fresh-tasting and filling.

Prep: 20 minutes   **Cook:** 7 hours on low plus 30 minutes on high or 4 hours on high   **Makes:** 4 main-dish servings

1. In a 3½-, 4-, or 5-quart slow cooker place drained beans, corn, onion, barley, green sweet pepper, carrot, and garlic. In a medium bowl combine vegetable or chicken broth, parsley, basil or oregano, salt, and pepper. Stir into vegetable mixture.

2. Cover; cook on low-heat setting for 7 to 8 hours or on high-heat setting for 3½ to 4 hours.

3. If using low-heat setting, turn to high-heat setting. Stir in the zucchini, tomatoes, and lemon juice. Cover and cook 30 minutes longer on high-heat setting.

Nutrition Facts per serving: 302 calories, 3 g total fat, 1 mg cholesterol, 1,199 mg sodium, 60 g carbohydrate, 18 g protein.

1 15-ounce can black beans, rinsed and drained
1 10-ounce package frozen whole kernel corn
1 cup chopped onion
½ cup regular pearl barley
1 medium green sweet pepper, chopped (¾ cup)
1 medium carrot, thinly sliced (½ cup)
2 cloves garlic, minced
1 14½-ounce can vegetable broth or chicken broth (1¾ cups)
2 tablespoons snipped fresh parsley
1 teaspoon dried basil, crushed, or ½ teaspoon dried oregano, crushed
½ teaspoon salt
¼ teaspoon pepper
1 medium zucchini, halved lengthwise and thinly sliced
2 medium tomatoes, coarsely chopped
1 tablespoon lemon juice

Herbed Mushroom-Tomato Sauce

To make this light tomato sauce heartier, brown some ground beef in a skillet and drain off the fat. Stir the browned meat into the tomato mixture before turning on the slow cooker.

Prep: 15 minutes   **Cook:** 8 hours on low or 4 hours on high   **Makes:** 6 main-dish servings

2 16-ounce cans whole
   tomatoes, cut up
2 cups sliced fresh
   mushrooms
1 6-ounce can tomato paste
½ cup chopped onion
2 cloves garlic, minced
2 tablespoons grated
   Parmesan cheese
2 teaspoons dried oregano,
   crushed
2 teaspoons brown sugar
1½ teaspoons dried basil,
   crushed
½ teaspoon salt
½ teaspoon fennel seeds,
   crushed (optional)
¼ to ½ teaspoon crushed
   red pepper
1 bay leaf
12 ounces spaghetti, linguine,
   or other pasta, cooked
   and drained
   Grated Parmesan cheese
   (optional)

1. In a 3½- or 4-quart slow cooker combine undrained tomatoes, mushrooms, tomato paste, onion, garlic, grated Parmesan cheese, oregano, brown sugar, basil, salt, fennel seeds (if desired), red pepper, and bay leaf.

2. Cover; cook on low-heat setting for 8 to 10 hours or on high-heat setting for 4 to 5 hours.

3. Discard bay leaf. Serve sauce over hot cooked pasta. Top with grated Parmesan cheese, if desired.

Nutrition Facts per serving: 310 calories, 2 g total fat, 2 mg cholesterol, 485 mg sodium, 62 g carbohydrate, 12 g protein.

California Vegetable Casserole

Take this creamy vegetable-and-rice dish to a potluck, and you'll bring home an empty pot.

Prep: 15 minutes **Cook:** 4½ hours on low **Makes:** 6 side-dish servings

1. Place frozen vegetables in a 3½- or 4-quart slow cooker. In a small bowl combine the soup, uncooked rice, cheese dip, milk, onion, water, and butter. Pour over the vegetables.

2. Cover; cook on low-heat setting for 4½ to 5½ hours or until vegetables and rice are tender. Stir before serving.

Nutrition Facts per serving: 292 calories, 17 g total fat, 36 mg cholesterol, 1,124 mg sodium, 26 g carbohydrate, 9 g protein.

- **1 16-ounce package loose-pack frozen California-blend vegetables (cauliflower, broccoli, and carrots)**
- **1 10¾-ounce can condensed cream of mushroom soup**
- **1 cup instant white rice**
- **½ of a 15-ounce jar process cheese dip (about 1 cup)**
- **⅔ cup milk**
- **⅓ cup chopped onion**
- **¼ cup water**
- **2 tablespoons butter, cut up**

Cheesy Cauliflower

Even kids will eat their vegetables when they're cooked in a delicious cheesy sauce.

Make this generous recipe when you've got a crowd coming for dinner.

Prep: 15 minutes **Cook:** 6 hours on low or 3 hours on high **Makes:** 10 to 12 side-dish servings

---

8 cups cauliflower florets

1 large onion, thinly sliced

½ teaspoon fennel seeds, crushed

1 14- to 16-ounce jar cheddar cheese pasta sauce

Cracked black pepper

1. In a 3½- or 4-quart slow cooker place cauliflower, onion, and fennel seeds. Pour pasta sauce over all.

2. Cover and cook on low-heat setting for 6 to 7 hours or on high-heat setting for 3 to 3½ hours. Stir gently. Sprinkle with cracked black pepper before serving.

Nutrition Facts per serving: 59 calories, 6 g total fat, 16 mg cholesterol, 329 mg sodium, 8 g carbohydrate, 3 g protein.

Confetti Corn

Although this pretty and appetizing creamed corn is delicious alongside almost anything, it is especially good with pork chops or roast beef.

Prep: 10 minutes   **Cook:** 8 hours on low or 4 hours on high   **Makes:** 12 side-dish servings

1. In a 3½- or 4-quart slow cooker combine corn, sweet pepper, onion, and black pepper. In a bowl combine soup, cream cheese, and milk. Whisk to combine. Add to cooker.

2. Cover; cook on low-heat setting for 8 to 10 hours or on high-heat setting for 4 to 5 hours.

Nutrition Facts per serving: **166 calories, 8 g total fat, 21 mg cholesterol, 280 mg sodium, 22 g carbohydrate, 4 g protein.**

2 16-ounce packages frozen whole kernel corn

2 cups coarsely chopped red or green sweet pepper

1 cup chopped onion

¼ teaspoon ground black pepper

1 10¾-ounce can condensed cream of celery soup

1 8-ounce tub cream cheese with chives and onion or cream cheese with garden vegetables

¼ cup milk

Cranberry-Orange-Sauced Squash

With its brightly colored rings of sweet winter squash, cranberries, and aromatic cinnamon, this is the perfect side dish to serve with the holiday turkey or ham.

Prep: 15 minutes **Cook:** 4 hours on low or 2 hours on high **Makes:** 4 to 6 side-dish servings

2 medium acorn squash
(about 2 pounds)
1 8-ounce can jellied
or whole cranberry sauce
⅓ cup orange marmalade
¼ cup raisins
1 teaspoon quick-cooking
tapioca
¼ teaspoon ground cinnamon

1. Cut squash crosswise into 1-inch-thick rings; discard seeds. Cut each ring in half to form wedges. Arrange squash in a 3½- or 4-quart slow cooker.

2. In a small bowl combine cranberry sauce, marmalade, raisins, tapioca, and cinnamon. Pour over squash rings.

3. Cover; cook on low-heat setting for 4 to 5 hours or on high-heat setting for 2 to 2½ hours.

Nutrition Facts per serving: 260 calories, 0 g total fat, 0 mg cholesterol, 29 mg sodium, 69 g carbohydrate, 2 g protein.

Green Beans in Cheesy Bacon Sauce

Is there anyone who doesn't like green bean casserole? This version is brightened by bits of pimiento and topped off with crumbles of crispy bacon.

Prep: 10 minutes **Cook:** 5 hours on low or 2½ hours on high **Makes:** 8 to 10 side-dish servings

1. In a 3½- or 4-quart slow cooker combine green beans, onion, pimiento, mushrooms, soup, cheese, and pepper. Sprinkle with crumbled bacon.

2. Cover; cook on low-heat setting for 5 to 6 hours or on high-heat setting for 2½ to 3 hours. Stir before serving.

Nutrition Facts per serving: **199 calories, 13 g total fat, 27 mg cholesterol, 536 mg sodium, 14 g carbohydrate, 10 g protein.**

- 2 16-ounce packages frozen cut green beans
- ½ cup finely chopped onion
- 1 4-ounce jar sliced pimiento, drained
- 1 4-ounce can sliced mushrooms, drained
- 1 10¾-ounce can condensed cream of mushroom soup
- 1½ cups shredded cheddar cheese (6 ounces)
- ¼ teaspoon pepper
- 6 slices bacon, crisp-cooked, drained, and crumbled

Simple Succotash

This thoroughly American concoction is a classic combination of lima beans, corn, celery, and sweet pepper. Serve it with roasted chicken.

Prep: 15 minutes **Cook:** 8 hours on low or 4 hours on high **Makes:** 6 side-dish servings

1 cup dry lima beans

1 16-ounce package frozen
   whole kernel corn

1 cup coarsely chopped red
   or green sweet pepper

½ cup chopped onion

½ cup sliced celery

2 cloves garlic, minced

¼ teaspoon pepper

1 bay leaf

1 10¾-ounce can condensed
   cream of celery soup

1 cup water

6 slices bacon, crisp-cooked,
   drained, and crumbled

1. Rinse beans; drain. In a 3½- or 4-quart slow cooker combine beans, corn, sweet pepper, onion, celery, garlic, pepper, and bay leaf. In a bowl combine soup and water. Add to cooker.

2. Cover; cook on low-heat setting for 8 to 10 hours or on high-heat setting for 4 to 5 hours. Discard bay leaf. Stir in bacon.

Nutrition Facts per serving: **255 calories, 7 g total fat, 10 mg cholesterol, 486 mg sodium, 40 g carbohydrate, 12 g protein.**

Creamy Corn and Broccoli

Stir together the ingredients for this saucy vegetable side in a large bowl before you place the mixture in your slow cooker.

Prep: 10 minutes   **Cook:** 5 hours on low or 2½ hours on high   **Makes:** 8 to 10 side-dish servings

1. Lightly coat the inside of a 4- to 5-quart slow cooker with cooking spray. In a very large mixing bowl combine all ingredients. Place in cooker.

2. Cover and cook on low-heat setting for 5 to 6 hours or on high-heat setting for 2½ to 3 hours.

Nutrition Facts per serving: **191 calories, 10 g total fat, 25 mg cholesterol, 548 mg sodium, 19 g carbohydrate, 9 g protein.**

Nonstick cooking spray
1 16-ounce bag frozen cut broccoli
1 16-ounce bag frozen corn
1 10¾-ounce can cream of chicken soup
1 cup shredded American cheese
½ cup shredded cheddar cheese
¼ cup milk

Caramelized Onions and Potatoes

Slow cooking transforms the humble onion into sweet, golden, aromatic bites of heaven. This mixture of caramelized onions and creamy potatoes is a perfect accompaniment to beef tenderloin or salmon.

Prep: 15 minutes **Cook:** 6 hours on low or 3 hours on high **Makes:** 6 side-dish servings

2 large sweet onions, thinly sliced (2 cups)

1½ pounds tiny new potatoes, halved

¼ cup butter, melted

½ cup beef or chicken broth

3 tablespoons brown sugar

½ teaspoon salt

¼ teaspoon freshly ground black pepper

1. In a 3½- or 4-quart slow cooker place onions and potatoes.

2. In a medium bowl combine melted butter, beef or chicken broth, brown sugar, salt, and black pepper. Pour mixture over onions and potatoes.

3. Cover and cook on low-heat setting for 6 to 7 hours or on high-heat setting for 3 to 3½ hours. Stir gently before serving. Serve with a slotted spoon.

Nutrition Facts per serving: 194 calories, 8 g total fat, 22 mg cholesterol, 356 mg sodium, 28 g carbohydrate, 3 g protein.

Cheesy Potatoes

Prosciutto is an Italian-style cured pork that is similar to ham, but not as salty.

Look for prosciutto that is sliced very thinly for this savory side.

Prep: 20 minutes **Cook:** 5 hours on low **Makes:** 12 side-dish servings

1. In a 3½- or 4-quart slow cooker combine thawed potatoes, soup, cheeses, milk, leek or green onion, prosciutto (if using), and pepper.

2. Cover and cook on low heat setting for 5 to 6 hours. Gently stir in chives and bacon (if using) before serving.

Nutrition Facts per serving: **216 calories, 14 g total fat, 39 mg cholesterol, 534 mg sodium, 16 g carbohydrate, 8 g protein.**

1 28-ounce package frozen
  loose-pack diced hash
  brown potatoes with onion
  and peppers, thawed
1 10¾-ounce can condensed
  cream of chicken
  with herbs soup
1 cup finely shredded smoked
  Gouda cheese (4 ounces)
1 cup finely shredded
  provolone cheese
  (4 ounces)
1 8-ounce package cream
  cheese, cut into cubes
¾ cup milk
¼ cup finely chopped leek
  or thinly sliced green onion
¼ cup chopped prosciutto
  or 4 slices bacon, crisp-
  cooked and crumbled
½ teaspoon pepper
2 tablespoons snipped
  fresh chives

Hot German Potato Salad

If you have the luxury of having two slow cookers, coordinate them to serve this tangy potato salad with Bavarian Pork Roast (page 150), steamed green beans, and a nice cold German beer.

Prep: 15 minutes **Cook:** 8 hours on low or 4 hours on high **Makes:** 8 side-dish servings

6 cups peeled potatoes,
  cut into ¼-inch slices
  (about 2 pounds)
1 cup chopped onion
1 cup chopped celery
1 cup water
⅔ cup cider vinegar
¼ cup sugar
2 tablespoons quick-cooking
  tapioca
1 teaspoon salt
¾ teaspoon celery seeds
¼ teaspoon pepper
6 slices bacon, crisp-cooked,
  drained, and crumbled
¼ cup snipped fresh parsley

1. In a 3½- or 4-quart slow cooker combine potatoes, onion, and celery.

2. In a bowl combine water, vinegar, sugar, tapioca, salt, celery seeds, and pepper. Pour over potatoes.

3. Cover; cook on low-heat setting for 8 to 10 hours or on high-heat setting for 4 to 5 hours. Stir in bacon and parsley.

Nutrition Facts per serving: **162 calories, 3 g total fat, 4 mg cholesterol, 371 mg sodium, 33 g carbohydrate, 4 g protein.**

Ranch Potatoes

Ranch dressing is equally good on crisp lettuce leaves or creamy potatoes. Your little buckaroos, especially, will yahoo for these yummy spuds.

Prep: 10 minutes   **Cook:** 7 hours on low or 3½ hours on high   **Makes:** 6 side-dish servings

1. Place potatoes in a 3½-quart slow cooker. In a small bowl combine cream cheese and salad dressing mix. Stir in soup. Add to potatoes.

2. Cover; cook on low-heat setting for 7 to 9 hours or on high-heat setting for 3½ to 4½ hours. Stir to blend before serving.

Nutrition Facts per serving: **315 calories, 14 g total fat, 45 mg cholesterol, 665 mg sodium, 40 g carbohydrate, 7 g protein.**

2 pounds small red potatoes, quartered

1 8-ounce package cream cheese, softened

1 envelope buttermilk ranch dry salad dressing mix

1 10¾-ounce can condensed cream of potato soup

Apple Spiced Sweet Potatoes

These golden, spiced sweet potatoes get crowned with candied pecans for a pleasing crunch and buttery flavor. They'd make a lovely side to a Thanksgiving turkey or holiday ham.

Prep: 20 minutes **Cook:** 6 hours on low or 3 hours on high **Makes:** 10 side-dish servings

Nonstick cooking spray

3½ to 4 pounds sweet potatoes,
　　peeled and cut into
　　2-inch chunks

1　20-ounce can apple
　　pie filling

⅔ cup golden raisins

3　tablespoons butter, cut up

1½ teaspoons apple pie spice

1　cup coarsely
　　chopped pecans

⅓ cup sugar

2　tablespoons butter

1. Lightly coat a 3½- or 4-quart slow cooker with cooking spray. Add sweet potato chunks, apple pie filling, raisins, 3 tablespoons butter, and apple pie spice; mix well.

2. Cover; cook on low-heat setting for 6 to 8 hours or on high-heat setting for 3 to 4 hours.

3. Meanwhile, for candied pecans, in a heavy large skillet combine pecans, sugar, and 2 tablespoons butter. Cook and stir over medium heat for 8 to 10 minutes or until sugar mixture clinging to nuts turns golden and starts to melt. Pour nut mixture onto a large piece of foil to cool completely. When cool, coarsely crush the nut mixture.

4. Top each serving of potatoes with some of the pecans.

Nutrition Facts per serving: **413 calories, 14 g total fat, 16 mg cholesterol, 109 mg sodium, 70 g carbohydrate, 4 g protein.**

Coconut-Pecan Sweet Potatoes

Got a big crowd coming over for a holiday dinner? Just double the ingredients and cook them in a 5- or 6-quart slow cooker.

Prep: 20 minutes **Cook:** 6 hours on low or 3 hours on high **Makes:** 4 to 6 side-dish servings

1. In a 3½-quart slow cooker combine sweet potatoes, brown sugar, melted margarine or butter, coconut, toasted pecans, and cinnamon.

2. Cover; cook on low-heat setting for 6 to 8 hours or on high-heat setting for 3 to 4 hours. Stir in coconut flavoring and vanilla. Sprinkle with toasted coconut, if desired.

Nutrition Facts per serving: **408 calories, 18 g total fat, 0 mg cholesterol, 157 mg sodium, 61 g carbohydrate, 4 g protein.**

- **2 pounds sweet potatoes,** peeled and shredded
- **⅓ cup packed brown sugar**
- **¼ cup margarine or butter,** melted
- **¼ cup coconut**
- **¼ cup broken pecans, toasted**
- **¼ teaspoon ground cinnamon**
- **¼ teaspoon coconut flavoring**
- **¼ teaspoon vanilla**
- **Toasted coconut (optional)**

Mashed Sweet Potatoes and Parsnips

Parsnips contribute their nutty flavor to this creamy dish of mashed sweet potatoes infused with sage.

Prep: 20 minutes **Cook:** 7 hours on low or 3½ hours on high **Makes:** 6 to 8 side-dish servings

Nonstick cooking spray

1½ pounds sweet potatoes, peeled and cubed (about 4 cups)

3 medium parsnips, peeled and cubed (about 2½ cups)

½ cup chicken broth

2 tablespoons butter or margarine, melted

½ teaspoon ground sage

½ teaspoon onion salt

1. Lightly coat the inside of a 3½- to 4-quart slow cooker with nonstick cooking spray. Add sweet potatoes, parsnips, broth, melted butter, sage, and onion salt.

2. Cover and cook on low-heat setting for 7 to 8 hours or on high-heat setting for 3½ to 4 hours or until very tender. Mash with potato masher.

Nutrition Facts per serving: **166 calories, 5 g total fat, 11 mg cholesterol, 273 mg sodium, 30 g carbohydrate, 2 g protein.**

Creamy Wild Rice Pilaf

Bits of sweet-tart dried apricot stud this nutty-flavored side dish. Serve it with roast chicken or broiled or grilled salmon and steamed broccoli.

Prep: 20 minutes **Cook:** 7 hours on low or 3½ hours on high **Makes:** 12 side-dish servings

1. In a 3½- or 4-quart slow cooker combine wild rice, brown rice, carrot, mushrooms, celery, onion, dried apricots, soup, thyme, poultry seasoning, salt, and pepper. Stir in water.

2. Cover; cook on low-heat setting for 7 to 8 hours or on high-heat setting for 3½ to 4 hours. Stir in sour cream.

Nutrition Facts per serving: **165 calories, 4 g total fat, 4 mg cholesterol, 339 mg sodium, 28 g carbohydrate, 4 g protein.**

1 cup wild rice, rinsed
    and drained
1 cup regular brown rice
1 cup shredded carrot
    (2 medium)
1 cup sliced fresh mushrooms
½ cup thinly sliced celery
    (1 stalk)
⅓ cup chopped onion (1 small)
¼ cup snipped dried apricot
1 10¾-ounce can condensed
    cream of mushroom with
    roasted garlic or condensed
    golden mushroom soup
1 teaspoon dried thyme,
    crushed
1 teaspoon poultry seasoning
¾ teaspoon salt
½ teaspoon pepper
5½ cups water
½ cup dairy sour cream

Maple Ginger Bean Bake

Choose one kind of bean or some of each kind for this simple side. Fresh ginger gives the dish a real kick.

Prep: 15 minutes **Cook:** 5 hours on low or 2½ hours on high **Makes:** 8 to 10 side-dish servings

3 15-ounce cans Great Northern beans and/or red kidney beans, pinto beans, black beans, butter beans, rinsed and drained

1 8-ounce can tomato sauce

¾ cup maple-flavored syrup

¾ cup diced fully-cooked ham or Canadian-style bacon (3½ ounces)

2 tablespoons prepared mustard

2 tablespoons vinegar

1 teaspoon grated ginger

¼ teaspoon pepper

1. In a 3½- or 4-quart slow cooker combine beans, tomato sauce, maple-flavored syrup, ham, mustard, vinegar, ginger, and pepper.

2. Cover; cook on low-heat setting for 5 to 6 hours or on high-heat setting for 2½ to 3 hours.

Nutrition Facts per serving: **253 calories, 1 g total fat, 7 mg cholesterol, 936 mg sodium, 51 g carbohydrate, 14 g protein.**

New England Baked Beans

The slow cooker is the perfect partner to make this slow-cooked American classic.

Prep: 1½ hours **Cook:** 10 hours on low or 5 hours on high **Makes:** 12 side-dish servings

---

1. Rinse beans; drain. In a large saucepan or kettle combine beans and the 8 cups water. Bring to boiling; reduce heat. Simmer, covered, for 1½ to 2 hours or until beans are tender.

2. Drain beans. In a 3½- or 4-quart slow cooker combine drained beans, onion, and salt pork or bacon. Add 1 cup water, molasses, brown sugar, dry mustard, and pepper. Stir to combine.

3. Cover; cook on low-heat setting for 10 to 12 hours or on high-heat setting for 5 to 6 hours. Stir before serving.

Nutrition Facts per serving: **257 calories, 8 g total fat, 8 mg cholesterol, 145 mg sodium, 39 g carbohydrate, 8 g protein.**

1 pound dry navy beans
  or dry Great Northern beans
  (2⅓ cups)
8 cups cold water
1 cup chopped onion
¼ pound salt pork, chopped,
  or 6 slices bacon, cooked,
  drained, and crumbled
1 cup water
½ cup molasses
⅓ cup packed brown sugar
1 teaspoon dry mustard
¼ teaspoon pepper

Sage Dressing

When the oven is stuffed with the Thanksgiving turkey and all the trimmings, this savory herbed dressing cooks on the countertop.

Prep: 20 minutes **Cook:** 4 hours on low **Makes:** 8 to 10 side-dish servings

---

 12 cups dry bread cubes
  2 cups sliced celery
 ½ cup finely chopped onion
 ¼ cup snipped fresh parsley
 1½ teaspoons dried sage,
     crushed
 ½ teaspoon dried marjoram,
     crushed
 ¼ teaspoon pepper
 1½ cups chicken broth
 ¼ cup margarine or butter,
     melted

1. In a large bowl combine the dry bread cubes, celery, onion, parsley, sage, marjoram, and pepper.

2. Pour chicken broth and margarine or butter over bread mixture and toss gently. Place bread mixture in a 3½-, 4-, or 5-quart slow cooker.

3. Cover; cook on low-heat setting for 4 to 5 hours.

Nutrition Facts per serving: 253 calories, 9 g total fat, 0 mg cholesterol, 568 mg sodium, 37 g carbohydrate, 7 g protein.

Fruit and Pecan Stuffing

Those who think the stuffing is the best part of the meal will be especially pleased with this fruit-and-nut-studded side flavored with sage, marjoram, and thyme.

Prep: 25 minutes **Cook:** 5 hours on low or 2½ hours on high **Stand:** 10 minutes **Makes:** 10 to 12 side-dish servings

1. In a small saucepan heat liqueur until boiling. Stir in dried fruit. Remove from heat; cover and let stand 10 to 15 minutes.

2. Meanwhile, in a medium saucepan cook celery and onion in margarine or butter over medium heat until tender but not brown; remove from heat. Stir in parsley, sage, thyme, marjoram, salt, and pepper.

3. Place dry bread cubes in a large bowl. Add undrained fruit, vegetable mixture, and pecans. Drizzle with enough of the broth to moisten, tossing lightly. Transfer stuffing mixture to a 3½- or 4-quart slow cooker.

4. Cover; cook on low-heat setting for 5 to 6 hours or on high-heat setting for 2½ to 3 hours.

Note: To prepare dry bread cubes, start with about 20 slices of bread for the 10 cups dry cubes. Cut the bread into ½-inch cubes and spread in a single layer in a large roasting pan. Bake in a 300° oven for 10 to 15 minutes or until dry; stir twice.

Nutrition Facts per serving: **282 calories, 14 g total fat, 0 mg cholesterol, 504 mg sodium, 32 g carbohydrate, 4 g protein.**

½ cup orange liqueur or water
1 6-ounce package mixed
   dried fruit bits (1½ cups)
1 cup finely chopped celery
½ cup sliced green onion
½ cup margarine or butter
2 tablespoons snipped fresh
   parsley
1 teaspoon dried sage, crushed
½ teaspoon dried thyme,
   crushed
½ teaspoon dried marjoram,
   crushed
½ teaspoon salt
¼ teaspoon pepper
10 cups dry bread cubes*
½ cup broken pecans, toasted
1½ to 2 cups chicken broth

desserts

Indulge in a double feature: Go out for a night at the movies, then come home for dessert. With the convenience of your slow cooker, you can choose from a roster of old-fashioned favorites: warm fruit cobbler, bread pudding, gooey brownies, or spicy and aromatic gingerbread.

Apple-Cherry Cobbler, page 258

Apple-Cherry Cobbler

Pick your dried cherries—either tart or sweet. Tart cherries are brighter red than sweet ones and add a pleasing tang to the taste of this old-fashioned dessert, but either variety works just fine.

Prep: 20 minutes **Bake:** 8 to 10 minutes **Cook:** 6 hours on low or 3 hours on high **Makes:** 6 to 8 servings

½ cup granulated sugar
4 teaspoons quick-cooking tapioca
1 teaspoon apple pie spice
1½ pounds cooking apples, peeled, cored, and cut into ½-inch slices (4½ cups)
1 16-ounce can pitted tart or sweet cherries
½ cup dried cherries
1 recipe Spiced Triangles
Ice cream, such as butter pecan or cinnamon, or half and half or light cream (optional)

1. In a 3½- or 4-quart slow cooker stir together sugar, tapioca, and apple pie spice. Stir in the apple slices, undrained canned cherries, and dried cherries until combined.

2. Cover and cook on low-heat setting for 6 to 7 hours or on high-setting for 3 to 3½ hours. To serve, divide apple-cherry mixture among 6 to 8 shallow dessert dishes. Top with Spiced Triangles and ice cream or half and half, if desired.

Spiced Triangles: In a bowl combine 1 tablespoon sugar and ½ teaspoon apple pie spice. Unroll 1 package (8) refrigerated crescent rolls. Separate triangles. Brush tops with 1 tablespoon melted butter and sprinkle with sugar-spice mixture. Cut each triangle into 3 triangles. Place on an ungreased baking sheet. Bake in a 375° oven for 8 to 10 minutes or until bottoms are lightly browned. Remove to a wire rack to cool.

Nutrition Facts per serving: **387 calories, 11 g total fat, 5 mg cholesterol, 333 mg sodium, 75 g carbohydrate, 4 g protein.**

Blueberry-Blackberry Cobbler

The cobbler will rise to the top of the slow cooker as it cooks. When dessert is served, spoon the fruit from the bottom of the cooker over the warm cake (and top it with cream or ice cream, if you like).

Prep: 20 minutes **Cook:** 2 hours on high **Cool:** 30 minutes **Makes:** 6 servings

1. In a medium mixing bowl stir together flour, ¾ cup sugar, baking powder, salt, cinnamon, and nutmeg. Combine eggs, oil, and milk; add to dry ingredients. Stir just until moistened. Spread batter evenly in the bottom of a 3½- or 4-quart slow cooker.

2. In a medium saucepan combine blueberries, blackberries, ¾ cup sugar, water, and orange peel; bring to a boil. Pour hot fruit over batter.

3. Cover; cook on high-heat setting for 2 to 2½ hours or until a toothpick inserted into the center of the cake comes out clean. Let stand about 30 minutes to cool slightly before serving.

4. To serve, spoon the warm cobbler into bowls. Serve with cream or ice cream, if desired.

Nutrition Facts per serving: 371 calories, 7 g total fat, 71 mg cholesterol, 177 mg sodium, 75 g carbohydrate, 5 g protein.

1 cup all-purpose flour
¾ cup sugar
1 teaspoon baking powder
¼ teaspoon salt
¼ teaspoon ground cinnamon
¼ teaspoon ground nutmeg
2 slightly beaten eggs
2 tablespoons cooking oil
2 tablespoons milk
1½ cups fresh
   or frozen blueberries
1½ cups fresh or frozen
   blackberries
¾ cup sugar
½ cup water
1 teaspoon finely shredded
   orange peel
   Half-and-half, light cream,
   whipped cream,
   or ice cream (optional)

Boston Brown Bread

If you don't have buttermilk, make sour milk. Stir together 1 tablespoon of lemon juice or vinegar, plus enough whole milk to make 1 cup. Let stand 5 minutes before using, then measure out what you need.

Prep: 15 minutes **Cook:** 2 hours on high **Cool:** 10 minutes **Makes:** 2 loaves (8 servings per loaf)

½ cup whole wheat flour

¼ cup all-purpose flour

¼ cup cornmeal

½ teaspoon baking powder

¼ teaspoon baking soda

⅛ teaspoon salt

1 beaten egg

¾ cup buttermilk
   or sour milk

¼ cup molasses

2 tablespoons sugar

2 teaspoons cooking oil

2 tablespoons raisins,
   finely chopped

½ cup warm water

1. In a mixing bowl stir together whole wheat flour, all-purpose flour, cornmeal, baking powder, baking soda, and salt.

2. In a small bowl combine egg, buttermilk or sour milk, molasses, sugar, and oil. Add egg mixture to flour mixture, stirring just until combined. Stir in raisins.

3. Pour mixture into 2 well-greased 1-pint straight-sided, wide-mouth canning jars; cover the jars tightly with foil. Set jars in a 4-, 5-, or 6-quart slow cooker. Pour ½ cup warm water into the cooker around the jars.

4. Cover; cook on high-heat setting about 2 hours or until a wooden toothpick inserted near the centers comes out clean. Remove jars from cooker; cool 10 minutes. Carefully remove bread from jars. Cool completely on a rack before cutting.

Nutrition Facts per serving: 64 calories, 1 g total fat, 14 mg cholesterol, 54 mg sodium, 12 g carbohydrate, 2 g protein.

Cherry Gingerbread with Lemon Cream

A sweet and spicy classic gets an update. The crystallized ginger and dried cherries give this homey dessert a sophisticated touch. Look for crystallized ginger in the baking section of your supermarket.

Prep: 20 minutes   **Cook:** 1¾ hours on high   **Cool:** 30 minutes   **Makes:** 6 servings

1. Generously grease the bottom and halfway up the sides of a 1-pint straight-sided, wide-mouth canning jar. Flour the jar; set aside. In a bowl stir together flour, baking powder, baking soda, cinnamon, salt, and allspice. In a mixing bowl beat shortening and brown sugar with an electric mixer on medium speed until combined. Add egg and molasses. Beat 1 minute more. Alternately add flour mixture and boiling water, beating on low speed after each addition. Stir in cherries or fruit bits and ginger. Pour into prepared canning jar. Cover jar tightly with greased foil, greased side down. Place in a 3½- or 4-quart slow cooker. Pour 1 cup water around jar.

2. Cover; cook on high-heat setting 1¾ hours or until a toothpick inserted near the center comes out clean. Remove jar from cooker; cool 10 minutes. Using a small spatula, loosen bread from sides of jar; remove from jar. Cool 20 minutes on a wire rack. Cut bread into 12 slices; place 2 slices on a dessert plate. If desired, combine the whipped cream and lemon peel; top each serving with whipped cream mixture.

Nutrition Facts per serving: **189 calories, 10 g total fat, 36 mg cholesterol, 104 mg sodium, 24 g carbohydrate, 3 g protein.**

¾ cup all-purpose flour
¼ teaspoon baking powder
¼ teaspoon baking soda
¼ teaspoon ground cinnamon
   Dash salt
   Dash ground allspice
¼ cup shortening
 2 tablespoons brown sugar
 1 egg
 3 tablespoons molasses
¼ cup boiling water
 2 tablespoons snipped
   dried cherries
   or mixed dried fruit bits
 2 teaspoons finely chopped
   crystallized ginger
 1 cup water
¾ cup whipped cream
   (optional)
 1 teaspoon finely shredded
   lemon peel (optional)

Pumpkin Bread

Round slices of this moist, spice-infused bread slathered with soft-style cream cheese are delicious for dessert, breakfast, or tea time.

Prep: 15 minutes **Cook:** 1½ hours on high **Cool:** 10 minutes **Makes:** 2 loaves (6 servings per loaf)

½ cup all-purpose flour
¾ teaspoon baking powder
½ teaspoon pumpkin pie spice
¼ cup packed brown sugar
1 tablespoon cooking oil
1 egg
¼ cup canned pumpkin
2 tablespoons raisins
 or dried currants, finely
 chopped, or dried cherries
 or cranberries, snipped
½ cup warm water

1. Grease well two ½-pint straight-sided, wide-mouth canning jars; flour the greased jars. Set aside.

2. In a small bowl combine flour, baking powder, and pumpkin pie spice.

3. In a medium mixing bowl combine brown sugar and oil; beat until well combined. Beat in egg. Add pumpkin; mix well. Add flour mixture. Beat just until combined. Stir in raisins or other dried fruit.

4. Pour mixture into the prepared canning jars. Cover the jars tightly with greased foil, greased side down. Place the jars in a 3½- or 4-quart slow cooker. Pour ½ cup warm water into the cooker around the jars.

5. Cover; cook on high-heat setting for 1½ to 1¾ hours or until a wooden toothpick inserted near the centers comes out clean. Remove jars from cooker; cool 10 minutes. Carefully remove bread from jars. Cool completely on a wire rack before cutting.

Nutrition Facts per serving: **58 calories, 2 g total fat, 18 mg cholesterol, 113 mg sodium, 10 g carbohydrate, 1 g protein.**

Caramel-Orange Pudding Cake

To finely shred the orange peel, use a citrus zester to remove just the orange part of the peel, then use a pair of clean kitchen shears to snip the strips into tiny pieces.

Prep: 20 minutes **Cook:** 2 hours on high **Stand:** 30 minutes **Makes:** 6 servings

---

1. In a mixing bowl stir together flour, ⅓ cup sugar, baking powder, ½ teaspoon orange peel, and cinnamon. Add milk and oil. Stir until batter is combined. Stir in pecans and currants or raisins. Spread batter evenly in the bottom of a 3½- or 4-quart slow cooker.

2. In a small saucepan combine brown sugar, water, orange juice, margarine or butter, and ½ teaspoon orange peel. Bring to a boil; boil 2 minutes. Pour evenly over batter in slow cooker.

3. Cover; cook on high-heat setting for 2 to 2½ hours or until a toothpick inserted 1-inch deep into center of the cake comes out clean. Let stand 30 to 40 minutes to cool slightly before serving.

4. To serve, spoon the warm cake and pudding into dessert dishes. Serve with half-and-half or light cream.

Nutrition Facts per serving: 423 calories, 19 g total fat, 21 mg cholesterol, 59 mg sodium, 61 g carbohydrate, 5 g protein.

- 1 cup all-purpose flour
- ⅓ cup sugar
- 1 teaspoon baking powder
- ½ teaspoon finely shredded orange peel
- ½ teaspoon ground cinnamon
- ½ cup milk
- 2 tablespoons cooking oil
- ½ cup chopped pecans
- ¼ cup currants or raisins
- ⅔ cup packed brown sugar
- ¾ cup water
- ¾ cup orange juice
- 1 tablespoon margarine or butter
- ½ teaspoon finely shredded orange peel
- Half-and-half or light cream

Brownie Cakes

If a little chocolate is good, more is better: Drizzle hot fudge topping over the cake and ice cream.

Prep: 20 minutes **Cook:** 2¾ hours on high **Cool:** 10 minutes **Makes:** 8 servings

---

1 cup all-purpose flour
1 cup sugar
½ teaspoon baking soda
¼ teaspoon ground cinnamon
    (optional)
⅓ cup margarine or butter
¼ cup water
3 tablespoons unsweetened
    cocoa powder
¼ cup buttermilk or sour milk
    (see page 260)
1 beaten egg
½ teaspoon vanilla
¼ cup finely chopped walnuts
    Vanilla ice cream
½ cup warm water

1. Grease two 1-pint straight-sided, wide-mouth canning jars; line the bottom of each jar with waxed paper. Set aside.

2. In a small bowl stir together flour, sugar, baking soda, and cinnamon, if desired. Set aside.

3. In a medium saucepan combine margarine or butter, water, and cocoa powder; heat and stir until margarine is melted and mixture is well combined. Remove from heat; stir in flour mixture. Add buttermilk or sour milk, egg, and vanilla; beat by hand until smooth. Stir in nuts.

4. Pour mixture into the prepared canning jars. Cover the jars tightly with greased foil, greased side down. Place the jars in a 3½-, 4-, or 5-quart slow cooker. Pour ½ cup warm water into the cooker around the jars.

5. Cover; cook on high-heat setting for 2¾ to 3 hours or until cakes spring back when touched and a long wooden toothpick inserted near the centers comes out clean. Remove jars from cooker; cool 10 minutes.

6. To serve, unmold cakes; discard waxed paper. Serve warm or cool with ice cream.

Nutrition Facts per serving: **393 calories, 18 g total fat, 56 mg cholesterol, 233 mg sodium, 53 g carbohydrate, 6 g protein.**

Chocolate-Peanut Butter Pudding Cake

Kids will love this yummy pudding cake that combines peanut butter and chocolate. As it cooks, a warm pudding develops under the cake layer. Eat it alone or spooned atop ice cream.

Prep: 25 minutes **Cook:** 2 hours on high **Stand:** 30 minutes **Makes:** 8 servings

1. In a mixing bowl stir together flour, the ½ cup sugar, the 2 tablespoons cocoa powder, and baking powder. Add the milk, oil, and vanilla; stir until batter is smooth. Stir in the peanut butter pieces. Spread batter evenly in the bottom of a greased 3½- or 4-quart slow cooker.

2. In another mixing bowl combine the ¾ cup sugar and the ¼ cup cocoa powder. Stir together boiling water and peanut butter; stir into the cocoa mixture. Pour evenly over the batter in the slow cooker.

3. Cover; cook on high-heat setting for 2 to 2½ hours or until a toothpick inserted 1 inch into the center of the cake comes out clean. Let stand, uncovered, for 30 to 40 minutes to cool slightly.

4. To serve, spoon pudding cake into dessert dishes. Sprinkle with peanuts. If desired, serve with ice cream.

Nutrition Facts per serving: 417 calories, 18 g total fat, 1 mg cholesterol, 196 mg sodium, 56 g carbohydrate, 10 g protein.

1 cup all-purpose flour
½ cup sugar
2 tablespoons unsweetened cocoa powder
1½ teaspoons baking powder
½ cup milk
2 tablespoons cooking oil
1 teaspoon vanilla
¾ cup peanut butter-flavored pieces
¾ cup sugar
¼ cup unsweetened cocoa powder
2 cups boiling water
½ cup chunky peanut butter
2 tablespoons chopped unsalted, dry-roasted peanuts
Vanilla ice cream (optional)

Raisin Pudding Cake

Let this homey dessert stand about 45 minutes before serving to give it time to cool slightly and for the center to finish firming up.

Prep: 15 minutes **Cook:** 2½ hours on high **Stand:** 45 minutes **Makes:** 8 to 10 servings

1 package 2-layer-size
    spice cake mix
⅔ cup milk
1 cup raisins
½ cup chopped pecans
1½ cups water
½ cup packed brown sugar
½ cup butter or margarine
1 teaspoon vanilla
    Vanilla ice cream (optional)

1. In large mixing bowl stir together cake mix and milk with a wooden spoon until smooth. Stir in raisins and pecans (batter will be thick); set aside.

2. In small saucepan combine water, brown sugar, and butter or margarine; bring to boiling. Remove from heat. Stir in vanilla. Pour into a 3½- or 4 quart slow cooker. Carefully drop large spoonfuls of batter into sugar mixture. Cover and cook on high-heat setting for 2½ hours (center may appear moist, but will set upon standing). Remove crock from cooker and let stand 45 minutes to cool slightly before serving.

3. Serve warm with ice cream, if desired.

Nutrition Facts per serving: 527 calories, 22 g total fat, 34 mg cholesterol, 548 mg sodium, 82 g carbohydrate, 4 g protein.

Mocha-Pecan Pudding Cake

Two kinds of chocolate and a warm mocha sauce make this pecan-studded pudding cake a chocolate-lover's dream.

Prep: 15 minutes **Cook:** 2 hours on high **Stand:** 30 minutes **Makes:** 6 servings

---

1. In a mixing bowl stir together flour, ½ cup sugar, 2 tablespoons cocoa powder, and baking powder. Add milk, oil, and vanilla. Stir until batter is smooth. Stir in chocolate pieces and pecans. Spread batter evenly in the bottom of a greased 3½- or 4-quart slow cooker.

2. Combine the ¾ cup sugar and ¼ cup cocoa powder. Dissolve coffee crystals in boiling water; stir in coffee liqueur, if desired. Gradually stir coffee mixture into the sugar-cocoa mixture. Pour evenly over batter in slow cooker.

3. Cover; cook on high-heat setting for 2 to 2½ hours or until a toothpick inserted 1-inch deep into the center of the cake comes out clean. Let stand 30 to 40 minutes to cool slightly before serving.

4. To serve, spoon the warm cake into dessert dishes, then spoon pudding over the cake. Top with a scoop of vanilla ice cream, if desired.

Nutrition Facts per serving: **434 calories, 15 g total fat, 2 mg cholesterol, 101 mg sodium, 72 g carbohydrate, 5 g protein.**

- **1 cup all-purpose flour**
- **½ cup sugar**
- **2 tablespoons unsweetened cocoa powder**
- **1½ teaspoons baking powder**
- **½ cup milk**
- **2 tablespoons cooking oil**
- **1 teaspoon vanilla**
- **½ cup miniature semisweet chocolate pieces**
- **½ cup broken pecans**
- **¾ cup sugar**
- **¼ cup unsweetened cocoa powder**
- **2 teaspoons instant coffee crystals**
- **1½ cups boiling water**
- **¼ cup coffee liqueur (optional)**
- **Vanilla ice cream (optional)**

Raspberry Fudgey Brownies

Chocolate paired with fruit such as oranges or raspberries is a classic combination. Dress up slices of these brownies with raspberries to take them from afternoon snack to elegant after-dinner dessert.

Prep: 15 minutes **Cook:** 3 hours on high **Cool:** 10 minutes **Makes:** 12 brownie slices

½ **cup margarine or butter**

2 **ounces unsweetened chocolate**

2 **eggs**

¾ **cup sugar**

⅓ **cup seedless red raspberry jam**

1 **teaspoon vanilla**

¾ **cup all-purpose flour**

¼ **teaspoon baking powder**

1 **cup water**

Vanilla ice cream (optional)

Chocolate ice cream topping (optional)

Fresh raspberries (optional)

1. Generously grease two 1-pint straight-sided, wide-mouth canning jars. Flour the greased jars; set aside.

2. In a saucepan melt margarine or butter and chocolate over low heat. Remove from heat. Stir in eggs, sugar, jam, and vanilla. Using a spoon, beat lightly just until combined. Stir in flour and baking powder. Pour batter into prepared jars. Cover jars tightly with greased foil, greased side down. Place jars in a 3½- or 4-quart slow cooker. Pour 1 cup water around jars.

3. Cover; cook on high-heat setting for 3 to 3½ hours or until a toothpick inserted near the centers of brownie rolls comes out clean. Remove jars from cooker; cool for 10 minutes. Using a metal spatula, loosen brownies from sides of jars. Carefully remove rolls from jars. Place rolls on their sides on a wire rack; cool completely. To serve, cut each roll into 6 slices. If desired, serve with ice cream, ice cream topping, and fresh raspberries.

Nutrition Facts per serving: **204 calories, 11 g total fat, 36 mg cholesterol, 109 mg sodium, 26 g carbohydrate, 2 g protein.**

Cranberry Bread Pudding

The holiday season is the perfect time to make this festive bread pudding that can bake unattended. White chocolate, dried cranberries, nuts, and ginger make it special enough for company.

Prep: 25 minutes **Cook:** 4 hours on low or 2 hours on high **Makes:** 6 servings

1. In a small saucepan heat half-and-half or light cream over medium heat until very warm but not boiling. Remove from heat; add chopped white baking bar and cranberries or cherries. Stir until baking bar is melted.

2. In a bowl combine eggs, sugar, and ½ teaspoon ginger. Whisk in the cream mixture. Gently stir in bread cubes and nuts. Pour mixture into a 1-quart soufflé dish (dish will be full). Cover the dish tightly with foil.

3. Pour 1 cup warm water into a 3½-, 4-, or 5-quart slow cooker. Tear off an 18×12-inch piece of heavy foil. Divide in half lengthwise. Fold each piece into thirds lengthwise. Crisscross the strips and place the soufflé dish in the center of the foil cross. Bringing up foil strips, lift the ends of the strips to transfer the dish and foil to the cooker. (Leave foil strips under dish.)

4. Cover; cook on low-heat setting for 4 hours or on high-heat setting for 2 hours. Using the foil strips, carefully lift dish out of cooker. Serve pudding warm or chilled. If desired, serve with whipped cream and sprinkle with grated white chocolate and additional ground ginger.

Nutrition Facts per serving: **360 calories, 17 g total fat, 98 mg cholesterol, 177 mg sodium, 45 g carbohydrate, 7 g protein.**

1½ cups half-and-half
   or light cream
½ of a 6-ounce package white
   baking bars or squares,
   coarsely chopped
⅓ cup snipped dried cranberries
   or dried cherries
2 beaten eggs
½ cup sugar
½ teaspoon ground ginger
3 cups dry ½-inch bread cubes
   (about 4½ slices)
¼ cup coarsely chopped pecans
   or hazelnuts
1 cup warm water
   Whipped cream (optional)
   Grated white baking bar
   (optional)
   Ground ginger (optional)

Fruit-and-Nut Bread Pudding

This warm and indulgent bread pudding has the taste of the tropics, with coconut, nuts, and candied pineapple. Crown it with caramel ice cream topping and serve it with a pot of fresh-brewed coffee.

Prep: 15 minutes **Cook:** 4 hours on low or 2 hours on high **Makes:** 6 servings

2 beaten eggs

½ cup sugar

½ teaspoon ground cinnamon

½ teaspoon vanilla

1½ cups whole milk,
   half-and-half,
   or light cream

3 cups dry cinnamon-raisin
   bread cut into ½-inch
   cubes (about 6 slices)*

⅓ cup raisins

⅓ cup chopped pecans

⅓ cup coconut (optional)

⅓ cup chopped candied
   pineapple (optional)

1 cup warm water

½ cup caramel ice cream
   topping (optional)

1. In a bowl combine eggs, sugar, cinnamon, and vanilla. Whisk in milk. Gently stir in bread cubes, raisins, and pecans. Add coconut and candied pineapple, if desired. Pour mixture into a 1-quart soufflé dish (dish will be full). Cover the dish tightly with foil.

2. Pour 1 cup warm water into a 3½- to 5-quart slow cooker. Tear off an 18×12-inch piece of heavy foil. Divide in half lengthwise. Fold each piece into thirds lengthwise. Crisscross the strips and place the soufflé dish in the center of the foil cross. Bringing up foil strips, lift the ends of the strips to transfer the dish and foil to the cooker. (Leave foil strips under dish.)

3. Cover and cook on low-heat setting for 4 hours or on high-heat setting for 2 hours. Using the foil strips, carefully lift dish out of cooker. Serve pudding warm or chilled with caramel ice cream topping, if desired.

Note: To make dry bread cubes, cut bread into ½-inch square pieces. You'll need about 4 cups fresh bread cubes to make 3 cups dry cubes. Spread in a single layer on a 15×10×1-inch baking pan. Bake, uncovered, in 300° oven for 10 to 15 minutes or until dry, stirring twice; cool.

Nutrition Facts per serving: **395 calories, 9 g total fat, 79 mg cholesterol, 63 mg sodium, 71 g carbohydrate, 12 g protein.**

Mexican Chocolate Bread Pudding

Kissed with cinnamon and chocolate, a familiar dessert becomes new and just a bit exotic.

Prep: 15 minutes **Cook:** 4 hours on low or 2 hours on high **Makes:** 6 servings

---

1. In a small saucepan heat half-and-half over medium heat until steaming. Remove from heat, add chopped chocolate and raisins, if desired. Stir occasionally until chocolate melts.

2. In a medium bowl whisk together eggs, sugar, and cinnamon. Whisk in cream mixture. Gently stir in bread cubes. Pour into a 1-quart soufflé dish. Cover the dish tightly with foil.

3. Tear off two 15×6-inch pieces of heavy foil. Fold each piece in thirds lengthwise. Crisscross the strips and place the soufflé dish in the center. Bringing up foil strips, lift the ends of the strips and transfer the dish and foil to a 3½-, 4-, or 5-quart slow cooker. (Leave foil strips under dish.) Pour warm water into the cooker around the dish to a depth of 2 inches (about 1 cup).

4. Cover; cook on low-heat setting about 4 hours or on high-heat setting about 2 hours or until a knife inserted near the center comes out clean.

5. Using foil strips, carefully lift the dish out of cooker. Serve bread pudding warm or chilled. If desired, top each serving with whipped cream and sprinkle with nuts.

Nutrition Facts per serving: **281 calories, 17 g total fat, 95 mg cholesterol, 124 mg sodium, 31 g carbohydrate, 7 g protein.**

1½ cups half-and-half
   or light cream
3 ounces unsweetened
   chocolate, coarsely chopped
⅓ cup raisins (optional)
2 beaten eggs
½ cup sugar
¾ teaspoon ground cinnamon
3 cups ½-inch bread cubes
   (about 4 slices)
   (see note, page 270)
1 cup warm water
   Whipped cream (optional)
   Chopped nuts (optional)

Caramel-Apple Nachos

These nachos get a cinnamon-and-sugar treatment, using either flour or corn tortillas to make the crisps. Good apple varieties to cook with include Granny Smith, Rome Beauty, or Jonathan.

Prep: 25 minutes (apples) and 15 minutes (crisps) **Cook:** 6 hours on low or 3 hours on high **Makes:** 8 servings

⅔ cup packed brown sugar

¼ cup granulated sugar

1 tablespoon quick-cooking tapioca

1 teaspoon ground cinnamon

1½ cups apple juice or apple cider

2 pounds cooking apples, peeled, cored, and cut into ½-inch-thick slices (6 cups)

1 tablespoon margarine or butter, cut up

1 8-ounce carton vanilla yogurt

¼ cup chopped pecans, toasted

1 recipe Cinnamon Tortilla Crisps

1. In a 3½- or 4-quart slow cooker stir together brown sugar, granulated sugar, tapioca, and cinnamon. Stir in the apple juice or cider. Add apple slices and margarine or butter; stir to mix.

2. Cover; cook on low-heat setting for 6 to 7 hours or on high-heat setting for 3 to 3½ hours. To serve, divide apples and syrup among 8 dessert dishes. Top each serving with vanilla yogurt and pecans. Serve with Cinnamon Tortilla Crisps.

Cinnamon Tortilla Crisps: In a bowl combine 4 teaspoons granulated sugar and 1 teaspoon ground cinnamon. Cut two 7- to 8-inch flour tortillas into 8 wedges each. (Or cut three 6-inch corn tortillas into 6 wedges each.) Lightly spray wedges with nonstick coating. Place wedges in a single layer on an ungreased baking sheet. Sprinkle with sugar-cinnamon mixture. Bake in a 350° oven about 12 minutes or until crisp. (Or bake corn tortillas about 8 minutes.)

Nutrition Facts per serving: 280 calories, 5 g total fat, 1 mg cholesterol, 85 mg sodium, 60 g carbohydrate, 3 g protein.

Chocolate-Almond Fondue

No fondue pot required to make this luscious chocolate dipping sauce. In the unlikely event

you have some left over, reheat it to serve over ice cream.

Prep: 10 minutes **Cook:** 2 hours on low **Makes:** about 4 cups

1. In a 3½- or 4-quart slow cooker combine milk chocolate, white baking bar, marshmallow crème, cream, and almonds.

2. Cover; cook on low-heat setting for 2 to 2½ hours or until chocolate melts, stirring once. Stir until smooth. If desired, stir in the amaretto.

3. To serve, spear cake cubes or fruit with fondue forks; dip into chocolate mixture.

Nutrition Facts per ¼ cup: 260 calories, 15 g total fat, 21 mg cholesterol, 38 mg sodium, 28 g carbohydrate, 3 g protein.

2 **7-ounce bars milk chocolate, broken into pieces**

3 **ounces white baking bar, chopped**

1 **7-ounce jar marshmallow crème**

¾ **cup whipping cream, half-and-half, or light cream**

¼ **cup finely chopped toasted almonds**

3 **tablespoons amaretto (optional)**
   Pound cake cubes
   Assorted fruit such as strawberries, bananas, orange segments and/or grapes

Gingered Fruit Sauce

A spike of fresh ginger brings out the sweetness of fresh fruit in this aromatic and versatile dessert sauce. Serve it over ice cream or angel food or pound cake.

Prep: 25 minutes **Cook:** 4 hours on low or 2 hours on high **Stand:** 10 minutes **Makes:** 8 servings

6 cups assorted thinly sliced
    fruit, such as peeled
    mangoes, apricots,
    peaches, pears, apples,
    and/or unpeeled nectarines
¾ cup apricot nectar
    or orange juice
¼ cup packed brown sugar
1 tablespoon quick-cooking
    tapioca
1 teaspoon finely shredded
    orange peel
1 teaspoon grated ginger
½ cup dried cherries
    Vanilla ice cream (optional)
    Toasted slivered almonds
    (optional)

1. In a 3½- or 4-quart slow cooker combine desired fruit, apricot nectar or orange juice, brown sugar, tapioca, orange peel, and ginger.

2. Cover; cook on low-heat setting for 4 to 5 hours or on high-heat setting for 2 to 3 hours. Add cherries; let stand, covered, for 10 minutes. If desired, serve over ice cream and sprinkle with slivered almonds.

Nutrition Facts per ½-cup serving: **134 calories, 0 g total fat, 0 mg cholesterol, 4 mg sodium, 34 g carbohydrate, 1 g protein.**

Lemony Strawberry Pears

When you want something sweet—and you want to keep it light—look to these refreshing strawberry-sauced pears that poach beautifully in your slow cooker.

Prep: 15 minutes **Cook:** 2 hours on high **Makes:** 5 servings

1. Peel pears. Core fruit from the bottom, leaving stems attached. Place pears upright in a 3½- or 4-quart slow cooker.

2. In a blender container blend strawberries until smooth. Add sugar, lemon peel, lemon juice, tapioca, and nutmeg to pureed strawberries. Pour strawberry mixture over pears in slow cooker, coating each pear. Add cinnamon stick.

3. Cover; cook on high-heat setting for 2 to 3 hours. Discard cinnamon. Serve pears warm or chilled.

Nutrition Facts per serving: **185 calories, 1 g total fat, 0 mg cholesterol, 2 mg sodium, 48 g carbohydrate, 1 g protein.**

- 5 medium pears
- 1 16-ounce package frozen strawberries, thawed
- ⅓ cup sugar
- 1 teaspoon finely shredded lemon peel
- 1 tablespoon lemon juice
- 1 teaspoon quick-cooking tapioca
- ⅛ teaspoon ground nutmeg
- 3 inches stick cinnamon

Cranberry-Raspberry Compote

This brightly hued and elegant fruit dessert can be served warm or chilled—and either alone in small bowls or spooned over angel food cake or ice cream.

Prep: 10 minutes   **Cook:** 8 hours on low or 4 hours on high   **Stand:** 10 minutes   **Makes:** 6 servings

---

3 cups cranberry-raspberry
   drink or cranberry
   juice cocktail
1 8-ounce package mixed
   dried fruit, cut into
   1-inch pieces
1 3-ounce package dried
   cranberries
   or ⅔ cup raisins
½ cup honey
6 inches stick cinnamon
1 tablespoon finely shredded
   orange peel
1 12-ounce package
   loose-pack frozen
   red raspberries

1. In a 3½- or 4-quart slow cooker combine the cranberry-raspberry drink or cranberry juice cocktail, dried fruit, dried cranberries or raisins, honey, stick cinnamon, and orange peel.

2. Cover; cook on low-heat setting for 8 to 10 hours or on high-heat setting for 4 to 5 hours. Stir in frozen raspberries; let stand 10 minutes. Discard cinnamon. Spoon compote into bowls.

Nutrition Facts per serving: **327 calories, 1 g total fat, 0 mg cholesterol, 17 mg sodium, 84 g carbohydrate, 2 g protein.**

Strawberry-Rhubarb Compote

This sweet-tart compote is delicious any time of year made with frozen fruit, but it's sublime when rhubarb and strawberries are in season. Try it served over individual shortcakes as well.

Prep: 15 minutes **Cook:** 5 hours on low plus 30 minutes on high or 3 hours on high **Makes:** 4 to 6 servings

1. In a 3½- or 4-quart slow cooker place rhubarb. In a bowl combine sugar, orange or lemon peel, and ginger; sprinkle over rhubarb. Add cinnamon stick. Pour grape juice, wine, or water over all.

2. Cover; cook on low-heat setting for 5 to 6 hours or on high-heat setting for 2½ to 3 hours.

3. Remove stick cinnamon. If using low-heat setting, turn to high-heat setting. Stir in strawberries. Cover and cook 30 minutes longer on high-heat setting. Spoon the warm compote into dishes. Serve with ice cream or yogurt.

Nutrition Facts per serving: 404 calories, 8 g total fat, 29 mg cholesterol, 63 mg sodium, 84 g carbohydrate, 5 g protein.

6 cups fresh rhubarb,
    cut into 1-inch pieces
    (about 2 pounds)
    or one 20-ounce package
    frozen unsweetened
    sliced rhubarb
1 cup sugar
½ teaspoon finely shredded
    orange peel or lemon peel
¼ teaspoon ground ginger
3 inches stick cinnamon
½ cup white grape juice,
    white wine, or water
2 cups fresh strawberries,
    halved or quartered
    Vanilla ice cream
    or frozen yogurt

Orange-and-Rum Apple Compote

Try this warm and homey fruit compote over butter brickle ice cream.

Prep: 15 minutes   **Cook:** 8 hours on low or 4 hours on high   **Makes:** 8 servings

6 cups peeled and cored
   cooking apples cut into
   ½-inch slices (about
   2 pounds)
1 6-ounce package mixed
   dried fruit bits
¼ cup sugar
2 teaspoons finely shredded
   orange peel
1 tablespoon quick-cooking
   tapioca
¾ cup orange juice
   or apple juice
3 tablespoons rum (optional)
½ cup whipping cream
½ cup toasted almonds,
   sliced

1. In a 3½- or 4-quart slow cooker combine the apples, dried fruit bits, sugar, and orange peel. Sprinkle with tapioca. Add the orange juice or apple juice and the rum (if desired).

2. Cover; cook on low-heat setting for 8 to 10 hours or on high-heat setting for 4 to 5 hours. Spoon compote into bowls. Top each serving with 1 tablespoon whipped cream and sliced almonds.

Nutrition Facts per serving: **256 calories, 9 g total fat, 20 mg cholesterol, 22 mg sodium, 45 g carbohydrate, 3 g protein.**

Old-Fashioned Rice Pudding

Start your day on a sweet note: Eat any leftovers of this delicious dessert for breakfast,

warmed up with a little milk or light cream on top.

Prep: 10 minutes **Cook:** 2 hours on low **Makes:** 12 to 14 servings

1. Coat a 3½- or 4-quart slow cooker with cooking spray; set aside. In a large bowl combine cooked rice, evaporated milk, milk, sugar, and water. Stir in butter, vanilla, cinnamon and raisins. Stir well to combine. Transfer to slow cooker.

2. Cover; cook on low-heat setting for 2 to 3 hours. Stir well before serving.

Nutrition Facts per serving: **204** calories, **6** g total fat, **18** mg cholesterol, **73** mg sodium, **34** g carbohydrate, **4** g protein.

Nonstick cooking spray
4 cups cooked rice
1 12-ounce can
   evaporated milk
1 cup milk
⅓ cup sugar
¼ cup water
3 tablespoons butter, softened
1 tablespoon vanilla extract
1 teaspoon ground cinnamon
1 cup raisins, dried cranberries,
   dried cherries or currants

Traditional Mincemeat

Serve warm mincemeat over ice cream or use it in your favorite recipe for mincemeat pie.

Excellent apple variety choices include Jonathan, Rome Beauty, and Golden Delicious.

Prep: 20 minutes **Cook:** 8 hours on low or 4 hours on high **Makes:** about 8 cups

¾ pound boneless beef chuck
    or round rump roast
2 pounds cooking apples,
    peeled, cored, and chopped
    (about 6 cups)
1¼ cups dark raisins
1¼ cups light raisins
1 cup currants
⅓ cup diced candied citron
⅓ cup diced mixed candied
    fruits and peels
2 tablespoons quick-cooking
    tapioca
2 tablespoons margarine
    or butter
1 cup sugar
¾ cup apple juice
½ cup dry sherry
¼ cup brandy
¼ cup molasses
2 teaspoons ground cinnamon
1 teaspoon ground nutmeg
1 teaspoon ground mace
⅛ teaspoon pepper

1. Trim fat from meat; chop meat. In a 3½-, 4-, or 5-quart slow cooker combine chopped meat, apples, dark raisins, light raisins, currants, citron, candied fruits and peels, tapioca, and margarine or butter.

2. Add sugar, apple juice, sherry, brandy, molasses, cinnamon, nutmeg, mace, and pepper. Stir well.

3. Cover; cook on low-heat setting for 8 to 10 hours or on high-heat setting for 4 to 5 hours. Skim off fat.

4. Divide mincemeat into 1-, 2-, or 4-cup portions. Use immediately. (Or place into freezer containers. Seal and label. Freeze up to 3 months. Thaw frozen mincemeat in the refrigerator overnight before using.)

Nutrition Facts per cup: **575 calories, 7 g total fat, 31 mg cholesterol, 65 mg sodium, 116 g carbohydrate, 13 g protein.**

Index

T-U

V

W-Z

Metric Information

The charts on this page provide a guide for converting measurements from the U.S. customary system, which is used throughout this book, to the metric system.

Product Differences

Most of the ingredients called for in the recipes in this book are available in most countries. However, some are known by different names. Here are some common American ingredients and their possible counterparts:

- Sugar (white) is granulated, fine granulated, or castor sugar.
- Powdered sugar is icing sugar.
- All-purpose flour is enriched, bleached or unbleached white household flour. When self-rising flour is used in place of all-purpose flour in a recipe that calls for leavening, omit the leavening agent (baking soda or baking powder) and salt.
- Light-colored corn syrup is golden syrup.
- Cornstarch is cornflour.
- Baking soda is bicarbonate of soda.
- Vanilla or vanilla extract is vanilla essence.
- Green, red, or yellow sweet peppers are capsicums or bell peppers.
- Golden raisins are sultanas.

Volume and Weight

The United States traditionally uses cup measures for liquid and solid ingredients. The chart below shows the approximate imperial and metric equivalents. If you are accustomed to weighing solid ingredients, the following approximate equivalents will be helpful.

- 1 cup butter, castor sugar, or rice = 8 ounces = ½ pound = 250 grams
- 1 cup flour = 4 ounces = ¼ pound = 125 grams
- 1 cup icing sugar = 5 ounces = 150 grams

Canadian and U.S. volume for a cup measure is 8 fluid ounces (237 ml), but the standard metric equivalent is 250 ml.

1 British imperial cup is 10 fluid ounces.

In Australia, 1 tablespoon equals 20 ml, and there are 4 teaspoons in the Australian tablespoon.

Spoon measures are used for smaller amounts of ingredients. Although the size of the tablespoon varies slightly in different countries, for practical purposes and for recipes in this book, a straight substitution is all that's necessary. Measurements made using cups or spoons always should be level unless stated otherwise.

Common Weight Range Replacements

Imperial / U.S.	Metric
½ ounce	15 g
1 ounce	25 g or 30 g
4 ounces (¼ pound)	115 g or 125 g
8 ounces (½ pound)	225 g or 250 g
16 ounces (1 pound)	450 g or 500 g
1¼ pounds	625 g
1½ pounds	750 g
2 pounds or 2¼ pounds	1,000 g or 1 Kg

Oven Temperature Equivalents

Fahrenheit Setting	Celsius Setting*	Gas Setting
300°F	150°C	Gas Mark 2 (very low)
325°F	160°C	Gas Mark 3 (low)
350°F	180°C	Gas Mark 4 (moderate)
375°F	190°C	Gas Mark 5 (moderate)
400°F	200°C	Gas Mark 6 (hot)
425°F	220°C	Gas Mark 7 (hot)
450°F	230°C	Gas Mark 8 (very hot)
475°F	240°C	Gas Mark 9 (very hot)
500°F	260°C	Gas Mark 10 (extremely hot)
Broil	Broil	Grill

*Electric and gas ovens may be calibrated using celsius. However, for an electric oven, increase celsius setting 10 to 20 degrees when cooking above 160°C. For convection or forced air ovens (gas or electric), lower the temperature setting 25°F/10°C when cooking at all heat levels.

Baking Pan Sizes

Imperial / U.S.	Metric
9×1½-inch round cake pan	22- or 23×4-cm (1.5 L)
9×1½-inch pie plate	22- or 23×4-cm (1 L)
8×8×2-inch square cake pan	20×5-cm (2 L)
9×9×2-inch square cake pan	22- or 23×4.5-cm (2.5 L)
11×7×1½-inch baking pan	28×17×4-cm (2 L)
2-quart rectangular baking pan	30×19×4.5-cm (3 L)
13×9×2-inch baking pan	34×22×4.5-cm (3.5 L)
15×10×1-inch jelly roll pan	40×25×2-cm
9×5×3-inch loaf pan	23×13×8-cm (2 L)
2-quart casserole	2 L

U.S. / Standard Metric Equivalents

⅛ teaspoon	= 0.5 ml
¼ teaspoon	= 1 ml
½ teaspoon	= 2 ml
1 teaspoon	= 5 ml
1 tablespoon	= 15 ml
2 tablespoons	= 25 ml
¼ cup = 2 fluid ounces	= 50 ml
⅓ cup = 3 fluid ounces	= 75 ml
½ cup = 4 fluid ounces	= 125 ml
⅔ cup = 5 fluid ounces	= 150 ml
¾ cup = 6 fluid ounces	= 175 ml
1 cup = 8 fluid ounces	= 250 ml
2 cups = 1 pint	= 500 ml
1 quart	= 1 litre